New Scarcity and Economic Growth
R. Hueting

North-Holland Publishing Company, Amsterdam

ERRATUM

The footnote on page 267 should read:

*Roman page numbers - references; italic page numbers - mentioned otherwise; p.i. - personal information.

NEW SCARCITY AND ECONOMIC GROWTH
More Welfare Through Less Production?

TO ERNA
WHO TAUGHT ME TO SEE A TREE

NEW SCARCITY AND ECONOMIC GROWTH

More Welfare Through Less Production?

ROEFIE HUETING

Netherlands Central Bureau of Statistics

translated by

TREVOR PRESTON

1980

NORTH-HOLLAND PUBLISHING COMPANY
AMSTERDAM · NEW YORK · OXFORD

ISBN: 0 444 85400 2

Publishers:

NORTH-HOLLAND PUBLISHING COMPANY
AMSTERDAM · NEW YORK · OXFORD

Sole distributors for the U.S.A. and Canada:

ELSEVIER NORTH-HOLLAND INC.
52 VANDERBILT AVENUE
NEW YORK, N.Y. 10017

PRINTED IN THE NETHERLANDS

PREFACE

It has become customary to preface national economic policy recommendations with a brief disclaimer acknowledging that Gross National Product (GNP) does not provide an adequate index of social welfare and that GNP growth is neither inevitable nor necessarily always desirable. Yet there is no widely accepted index of welfare to use in the place of GNP, and even if other indices of social well-being were available, the data required to assess them would be largely unavailable. National economic statistics have been primarily designed to permit the evaluation of GNP. As a consequence, policy recommendations continue to be based upon the erroneous assumption that the quality of life will always rise in any nation that succeeds in increasing its GNP. This fact is distressing to those who perceive that GNP accounts for a very small fraction of the costs and benefits accompanying man's actions and who realize that blind pursuit of short-term gains in GNP have led many nations to seriously deplete the institutional, cultural, environmental, and mineral resources required for their long-term development.

Decision makers cannot be expected to attend to problems about which they have no information. Thus vague diatribes against the concept of GNP and the cult of economic growth will have little day-to-day effect until alternative measures of progress and new social goals are brought to private and public decision makers in some concrete form. Those engaged in the attempt to define new social indicators and to design improved techniques for assessing the social implications of alternative technologies are striving to satisfy that goal. However, until these new approaches can be coupled directly with the traditional methods of national income accounting their influence will be limited. The work of Hueting and his associates illustrates how macro economic accounts may be revised. The group's painstaking work at the Netherland's Central Bureau of Statistics defines and implements a new set of welfare concepts and analytical procedures that can help separate the environmental costs and the economic benefits previously confounded in GNP. Their work is an important contribution to the knowledge and tools that maybe once will permit decision makers to balance the benefits of immediate economic growth against the decline in national environmental wealth that generally accompanies material production.

In addition to its theoretical contributions, the book provides a useful analysis of the debate over economic growth and points to the major areas of current disagreement. At this point in the growth debate, as the initial rhetoric is quieting down and the hard work to refine our understanding has begun, *New Scarcity and Economic Growth* is an important contribution to our information on the long-term consequences of material growth and to the knowledge that will be required to manage the transition from growth to equilibrium.

Dennis L. Meadows
Dartmouth College

FOREWORD

Dr Hueting and his associates have been at work for some years now collecting statistics on the nature and extent of air and water pollution. This is a subject about which much has been said and written in recent years, but which in many respects is new and consequently leads to utterances whose meaning is not always clear. Thus an exploration of the field was necessary, proposing concepts which define the nature of the above phenomena in an exact and where possible measurable manner. For this purpose Dr Hueting has distinguished the following concepts: functions of air and water, loss of function and agents as causes of loss of function. He has then endeavoured to fit these in with existing economic concepts, such as costs, prices and shadow prices. Moreover, he has conscientiously sought a tie-in with existing economic literature on environmental pollution, in which process he has in my opinion quite rightly regarded environmental scarcity as something inside, not outside, economics.

Further scientific discussion will have to pass judgment on the concepts proposed by him and his associates. But the numerical evaluations based on their definitions have already yielded one important proof, that – to use an apposite phrase – the proof of the pudding is in the eating. (Here eating does not mean drinking impure water or inhaling smog.) Moreover, in at least one case the shadow price has been calculated.

As the author deals with the already familiar concepts of economic science in clear and highly readable explanations, his attempt at extending the set of concepts in a new field can only be applauded, even though in the future amendment or further treatment in depth, or alternatively integration or aggregation, may be desirable.

Reasons not pertinent to the reader have delayed the publication of the English version, but sad to say the book has not lost its relevance. The attitude of large numbers of the world's inhabitants testifies to the invariably intensive need for the information and the education with which the book intends to provide us. Progress made in the legislation needed to save our natural environment has been slow enough for the intensity of the need just mentioned to have hardly changed.

Jan Tinbergen
Rotterdam

INTRODUCTION BY THE AUTHOR

This study endeavours to describe the connection between environment, economics and economic growth. In addition the possibilities of statistical measurement have been explored throughout. A separate study has been devoted to the relation between energy, growth of production and environment.

The author does not feel himself an epigone. The Dutch edition, which was published at the beginning of 1974, may be regarded as the elaboration of a number of ideas incorporated in a collection of articles from the period 1967–69. With the aid of the World Wildlife Fund the English translation was completed in 1975. Through causes that are irrelevant to the reader, publication of the latter has been delayed for five years. However, the text has been updated to mid 1978. This offered the particular advantage that the energy problem could be considered more closely (see 2.11: The energy problem and growth of production). For the problems of environment, energy and growth are closely bound up with each other, and the energy problem has intensified in recent years. The tables with losses of function and the quantitative results have been abridged and placed in appendices, which makes the book more readable for the layman.

However, a more important point is that the problem of the environment has been anything but solved in recent years and, in my expectation, will increase in severity in the years to come. After all, the a priori of continuing growth of production, which is the cause of the problems, is still adhered to by the governments of the 151 countries of this world, their international organizations and the whole of business. The same arguments are still used for this. These arguments are disputable from the point of view of economic theory or quite simply incorrect. A painstaking refutation of them in a form accessible to everybody therefore seems no less necessary in this day and age than 10 or 20 years ago.

The central idea of this study is as follows. Economic theory does not call for continuing growth of production. Economic growth can mean nothing more than an increase in welfare. This depends not only on goods and services produced but also on environmental goods that have become scarce. The simplest economic datum is the following: when goods are scarce, more of one means less of another. Investing in energy-saving measures, in the development of clean, riskless forms of energy or in treating plants, switching to a kind of agriculture offering better chances of survival to plant and animal species and changing to methods of production and patterns of consumption (usually on a smaller scale) that spare the environment thus slow down the growth of production. They are measures for the preservation of non-market goods which by definition have no return in market terms but are quite certainly justifiable from the economic point of view, insofar as people attach greater importance to these goods for themselves and for coming generations than to continuing cumulative growth of production. All these measures create very considerable employment but — again by definition — are at the expense of growth of the real wage rate. For wage is a claim to produced goods; non-market goods do not come under it. Since a shadow price can be constructed for environmental goods only exceptionally it cannot be established whether our activities still lead on balance to economic growth or already to economic decline.

The study may be summarized as follows. The deterioration of the environment is described as a rapidly spreading new variety of scarcity. This scarcity is caused by the increasing calls made on the functions (possible uses) of the environment, on which man is entirely dependent. A conflict is being waged between growth of production and population on the one hand and the environment on the other. The new scarcity is manifesting itself in increasingly severe competition between the activities utilizing the various environmental functions; the use of an environmental function is at the expense of the use of other functions or, to put it another way, leads to loss of function. The environmental functions now in short supply are economic goods. Deterioration of the environment may be defined as the occurrence of losses of function. The latter may be regarded as costs.

The functions and the losses of function are classified in this study per environmental component (water, soil and air). A distinction has been made between quantitative, spatial and qualitative competition of functions. This makes quantification possible, since the extremely complex whole of environmental deterioration is subdivided in this way into a large number of subproblems. Both the classification and the quantification have been worked out by the multidisciplinary team of the Department of Environmental Statistics of the Netherlands Central Bureau of Statistics, under the direction of the author.

Losses of function differ among other things on the following points of external effects. By definition the government cannot cause any external effect, but can cause losses of function, even when interests are weighed perfectly against one another. With losses of function one cannot, on the analogy of 'unintended side effects', speak of 'main functions' and 'subsidiary functions'. There are no 'positive gains of function': scarcity in the environment does not occur until functions are in competition with each other. In concept of function the environment occupies the central position, and not production.

In the attempt to establish the shadow prices of the environmental functions, the costs of elimination of the agent are plotted against the resultant benefits. The point of intersection of the marginal cost curve and the marginal benefit curve yields the shadow price of the function. At this point the social costs are minimum, whereas the difference between benefit and cost is maximum. The point indicates the optimal degree of purification.

The investigation has shown that in general the costs of elimination can in fact be estimated. Great difficulties occur on the benefit side. Part of the benefits can be established by estimating the reduction in compensatory costs (desalination canals, facilities at waterworks, etc.) and financial damage (losses suffered by market gardening, losses caused by corrosion, etc.). These costs are engendered by losses of function and disappear upon restoration of function. The expenditure on compensatory measures and the financial loss reflect needs for the environmental functions. These amounts may be derived from market data. The greater part of the needs for environmental functions cannot be expressed in market quantities. Even with the aid of simulated market behaviour the needs for environmental functions can be quantified in terms of money in only a few cases (recreation).

When the preferences for environmental functions cannot be established, in the conflict between production and environment, either the shadow prices of the functions should be explicitly assessed (so that the public can see which weights have been given to the several functions by the decision makers) or the utility of the two categories of goods should be directly weighed the one against the other, with due observance of their production costs (the costs of elimination are the 'production costs' of the functions). The prices of market goods are irrelevant here, because they do not give the slightest information on the ranking of the needs with regard to market goods *and* environmental functions; they may even be misleading.

The classification of functions and losses of function has been performed for quantitative and qualitative competition in water and qualitative competition in air. In addition, the utility of the functions and the consequences of the losses of function occurring in the Netherlands have been indicated in words. In this way the classification already gives some information for the weighing process mentioned above. Moreover, the elimination cost curves of several agents (biodegradable organic material, salination, eutrophy and the agents released in the combustion of fossil fuels) have been estimated. For salination the curve of compensatory costs and financial loss was also estimated. For this agent it was therefore possible to draw up a complete cost–benefit analysis.

Environmental deterioration has important consequences for economic growth. In this study economic growth is defined as the extent to which society succeeds in increasing the availability of economic goods (in the broad sense) desired by its members. Environmental functions supply essential needs of man. Losses of function therefore form an aspect of 'negative growth'. Growth is still generally defined as an increase in the real national income. This amounts to an increase in production. No allowance is made for the loss of scarce environmental functions. The author advocates correcting national income for the costs of measures of elimination and compensation which, in the present method of calculation and definition of growth, are wrongly considered to contribute to economic growth. In that case a new series of figures would appear alongside the existing series of traditional national income. Comparison of the two series can form one of the indicators giving greater insight into the final result of our economic activities. For a correct insight into economic growth the losses of function, valued against the shadow prices, ought to be subtracted from national income. However, the shadow prices of these losses usually remain unknown because the preferences are expressed only partly in market quantities. As a result, it cannot be said whether we are enjoying economic growth or suffering an economic decline.

As a lead-in to the problems of growth the advantages and disadvantages of the growth of production are recalled. Disadvantages (such as erosion) prove to have existed as long as human culture. However, there are essential differences between former times and the present: the increase in scale and the accelerated rate of environmental deterioration, and a drastic change in the relative scarcity of goods produced and environmental functions. The various forms of criticism of growth are considered. The ecological form is regarded as the most important one. The principal economic literature on environmental deterioration and growth is dealt with, and biological literature is also given.

BASIC CONCEPTS

CONTENTS

Chapter 1

INTRODUCTION

1.1. The Problem

The purpose of this book is to clarify the theoretical background of the work done since the end of 1969 by the Department of Environmental Statistics of the Netherlands Central Bureau of Statistics. This department is a multidisciplinary team under the direction of the author; it is trying to introduce some order into environmental data. The first products were the reports *Waterverontreiniging met afbreekbaar organisch en eutrofiërend materiaal* (Water pollution by biodegradable organic and eutrophicating materials), July 1972; *Waterverontreiniging ten gevolge van verzilting, 1950–1970* (Water pollution caused by salination, 1950–1970), February 1973; *Algemene Milieustatistiek, 1973* (General environmental statistics, 1973), July 1974;* and *Luchtverontreiniging door verbranding van fossiele brandstoffen, 1960–1972* (Air pollution resulting from the combustion of fossil fuels, 1960–1972), December 1974. These reports are based on a classification system designed to pinpoint environmental deterioration. However, no explanation is given in the reports of how this system came about and what the theoretical aspects are. It is the intention of this book to do just that.

The point of departure of the classification system is that environmental deterioration also forms an economic problem. It is not generally regarded as such: many contrast 'the environment' with 'economics', which is why the next section recalls a number of basic economic concepts, notably that economics is primarily concerned with scarcity. In this study the environment is regarded as a scarce resource, and its deterioration is approached in the first instance as the problem of the 'new scarcity'. This new scarcity of environmental goods is then defined as a loss of function. This is the central concept of the book. The environment fulfils a number of functions for man in his productive

*This publication, which will be issued annually, contains all relevant data – both from own investigation and from other sources – which are important to a quantitative insight into the condition of the environment.

and consumptive capacity; as a result of the pronounced increase in human activities these functions enter into competition with one another, so that losses of function occur. The heart of this study consists of the classification of these functions and losses thereof. In this process the environmental problem, which is often regarded as one overall field, is broken down into a large number of sub-problems.* The author has not come across such an approach to the environmental problem in the literature.

Losses of function are costs to the community. This fact is concealed by the way in which our society is organized: the market mechanism gives inadequate expression to these costs. It is therefore necessary to try to quantify them in another way. This idea formed the basis for the work of the Department of Environmental Statistics. We started by grouping the losses of function; this classification was an important part of the work. The most difficult and important problem is how environmental functions are to be valued in terms of money. It will be found that in principle only part of environmental costs can be expressed in terms of money.

Needless to say, the advent of the new scarcity is of importance to economic growth. One particular aspect is that in the conventional calculation of national income no allowance is made for the environment's losses of function caused by the growth of production. To get an exact picture of growth, these costs ought really to be subtracted. But here we encounter serious difficulties, for only that part of the losses of function which can be valued in terms of money can be subtracted. The author advocated that this correction to national income should be made in practice. Thus the figure for national income calculated in accordance with present conventions is supplemented by a second figure. Comparison of the two figures may increase insight into the economic development of society.

It will already be evident that a sharp distinction must be made between the deterioration of the environment that can be quantified in terms of money and that which cannot. The criterion of this distinction is to be found in market behaviour. Insofar as people give expression to their preferences in the market, conclusions can be drawn from their behaviour regarding the value of the goods and services that they buy. Insofar as people do not give expression to their preferences in the market, we have no straightforward method of estimating the intensity of their wants. Unfortunately, preference for a clean, healthy

*It will prove in Chapter 4 and in Appendix II that these sub-problems cannot be tackled separately in research practice. However, they can be classified, which has been done for water and air in Appendix I.

environment and its future stability may be derived only very partially from market behaviour. This is the essential difficulty that every attempt to evaluate environmental deterioration comes up against.

Meanwhile, it is important to estimate those parts of the loss of function that *can* be quantified in terms of money. However, this still requires a great deal of statistical work and theoretical consideration. The Department of Environmental Statistics has merely made a modest start. For example, it is at present working on a quantification of the emissions by the process industry, a study of emissions of substances injurious to the environment (notably heavy metals), a determination of the fertilizer surplus by means of emissions and also the absorptive capacity and requirement of the soil and crops, a quantification of emissions of solid industrial waste, on the compilation of a phosphate balance, on indicators such as concentrations of substances and the occurrence of species of animals and plants, and on a classification of areas according to the extent to which the natural environment is being disturbed (biological criterion) and people can enjoy peace and quiet (psychohygienic criterion). An extensive programme for further research is also scheduled. The author hopes that meanwhile the publication of this study, and more especially the description of the classification system, will lead other institutions to follow the methods outlined below. The task that lies before us is a gigantic one.

1.2. The Subject Matter of Economics; Production, Environment and Welfare

Briefly formulated,* economic problems are born of the scarcity of means of satisfying wants compared to the wants. It follows immediately from this definition that deterioration of the environment is also an economic problem. After all, man needs environmental goods for the direct satisfaction of his wants (consumption) and for production. Fairly clean water, fairly fresh air, a properly functioning soil, an environment with a wide diversity of species, space, a certain degree of quiet and a varied landscape are all essential to human life. But at the same time they are scarce and they are becoming scarcer with great rapidity. If the environment were abundantly available in undamaged form, it would not present any economic problem and the marginal value (the price) of environmental goods would be nil. Unfortunately, reality displays a different picture. The new scarcity is impinging painfully on more and more people.

*See p. 6 for a full definition.

In the light of these simple truths it is remarkable that some authors with great obstinacy construe a contrast between 'economics' and 'the environment'. This misunderstanding, which can adopt a variety of forms, may be traced back to two main causes: an outmoded idea of what constitutes the subject matter of economics and an outmoded diagnosis of the environmental situation. The first occurs more frequently than the second.

The old-fashioned idea of the subject matter of economics has its roots in the eighteenth and nineteenth centuries. Adam Smith was interested in material, marketable goods – after all, in his opinion they form the 'Wealth of Nations'. Even services – they are 'immaterial' – fall outside this category,[1*] as does the environment. The material goods are valued in accordance with the costs of production – the value is created by production. In other words, this is a productivistic point of view, and one in which the concept of production is interpreted very narrowly, viz. as the production of material goods.

In the course of the nineteenth century three changes in this point of view occurred. In the first place it came to be seen that the distinction between material goods and immaterial services is not relevant to an overall economic viewpoint. Both are scarce means for the satisfaction of human wants. Government services also come under this category. In the second place the concept of wealth was replaced by that of welfare. This means the satisfaction of wants evoked by the scarce means. In other words, it is a psychical and subjective quantity. When economists presume that 'welfare has to be maximized', they simply mean that scarce resources have to be used in such a way that the resultant satisfaction of wants is as great as possible. In the third place, the concept of value evolved. While for Adam Smith and the English classicists value was determined by the costs of production, since 1870 it has been realized that a good derives its value primarily from the fact that it can satisfy wants. The subjective value is caused by the discrepancy between want and the means of satisfying want, i.e. by scarcity. Of course the marginal utility school, which brought about this shift in thought, did not forget that there are also such things as the costs of production; their relevance to value is that the costs help to

*John Stuart Mill makes a distinction between directly productive, indirectly productive and unproductive work. Mill describes as indirectly productive that work which causes the productivity of the directly productive sector to increase (e.g. the government's work insofar as this contributes to the proper functioning of industry and the – medical – work devoted to saving a productive worker). This is reminiscent of the view sometimes heard today that measures on behalf of the environment are 'economically justified' only if they further productivity.

determine the volume of production, and thus the ultimate scarcity of the goods and services produced. As a result, production acquired a more modest place in the overall economic picture than with Adam Smith and the English classicists. Welfare can be increased (or in other words scarcity can decrease) by production, but also by a reduction in the level of wants. Welfare can even be increased by reduced production, for instance when leisure time is valued more highly than the produced good sacrificed for it. In this way the productivistic idea has been abandoned.

Those who construe a contrast between 'economics' and 'environment' are often still assuming that the production of material goods is the only concern of economics. They believe that economics calls for more and more production, whereas in fact economics assumes that man aims at an increasingly high level of welfare (that is, the satisfaction of wants).

Now it must immediately be remarked that greater production and increased welfare often do in fact run parallel. If great poverty prevails, it may safely be assumed that additions to production increase welfare within broad limits (though allowance should definitely be made here for the fact that inhumanly long working hours, child labour, etc. reduce welfare!) But as soon as production has attained a certain level and the injurious side-effects of production make themselves felt, this parallelism may cease. It is extremely difficult to say when exactly this is the case. A sound 'scientific' answer cannot be given; it is a matter of an extremely subjective appraisal, which may differ from person to person. But everything points to the fact that continuing growth of production in a finite world leads to increasingly serious bottlenecks in the environment and probably even to catastrophes. As a result, the environmental problem is above all one of the needs by the present generation for a world fit for future generations to live in. This thorny problem turns up at various points in the study; a personal point of view is given in Chapter 6.

Any attempt to weigh the growth of production against harm to the environment was unknown in economic literature until recently. Economic textbooks describe water and air as typical examples of abundant and free goods. There are exceptions: F.W. Taussig gave evidence in his 1915 textbook of a progressive outlook when he said that fresh air might one day become scarce.[2]

The view that the 'environment' contrasts with 'economic interests' may for the greater part be explained by a misplaced identification of 'economics' with production. In part, however, the view challenged here may perhaps be a hangover from the time when the environment seemed to be a free good, abundantly available in respect of the existing wants, with a marginal value equal to nil, and therefore not relevant to economic discussion.

The transition to the theory of subjective value opened the way to the development of welfare economics. For in the subjectivistic view it is the greatest possible satisfaction of wants, the maximum welfare of individuals, not the maximization of national product, that is of primary importance. True, as a result economic theory loses the objective criterion against which the result of economic effort may be judged, but it does gain in reality to a considerable extent. Scarcity, interpreted as the discrepancy between wants and means, now occupies a central position in the definition of the subject matter of economics and thus as an explanation of the value phenomenon.* Following the above reasoning, the subject matter of economics may be defined as the problem of choice with regard to the use of scarce, alternatively applicable means for the satisfaction of classifiable wants.

This definition is an obvious widening of the earlier theory. In principle the one-sided coupling of economics to the phenomenon of production has been abandoned. In modern economic theory production is regarded as only one of the means that can contribute to the satisfaction of wants – the welfare – of man. Production thus ceases to be the central objective of economic action and is regarded as only one of the means of attaining a given end.

Of the authors who have constantly reflected on the points of departure of economic theory, P. Hennipman occupies a special position, in my opinion. Hennipman defines the view referred to here as the point of view that 'the common heart of the problems concerning economic science lies in the relations between relatively scarce, alternatively usable goods and the whole of the wants or purposes, whatever their nature, served by the goods'.[3] It emerges from the context of Hennipman's view that this definition contains a broad concept of goods which in fact can better be designated by the term 'means'. The ends themselves are metaeconomic and are not for economists to judge. Ends or wants are given, and are discussed only insofar as their achievement or satisfaction depends on the use of scarce means. Maximizing or even just increasing the size of the social product is no longer a necessary aim that can lay claim to a logical priority. All the objectives in conflict with this desired by individuals form a logical

*Ricardo describes scarcity – in addition to the amount of work required – as a determining factor for the value in exchange of goods. From the context of his argument scarcity proves to mean to him the degree of availability. There is no question of a subjectivistic explanation of the value phenomenon in Ricardo (D. Ricardo. *The Principles of Political Economy and Taxation*. London, 1969, p. 3 et seq.).

and complete part of economic policy. When they are given preference above production this does not mean a sacrifice of welfare on the strength of 'non-economic' considerations.[4]

Of course, this view does not mean a denial of the importance that production may have to society's welfare (satisfaction of wants). But the fundamental difference from the old productivistic interpretation is that the modern approach likewise regards the use of scarce means for the satisfaction of wants outside production, or possibly even at the expense of production, as an economic choice that can contribute to welfare.

It is L. Robbins in particular who has pointed to the importance to human activity of the phenomenon of scarcity. 'Scarcity of means to satisfy ends of varying importance is an almost ubiquitous condition of human behaviour', Robbins writes.[5] The economist studies the disposal of scarce means. He is interested for instance in the way different degrees of scarcity of different goods give rise to different ratios of valuation between them. He is also interested in the way in which changes in conditions of scarcity – whether coming from changes in ends or changes in means – affect these ratios. Economics is the science which studies human behaviour as a relationship between ends and scarce means which have alternative uses.[6]

The view now accepted by the mainstream of economic thought is that the phenomena emanating from scarcity, irrespective of the end for which the scarce means are used, form a logical entity. This view is designated as the formal or indifferent concept of welfare. This nomenclature was probably introduced for the first time in the essay *Grenznutzen* by P.N. Rosenstein-Rodan. 'Der subjektive Wohlfahrtszustand oder der Gesamtwirtschaftsnutzen, den die wirtschaftenden Menschen anstreben, ist in der moderne ökonomischen Theorie rein formal bestimmt: er umfasst alles Erstrebte – natürlich nur soweit für dessen Erreichung Aufwendungen wirtschaftlicher Güter erforderlich sind – , gleichviel ob es aus egoistischen oder altruistischen, ethischen oder unethischen Motiven, 'wirklich bestehenden' oder nur 'eingebildeten' Bedürfnissen entsteht', Rosenstein-Rodan writes,[7] and L. Robbins states: 'There are no economic ends as such; there are only economic problems involved in the achievement of ends'.[8] In the Netherlands a clear-cut definition of the formal concept of welfare is given in P. Hennipman's work – not only in the already mentioned essay 'Doeleinden en criteria', but also in his dissertation *Economisch motief en economisch principe*,[9] and in the article 'Welvaartstheorie of welzijnstheorie?'. According to Hennipman, when the field of economics is demarcated by means of the scarcity criterion, it is only logical and consistent to interpret welfare, the end and result of the economic process, in a corresponding sense, i.e. like any satisfaction of wants pursued or obtained with economic goods or, more precisely, as the balance of the positive utility over the negative utility caused by external effects or productive efforts.[10]

In the light of the modern definition given above of the subject matter of economics, there can be no doubt that the problem of environmental deterioration has a clearly economic facet. In view of the great social importance of the problem, the resultant problems of choice deserve the full attention of economic theory. For it is clear that the development in the industrialized countries on the one hand makes some scarce goods less scarce (and creates new wants alongside existing ones), but on the other hand makes certain originally free goods scarce and other scarce goods scarcer than before.

As regards the environment, a considerable degree of new scarcity has occurred. There is no denying the fact that there is a need for clean water, fresh air, unpolluted soil, peace and quiet (interpreted as freedom from noise), recreational areas, a natural environment with a wealth of species, room for children to play and room in general. In addition, there is a need to leave a livable environment for future generations. Large groups of people consider it unacceptable for biological, ethical or religious reasons that human activities are impoverishing the earth, with species of animals or plants dying out and remaining natural areas being damaged or even destroyed. On the other hand everyone can see that the new scarcity is caused by the production and consumption of man-made goods and services. The restoration of a proper quality of our environment calls for measures and provisions of many kinds or, to put it another way, for the utilization of scarce means. A problem of choice thus occurs with regard to the use of scarce means, either in the direction of the further increases in the amounts of goods and services becoming available, or of improvements to the environment. This problem comes under the subject of economic study.

As a result of the deterioration of our environment we are now faced with a problem of choice or conflict between production and environment.* Since both contribute to our satisfaction of wants (welfare), the renunciation of a further increase in production cannot be defined as the weighing of an economic disadvantage (the abandonment of potential production) against a non-economic advantage (improvement of the environment). When, for whatever reason, it becomes the general

*The construction of treatment plants etc. is performed on behalf of the environment and does not, of course, contribute to increasing the quantity of goods and services becoming available to us. This will be further elaborated on in the chapter on economic growth (Chapter 5).

feeling that the situation of our environment is unacceptable and the government proceeds to lay down measures relating to production processes and consumption habits leading to a smaller quantity of available goods and services, but to improvement in the environment, then the overall satisfaction of wants obtained from economic goods is enhanced as a result. In that case, less production leads to greater welfare.

The problem of environmental deterioration is, from the economic point of view, an allocation problem. This is the case in a dual respect. In the first place some products impose a greater burden on the environment than others. This fits in entirely with the traditional concept of allocation: allotment of scarce means to products. In the second place the total level of production – which traditionally is regarded in detachment from allocation – may be viewed as an allocative problem, in the sense that more production may entail a greater burden on the environment. Here again the rule is that more of the one means less of the other – the heart of economics. The well-known difficulty is finding the optimal combination. That difficulty already exists with individual goods distributable via the market mechanism. For, as we know, the market mechanism operates imperfectly and prices are often a deficient indicator of scarcity. The problem is all the greater when decisions on the collective and unpriced goods of our environment must be taken via the budget mechanism. We come up against even greater difficulties when we have to take decisions about the most desirable total level of production in relation to the overall state of the environment.

After the above digression on the subject matter of economics, which has been undertaken with the aim of clarifying a number of persistent misunderstandings about environment and economics, it will be clear that the contrast between 'material welfare' and 'immaterial well-being', made repeatedly in the discussions, obscures the harsh problem of choice confronting society. In this contrast, material welfare designates the goods produced, or 'economics', while immaterial well-being relates to the environment.

Of course, this is not right at all. It emerges from the above that welfare is a psychical quantity (an aspect of one's personal experience) and therefore 'immaterial'. In addition, from the economic point of view it makes no difference whether man's wants are met by material goods or 'immaterial goods'. But the remarkable thing is that precisely the new scarcity in the environment resulting from the growth of production, consumption and population relates to material goods *par excellence*. Birds and fish, for instance, are material things. When they lie on the beaches in their thousands as victims of oil or float dead in the rivers, you can take hold of them, though not everyone likes to do so. A forest is a material thing. As long as the trees are still standing you can bump your head against them; as proof of their hard matter a lump develops. Clean *and* polluted air is no less material than manufactured perfume. Polluted *and* unpolluted soil is likewise material. Noise nuisance is a physical phenomenon (vibrations in the air) and damage to hearing is a physical thing. The streets where children can no longer play are with good reason now as hard as stone. Irrefutably, the new scarce goods are no less material than the goods that are produced at their expense.

For an economic approach to the environmental problem the use of the term well-being alongside welfare may merely add to the confusion. Nevertheless, the contrast between well-being and welfare may be meaningful if well-being is defined as the psychical state (where appropriate, satisfaction of wants) which does not resolve itself into the use of scarce resources. In this definition well-being is not an economic category. It may relate to love and friendship, which after all 'money can't buy'. Insofar as the environment is still abundantly present and functions perfectly, well-being can be derived from it. But unfortunately the days when the saying 'the best things in life are free' also applied to the environment are gone for ever.

1.3. The Concept of Economic Growth

Economic growth is usually defined as the increase in real national income. In fact this amounts to an increase in the volume of goods and services produced, calculated in constant prices. For national income is equal to the added value created in production by firms and by the government.

The definition of economic growth as an increase in the volume of production once again shows the after-effect of the old productivistic conception. Starting from the criterion of scarcity, and given the wants, economic growth is possible only if and to the extent that the scarcity of the goods desired by individuals is successfully countered. In other words, economic growth is possible only insofar as there is an increase in the means of satisfying wants. The basis here must be the broad concept of goods used in economics; economic goods are scarce, alternatively applicable 'instruments', deriving their utility from their ability to meet existing wants. The now scarce environmental functions fit into this concept of goods. Thus the inroads made into these functions by producers and consumers are costs. In the calculation of traditionally defined growth no allowance is – wrongly – made for these environmental costs.

In the system of National Accounts some costs and proceeds are not counted, as is generally known. This is due in part to the fact that certain costs and proceeds do not go via the market and as a result evade the usual calculation methods. Another reason is the fiction that government services as a whole are considered to be an addition to the net result of production. However, some government services are of an intermediate nature, performed solely to neutralize the adverse effects of economic activities. The authors who concerned themselves with the concept of national income – especially in the thirties – drew attention to this aspect at quite an early stage. After all, a part of private production itself, which is normally purchased on the market by private persons and thus normally counts in the calculation of national income, is also directed towards neutralization of adverse effects of economic activities elsewhere. These issues are considered in greater detail in Chapter 5.

The danger that statistics will give a favourable picture of the actual addition of value is increased above all by the failure to consider environmental deterioration and the exhaustion of natural resources. Moreover – and this is worse – the costs referred to here are also left out of consideration in the decisions that producers and consumers take, so that the allocation of the factors of production is distorted.

There is in fact reason to return to this question now. In the days when the system of National Accounts was being set up, environmental deterioration did not as yet play a major part. Perhaps it might then have been assumed that the costs and proceeds which did not figure in the calculations were not too great in size, or that they more or less cancelled each other out. But gradually it came to be believed that in particular the environmental costs which are not counted weigh so heavily that they make the utility of further expansion of production dubious. The guiding idea in setting up this study was that we now live in a critical phase. It is possible that the growth of national income, interpreted in accordance with the traditional definition, has still to be viewed positively in Western countries. This is not certain. It might be that a method of calculation in which environmental deterioration, the exhaustion of natural resources and the duplications are deducted, already yields a negative balance. If this were the case, the growth of production would in fact entail a negative addition of value. As we shall see later, the answer to the extremely important question whether we are already in this phase cannot be given. The result depends on the value we attach to the losses of environmental functions and on the need to leave future generations a world fit to live in. We do not have the instruments for measuring these. However, it may be concluded from the literature to be discussed that continuing growth of production will in the long run lead in all probability to catastrophic scarcity of essential environmental functions and natural resources, and must therefore be appraised negatively.

1.4. The Set-Up of the Book

The substance of the rest of this book is a description and discussion of environmental deterioration as a loss of functions (Chapter 4). The resultant statistical classification system is discussed in Appendix I, and a number of results of statistical survey are given in Appendix II.

By way of introduction to Chapter 4 a summary of the forms of new scarcity that have been caused by the growth of production is given in Chapter 2. The advantages of growth are also recalled there. It goes without saying that it would be desirable to weigh advantages and disadvantages in an unambiguous manner. However, this cannot be done, as a matter of principle – a common denominator for the pros and cons of growth does not exist. The concept of national income yields such a common denominator only in appearance. This fundamental problem is described in Chapter 2 and is further discussed in Chapter 5.

Chapter 3 contains a survey of some pioneering works in this field. The following authors are discussed in chronological order: A. Marshall and A.C. Pigou, K.W. Kapp, K.E. Boulding, E.J. Mishan, W. Isard, A.V. Kneese et al., W.W. Leontief, J.W. Forrester and D.L. Meadows, D. Arthur et al. and B. Commoner.

Chapter 4 forms the heart of this study. In Section 4.1 environmental goods are defined as the functions of the environment; a 'function' is a possible use of an environmental component possessing utility. Environmental deterioration is defined as a reduced availability of functions. As a result of the growth of production and population, the functions have come to compete with one another: the use of one function is at the expense of one or more other functions. This reflects the limitation of the possible uses of the environment. An essential element in the reasoning is the distinction between quantitative, physical and qualitative competition between functions.

In Section 4.2 the agreements and differences between the concept of environmental function and the concepts of collective good and external effect are discussed.

Sections 4.3 to 4.6 investigate to what extent it is possible to quantify the losses of function as a result of qualitative competition in terms of money. In qualitative competition the function of the environment as a place in which to dispose of refuse is in competition with all other possible uses. This form of competition thus proceeds via the discharge of substances (agents), which interfere with the remaining use of an environmental component. Consequently, the quantification in terms of money should in any case be preceded by a measurement of emissions and if possible of ambient concentrations. This point is dealt with in Section 4.3.

Section 4.4 shows how shadow prices of environmental functions can be constructed. For this a distinction is made between the costs of eliminating the agent on the one hand and the costs of compensation and financial damage on the other. As a result of elimination measures the costs of compensation and financial damage lessen. This decrease in costs may be interpreted as a benefit of the abatement measures. The costs of compensation and financial damage are regarded as preferences derived from the market. When, as is seldom the case, all individual preferences are reflected via the market, the shadow price is to be found at the point of intersection of the marginal curve of the costs of elimination and the marginal curve of costs of compensation and financial damage. This point of intersection then indicates at the same time the optimal degree of restoration of function. In this way, the loss of function occurring with the optimal situation has in principle been quantified in terms of money.

Section 4.5 deals with the ticklish problem of the needs for environmental functions that are not reflected in compensatory measures and financial damage. It is shown that there are various ways of dealing with these preferences. Which method is to be recommended depends on the environmental function under consideration. For example, in the case of the environmental functions which largely relate to consumption by the present generation, such as recreation, there is in principle the possibility of tracking down the individuals' preferences by simulated market behaviour. The shadow price may in principle be derived from the price that one is prepared to pay. This already becomes more difficult in the case of productive functions because people have no insight into the extent to which the environmental functions concerned are necessary for the production process. There is the danger here that the value of the environment will be underestimated. This danger will be all the greater when the objective possibility of disasters exists but is inadequately included in the estimate from a subjective point of view. A fortiori this underestimation applies in the case of large-scale catastrophes creeping up on us, such as pollution of the seas and the impoverishment of ecosystems.

The latter possibility introduces an entirely new element into the shadow price; if drastic environmental losses of function occur, the future of our civilization is endangered. This impending disaster cannot be translated into a monetary value via the preferences of the present generation. The interests of the future generations must be served by a normative value judgment based on as realistic as possible an estimate of the dangers threatening us. This leads to the view that a number of environmental functions are merit goods and must be treated as such. The valuation will have to be made by the authorities. In all cases of loss of function the authorities are the only agency that can bring the shadow prices into effect by taking appropriate action. This problem is dealt with in Sections 4.6 and 4.7.

The latter idea – an unknown, but very high shadow price – also dominates the chapter on economic growth (Chapter 5). The conclusion of this study is that only part of the environmental costs can be pinned down statistically; the really decisive monetary values cannot be established by exact methods. However, this does not alter the fact that everything possible must be done to estimate at least the monetary values that *can* be tracked down.

1.5. References

[1]This is in fact also the case in: J.S. Mill. *Principles of Political Economy*. Volume I. London, 1862, Book I, Chapter III, pp. 55–66.
[2]F.W. Taussig. *Principles of Economics*. Volume I. New York, 1915, p. 5.
[3]P. Hennipman. Doeleinden en criteria. In: *Theorie van de Economische Politiek*. Leiden, 1962, p. 48.
[4]P. Hennipman. Loc. cit., p. 50.
[5]L. Robbins. *An Essay on the Nature and Significance of Economic Science*. Second Edition. London, 1952, p. 15.
[6]L. Robbins. Loc. cit., p. 16.
[7]P.N. Rosenstein-Rodan. Grenznutzen. In: *Handwörterbuch der Staatswissenschaften*. Fourth Edition. Volume IV. Jena, 1927, pp. 1195 et seq.
[8]L. Robbins. *The Economic Causes of War*. London, 1939, pp. 116–117. Further *An Essay on the Nature and Significance of Economic Science*. Second Edition. London, 1952, pp. 24 et seq. and p. 145 (First Edition, 1932).
[9]P. Hennipman. *Economisch Motief en Economisch Principe*. Amsterdam, 9 July 1940, pp. 71–82. Further, in the adapted edition, 1945, pp. 73–80 and pp. 189–210.
[10]P. Hennipman. Welvaartstheorie of Welzijnstheorie? *Economisch-Statistische Berichten*, 26 January 1972, p. 81.

Further:

A. Smith. *The Wealth of Nations*. Volume I. London, 1970 (First Edition, 1776).
A. Smith. *An Inquiry into the Nature and Causes of the Wealth of Nations*. Volume II. Homewood (Ill.), 1963.
D. Ricardo. *The Principles of Political Economy and Taxation*. London, 1969, pp. 3 et seq.

Chapter 2

CHANGING VIEWS ON GROWTH OF PRODUCTION

2.1. Positive View of Growth

Until recently the increase in production was viewed favourably by more or less everyone. Of course, nobody took the attitude that production had to be forced up regardless of the accompanying sacrifices of labour, but, given the effort, a higher level of production was usually considered better than a lower one. This is not surprising, since production per head of the population roughly determines the average real income per head. Thus, other things being equal, with given wants, given income distribution and the absence of external effects, production determines welfare. This view is self-evident, certainly in times when there are still many unsatisfied wants of basic necessities and the environment is predominantly a free good. It is nowadays sometimes suggested that the growth of production is a strange objective, a fetish or myth propounded by economists or industrialists. The truth is that the cry for a higher income can be heard among all kinds of individuals and groups. Admittedly, not at all times and not in all cultures – there are static cultures, often with a religious tendency, that are satisfied today with what they had yesterday – , but in Western nations most people want more. In itself this endeavour may be viewed positively; by the standards to which most of us adhere, it is preferable to the apathy and apparent absence of wants which the most poverty-stricken section of the working class (the 'lumpenproletariat') had displayed in the previous century, a state rightly criticized by Marx.

The objections to the growth of production to be discussed below must therefore probably be explained not by a tendency of Western society to turn against more quantity, quality and variety, but by a growing awareness that the loss of the functions of the environment has become greater than the gain in goods achieved at the expense of this loss and that the loss of diversity in our environment is no longer compensated for by a still greater variety in the package of goods.

Growth percentages are, as the reader will know, often used as indicators of the success of a country (Japan!), of an economic system (such as Western capitalism or Soviet state socialism), or of a government's policy. Some examples follow. They relate to the average annual growth of real income (net market prices).

For the Netherlands, growth was 5% in the period between 1950 and 1970; per head of the population the increase amounted on average to $3\frac{1}{2}$% per annum. Uncorrected for population growth this amounts to an increase of some 150%, or a doubling per head of the population in a twenty-year period. By way of comparison it may be stated that in the period from 1910 to 1930 the average real growth was $3\frac{1}{4}$% per annum ($1\frac{3}{4}$% per head). In the thirties, as a result of the severe depression, there was barely any increase in national income, while the income per head even fell. In the period 1900–10 the average annual real growth was 2% ($\frac{1}{2}$% per head).[1]

A similar development occurs in all industrialized countries. As an illustration, the following figures for the period 1950–70 may be stated:[2] Sweden 4% ($3\frac{1}{4}$% per head), United Kingdom $2\frac{5}{8}$% ($2\frac{1}{8}$% per head), South Africa 5% ($2\frac{5}{8}$% per head), Canada $4\frac{3}{4}$% ($2\frac{3}{8}$% per head), United States $3\frac{1}{2}$% ($2\frac{1}{8}$% per head), Japan $9\frac{3}{4}$% ($8\frac{1}{2}$% per head),* Hungary $5\frac{3}{4}$% ($5\frac{1}{4}$% per head), Soviet Union $8\frac{3}{4}$% (7% per head).

The growth rates given above for a number of industrialized countries are not entirely comparable.** Allowance must also be made for the fact that an identical absolute increase from a point of departure with a

*1952–70; the figures for 1950 and 1951 are not available.

**In this list the national incomes of the first six countries come under the convention of the System of National Accounts (SNA) of the United Nations, whereas in the last two countries the Material Product System (MPS) is used. SNA defines national income as the 'sum of the incomes accruing to factors of production supplied by normal residents of the given country before deduction of direct taxes' (*Yearbook of National Accounts Statistics, 1969*, Volume I, p. XI). Under the concept of production come in this system all goods and services that are exchanged for money (*A System of National Accounts and Supporting Tables, 1953*, p. 4). MPS defines the Net Material Product as the 'total net value of goods and "productive" services, including turnover taxes, produced by the economy in the course of a year' (*Yearbook of National Accounts Statistics, 1969*, Volume I, p. 733). The difference between the two systems relates to the economic activities that do not directly contribute to material production, such as general administration and defence, social and personal services (*Yearbook of National Accounts Statistics, 1969*, Volume I, p. 733). In the Net Material Product of Hungary service activities such as passenger transport, communications and laundries have been regarded since 1959 as part of material production (*Yearbook of National Accounts Statistics, 1969*, Volume I, p. 304); and as a result, the difference between Hungary's figures and those of the SNA has decreased since 1959. This difference in definition leads to an overestimation of growth rates in the East European countries. Thus in the USSR for industry – and in particular the new rapidly growing branches of industry – a relatively high weighting coefficient has been built into the NMP, whereas small concerns growing less quickly, which usually supply local needs, and services not growing quickly are left out of the NMP.

low absolute level leads to a greater relative (percentage) growth than from a point of departure with a high absolute level. Nevertheless, the figures do suggest that growth of national income is connected above all with the degree of industrialization of a country and proceeds independently of the existing economic order and the prevailing political system. In the non-industrialized countries (the developing countries) there is considerably less growth in the package of goods and services becoming available. This statement is of importance in the context of this book, for two reasons. Firstly, the disadvantages that the growth of production entails for the environment were initially most apparent in the industrialized countries, manifesting themselves strongly in the fifties and sixties, precisely when the growth of production was greater than ever before. Secondly, it demonstrates that the choice to be discussed below between continuing growth of production on the one hand and a restoration of the quality and quantity of the environment on the other is an economic problem confronting all industrialized countries, irrespective of their economic order and political system.

2.2. *Advantages of the Growth of Production*

Until recently almost everyone was in favour of the increase in the package of goods and services. The following arguments can be adduced for this:

(1) Through the growth of production most of the population of the industrialized countries have been freed from the material distress that they had suffered since time immemorial. Most people can now satisfy their basic requirements for food and clothing. The housing situation has been greatly improved, despite the fact that limited sections of the population are still affected by a housing shortage. Sanitary provisions are much better than fifty years ago, not to mention the nineteenth century. Households possess more consumer durables than formerly.

(2) Growth has created scope for more education and better medical facilities. The level of schooling is much higher than before, and the school-leaving age has been raised. Hospital accommodation has been improved, serious epidemics are practically a thing of the past. Patients can now recover from a number of diseases which once were incurable, and the death rates in the industrialized world have fallen sharply.

(3) The consumer's choices have increased. This is a result of the fact that scope has been created above the minimum level of subsistence; moreover, the supply of goods is much more varied than

before. In addition, leisure time has increased,* as has the extent to which people can choose between work and leisure time. In connection with this the package of services has been greatly expanded, so that, for instance, many sections of the population can broaden their horizons by travel, and keeping up with fashion is no longer reserved for a small percentage of wealthy people. Sports facilities have been improved in quality and quantity. Active participation in sport, especially among young people, has increased. Perfected reproduction of sound and of paintings has brought music and art into the living room. The TV has done the same for the theatre and cabaret. Live performances are available for all. The paperback has brought literature within everyone's reach. Young people have their own pop culture. Many can choose between public transport, private car, bicycle or walking. The great variety in furnishings is striking in contrast with the former monotony. A complete hobby industry has sprung up to serve a wide range of pastimes.

(4) In the fourth place, experience indicates that with growth, income distribution becomes more uniform. This has the following causes:

(a) Growth of production is caused by greater capital intensity. At a low elasticity of substitution between labour and capital, a higher capital intensity leads to a lower share of capital in national income. And since many owners of capital are to be found in the category of the rich, this development leads to a levelling of personal income distribution. In the Netherlands the 'passive' income from wealth fell between 1930 and 1969 from 25% to 5% of national income.[3]

(b) Growth coincides with a higher degree of schooling. This leads to better opportunities for development and a higher income from work.

(c) Growth makes unskilled labour relatively scarcer. The result is a relatively rapid rise in lower incomes.

(d) With an increase in the package of goods and services, scope for income transfers is created. The incomes of those not participating in the production process, such as the elderly, the sick, the disabled and the jobless, are considerably increased. Since these categories usually belong to the lowest income groups, this development leads to a more uniform income distribution.[4]

The above trends are not the only ones; the relation between growth and income distribution is a highly complex one. In some respects

*This is one of the positive points that are not measured in national income; this is discussed further in Chapter 5.

growth encourages a greater inequality. It is notably of importance that technical development leads to bonuses for being ahead, which assume the form of personal incomes which are sometimes very high. In the service sector too, increasing production sometimes yields excessively high incomes.

(5) Growth and, more in particular, increased mechanization and automation, has alleviated human work. Arduous and dull work has certainly not disappeared, but working conditions have improved in many respects.

(6) Finally, growth of production can absorb involuntary unemployment and thus contribute to more or less full employment, Conversely, stagnation in growth may lead to unemployment. However, two comments should be made on the relation between growth of production and employment that is often brought up. In the first place work is a sacrifice. The utilization of labour is a cost factor in production. Although, as the term implies, involuntary unemployment is an undesirable phenomenon and extensive unemployment a social evil of the first order, it is not correct to regard a continual increase in the level of employment as a desirable objective in itself for all individuals. In the second place, full employment without growth is quite feasible. This situation can be achieved in principle by shortening working hours, sacrificing potential growth for the sake of more leisure.*

Progress in the growth of goods and services probably presupposes a certain frame of mind, in particular among those in charge of the process of progress. In this connection the following factors, among others, may be mentioned: the desire for a larger and more differentiated package of goods or, in other words, dependence on the level of supply of goods and services in order to attain the desired degree of satisfaction; further, willingness to take risks, interest in technology, perseverance, readiness to work hard, ability to co-operate (necessary in a far-reaching division of labour) and receptiveness to new ideas. Each of these factors can of course differ according to period and country. It seems as if in recent decades all these factors worked

*It should be pointed out in passing that the commonly-heard argument that protection of the environment is at the expense of employment is not proven. Measures of all kinds necessary for restoring or maintaining the quality of the environment will lead to a considerably higher utilization of factors of production for attaining the same package of goods and services as is available at present. In addition, supervision of the performance of measures and compliance with prescribed different methods of production and habits of consumption will tend to increase employment. Introduction of ecologically sound agricultural methods will greatly expand employment in farming. Only direct reduction of the level of activities for the environment reduces employment.

together in Western and Eastern Europe, North America and Japan, in a cultural climate which came to maturity in the immediately preceding period and which made this combination of factors possible – technically, organizationally and scientifically, and also with respect to mental attitude.

There are reasons enough for the fact that this culture looks with favour on one of its most striking characteristics. A number have been listed in this section. The highly positive view that our society has of the growth of production is reflected in many fields. It is no exaggeration to say that nothing short of a growth ideology has developed.

In economic policy the growth of national income has enjoyed high priority for some considerable time now, perhaps the highest priority having been accorded to it by orthodox Communism and Western capitalism after the Second World War. In both economic policy and literature the annual increase in real national income is taken without reservation as a criterion of economic growth and accepted, though with some restrictions, as a broad indicator for the increase of welfare. In political and journalistic language and in daily speech, growth of the quantity of goods and services was – and still is – identified with economic progress or even with progress pure and simple.

In this way growth rates were also able to become indicators of success. From economic progress to progress in general is only a small step – and in journalism and politics larger steps are quite a common occurrence. Growth rates have thus become an obvious subject of national and international rivalry. They form an important feature of election manifestos in Western countries. They even form a major criterion of the success of the economic order of a country. The Western democracies are growing fast. But, to judge by their rates, the Communist countries are growing even faster. This faster growth is adduced by some as proof of the superiority of the Communist system. There is an unconcealed growth race going on between the United States and the Soviet Union.[5] Japan, the fastest-growing country in the world, owes its esteem in Asia and elsewhere largely to the unprecedented speed with which its production has developed. Growth has become a symbol of national greatness.

2.3. Objections to the Growth of Production

The criticisms of growth have historically consisted of various currents of thought, which will be touched on here; the intention is to indicate those that will be dealt with in detail later and those that will not.

In the first place there are objections of a spiritual and religious nature. This criticism does not deny that economic growth brings more welfare, but points out that the pursuit of welfare interferes with other, more essential properties of the human spirit. A characteristic of this current of thought is that all forms of hedonism are rejected. Man should concentrate on spiritual and religious values; attention to worldly and material things may disturb that concentration. This reasoning is inherent, for example in Buddhism, in asceticism in its various versions, and also in some forms of Christianity. As regards the latter, matters are sometimes fairly complicated; Calvinism, for instance, is imbued with a positive appreciation of austerity on the one hand, but on the other it prompts unflagging industry, and the resultant economic success is sometimes interpreted as a sign that a blessing is bestowed on this hard work. One thing is certain – a steadily continuing growth of consumption is not reconcilable with Christianity.

In the second place there are objections of a more psychological nature. These do not reject hedonism, but doubt or deny that growth is conducive to human happiness. In this reasoning increasing consumption does not lead to a steadily greater satisfaction of wants but to a dulling of the senses, to a forced search for new wants, to empty luxury and selfishness. Especially in former times, this criticism has occasionally been of a reactionary nature: the poor, or the workers, would merely squander higher incomes. Nowadays it is realized that people have gradually to get used to new possibilities of consumption, but at the same time it is argued that this growth of wants reaches a limit beyond which human happiness is harmed rather than served. Opinions differ as to whether large sections of the population have now reached this limit. It is further remarked that the growth of production calls for a constant effort on the part of the individual; this effort may become too much for him. The pursuit of success breeds the fear of failure; that is how the typical neuroses of industrialized society are born. This vicious circle of consumption and ambitions is often called the rat race.

Unlike the objections of a religious and spiritual nature, which will not be considered further, the psychological objections to growth will be discussed in more detail below (in Section 2.5 and in the last part of Section 2.9, which deals with Marcuse and the student protest). At this point it may be remarked that arguments have long been heard that interpret economic growth as an increase in the flood of material goods; it is pointed out that greater consumption does not benefit people, and the superior importance of more education, more culture, more spiritual life is contrasted with this. Although this trend is closely related to the two preceding ones, it often derives from the mistaken notion that 'growth' consists only of more material goods. This identification of 'economics' with 'material goods' (or with 'money'!) is incorrect. The misunderstanding is illustrated by those advocating restraints on growth for the benefit of, for instance, more education, forgetting that more education is also a form of economic growth.

Finally – and that is the particular subject of this book – there is a form of criticism of growth that starts from the finite nature of this earth of ours. Thomas Malthus' pessimistic view of growth was of this kind; the limited availability of agricultural land would bring constant trouble down on mankind. The point is raised by all those who predict the mischief that could be done by man-made erosion; this will be dealt with in the following section. The reader will also be reminded of the various worrying predictions of the exhaustion of various natural resources.

This concern with the finite nature of the planet has gained enormously in strength in the last decades. This is due mainly to the work of biologists, who are used to thinking in terms of the equilibrium that exists among species of animals and between these species and their environment. It is this ecological approach that has produced the typically modern criticism of growth which came so much to the fore in the sixties. It culminates in the report *The Limits to Growth*, made by D.L. Meadows et al. to the Club of Rome in 1971.*

The economic interpretation of this criticism of growth, to which the rest of this book is devoted, amounts to the fact that in the course of the growth process costs are incurred which are not, or insufficiently, taken into account in the economic process. Systematic errors of calculation are made. Thus it is not a matter of rejecting growth as such; the argument is that what we call growth is not always growth upon further consideration. If the necessary corrections are made to the calculations, a number of phenomena of growth appear in quite a different light.

2.4. Some Warning Voices from the Past

Environmental pollution, erosion and ecological disturbance are no new concepts. From long before the Christian era right up to the present day voices have always been raised against the adverse effects of production. The saying 'there's nothing new under the sun' is applicable here too. It has at all times been recognized by some that production and consumption of products may entail disadvantages not allowed for in the price.

*This work is discussed in Chapter 3.

Erosion as a result of farming and lumbering has for millennia been identified by a number of authors as an encroachment upon the environment, the adverse effects of which weigh on later generations. The erosion in the Mediterranean region is well known. Mount Lebanon, now bare, was celebrated in the pre-Christian era for its cedar forests. The Bible mentions in I Kings 5:6–17 and in II Chronicles 2:8–18 the large-scale commercial transaction between King Solomon and King Hiram of Tyre, by which Hiram, in exchange for agricultural produce, agrees to supply cedar and fir trees from his well-stocked forests for the construction of the temple in Jerusalem. Solomon's reign was around 1000 B.C.[6] Lebanon now consists mainly of bare, stony slopes. Palestine, once 'the land of milk and honey', has been transformed into a desert. Where the Libyan desert now extends, there was flourishing viniculture along the coast in Roman days; in the hinterland were woods. In North Africa there are many remains of towns in the desert sands as mute testimony to squandered natural resources.[7]

Though no deserts have been created on the European side of the Mediterranean, the vegetation there has become greatly impoverished. Plato (427–347 B.C.) wrote in the *Critias*: 'Once Attica was covered by a layer of fertile soil with many woods. The trees have disappeared; what remains is like the skeleton of a seriously ill man. The rich and soft earth has been squandered, and only the bare bones are left'.[8] Theophrastus (fourth century B.C.) is known to have compiled a survey of the forests, stating the quality. Later authors still sing the praises of the gigantic forests of Spain, Crete and Cyprus. Marseilles and Genoa were favourably situated in respect of dense forest for ship-building. The basin of the Po was covered with dense forests of oak trees, where the pigs were fattened for shipment to Rome.[9] As we know, ancient Rome's aquaducts gave an ample supply of water which, after use, was conducted via a sewer into the Tiber. However, this had disastrous consequences for the vicinity of Rome, since as a result too much water was withdrawn from the surrounding countryside. Together with the deforestation, this led to erosion of the land. The discharge of nutrients into the sea via the sewage system impoverished the soil. All this may well have helped to bring about the fall of Rome.[10]

A more recent example of extensive erosion is the well-known dust bowl in the United States. It should be remarked that the cases of erosion that have been mentioned so far extended over hundreds of years, whereas the large-scale dust storms in Colorado, Kansas, Oklahoma and Texas in the thirties blew away millions of tons of fertile earth in just a few years.[11] In 1939 the loss of useful agricultural land as a result of erosion in the United States was estimated at 280 million acres.[12]

Lack of foresight, inability to make decisions and the fact that tomorrow's scarcity is not reflected in today's price have repeatedly led in the course of history to exhaustion of the natural resources of a society and thus contributed in some cases to its downfall.

The advent of the cities brought in its train not only an increase in the quantity and variety of products – bound up with extensive division of labour – and the rise of art and science, but also problems of waste disposal, hygiene, dust and noise.

Juvenal (ca. A.D. 60–140) complains about noise nuisance in the city of Rome and remarks that nothing is more valuable to a Roman than silence – to get peace and quiet it is necessary to build a country house outside the city: 'Many a sick man dies here (in Rome) because he cannot fall asleep . . . For which rented dwelling allows of sleep? Only for a great deal of money can one have a night's rest in this city. That is the main cause of our illnesses. The passage of the wagons through the narrow, twisty streets and the curses as a convoy grinds to a halt would awaken a Claudius'.[13] It follows from the context that the first sentence of the quotation has to be taken literally. During the day Rome was a noisy place as a result of workshops, markets and schools; at night goods traffic, which was forbidden during the day, supplied the din. Thus recovery from a severe illness could be hampered by lack of quiet and sleep.

Martial (ca. A.D. 40–105) likewise describes in detail the main sources of noise nuisance in Rome. He tells a certain Sparsus that he has purchased a humble cottage in dreary Nomentum (a suburb of Rome) so that, 'exhausted by annoyance', he could occasionally get a little peace and sleep. 'All Rome stands by my bed', writes Martial. Sparsus is described as rich and spoilt, because he lives on Petilius' property, where part of the city has been converted into countryside, so that silence prevails and one can sleep undisturbed.[14]

Erasmus called for a drastic programme of city cleansing, the countering of slums and the draining of swamps by the city authorities to prevent epidemics.[15] Hygiene in the cities of Europe must have been very bad indeed from about the year A.D. 500 into the nineteenth century. All human and animal waste was simply thrown into streets, squares and courtyards. There must have been an unbearable smell in the densely populated districts.[16] Although it was not until around 1850 that bacteria were discovered to be the causal agent of infections (Koch, Pasteur), long before then people had been aware that the unhygienic conditions were largely responsible for the poor state of health of the population.[17]

G.M. Trevelyan mentions at various places in his works on the social history of England the phenomenon of the concentration of people in poor accommodation with inadequate sanitary facilities and the air and water pollution in the period of the Industrial Revolution.[18] The English industrial areas in those days were black with soot. George Diggle recounts in *A History of Widnes* that in the town of Widnes, near Liverpool, the Leblanc chemical works polluted the air with fumes and the streams with effluent, while smelly hills of sulphide overwhelmed the countryside. The Alkali Acts of 1863 and later years brought increasingly efficient public inspection and control,[19] but as late as 1876 the Vicar of Widnes complained that the soda makers, having contributed to his endowments, seemed to think that they had a right to stifle him, crumble the slates on the church roof and drive away prospective curates.[20] I consider the comments of this nineteenth century observer so striking because they weigh the harm done by industry to (church) property against the compensation which industry paid for this.

François Raspail describes the adverse effects of air pollution by factories in France in the mid nineteenth century. According to Raspail, the proximity of certain factories was a scourge to the surrounding vegetation, whatever efforts were made to build high stacks; the acids, which are heavier than air, after all, end up on the ground again. It is clear that the health of those living in the vicinity must suffer just as much harm as is done to the tall trees that dry out at the base and to the grass that withers as it sprouts. How could the respiratory organs fail to suffer an adverse effect while over a large area everything that is green turns yellow and the surface of walls and of the ground is covered by nitrous scum? The local authorities, says Raspail, should realize firstly that children above all are susceptible to harmful emissions – not only through their greater sensitivity on account of their youth but also because the density of the stinging vapours is the greatest close to the ground – and secondly that the harvest is severely harmed.[21]

In the Netherlands the pollution and the stench of the water in the Fen Colonies was so bad at the end of the last century that in 1897 a State Commission was appointed by Royal Decree to examine the problem.[22]*

2.5. *Psychological Criticism of Growth*

Criticism of the level of production and consumption and their effects was also voiced in the fifties and early sixties by the proponents of social

*This may be regarded as the start of statutory regulation of water pollution.

medicine and social psychiatry. These objections acquired wider publicity through the books *Crisis in our Cities* by Lewis Herber[23] and *Die Unwirtlichkeit unserer Städte* by Alexander Mitscherlich,[24] both published in 1965. As the titles indicate, both books relate to the deterioration of the urban environment as the result of concentrations of industrial establishments and the accompanying agglomerations of people.

Herber, not a doctor himself but drawing mainly on medical material, and co-operating closely with a number of American scientific and government institutes of public health, describes many elements of environmental deterioration in his work. For instance, he points to disorders of the respiratory organs caused by air pollution, the degradation of drinking water and water for swimming by the transformation of the rivers into open sewers, the physical and mental harm caused by noise, the advance of cardiac infarction through lack of exercise and an excess of stress through the nerve-racking existence of the crowded masses of people in the cities. Mental stress and pollution of the human environment are not solely city problems, but the factors causing the health problems mentioned are being brought to refined perfection in the modern metropolis. We are being confronted by an epidemic of urbanization. This calls for strict quarantine and for permanent measures to keep the causes under control.

Mitscherlich, who is a psychoanalyst, is opposed above all to the extreme satisfaction of individual wants that manifests itself in a miserable urban environment. Modern housebuilding illustrates that man has lost his feeling for interaction between the individual and society. Egoism curbed by no civic obligation and wild quantitative growth prevail. The modern city has lost the characteristic of contrast essential to man. The urban area is noisy and congested by traffic. Contact with animals and nature has been broken. A resident of New York City has to drive 120 miles to find nature and peace and quiet. Few can still afford to buy a small piece of 'nature' in order to play the unnatural game of 'country-man', an expensive way of being asocial, since the proliferating suburbs encroach increasingly upon nature. There is no question of progress, according to Mitscherlich. You can't say it's better or worse than before – it's different.

The literature of social medicine stresses the adverse effects that the loss of facilities for play, of the characteristic of contrast and of adventure in the urban environment have on the child's development; the 'paved playgrounds with climbing racks' provided by the local authorities are a poor substitute. Motor disturbances and difficulties in learning may result from such deprivation. Causes mentioned include the unlimited use of private cars and the monotony of high-rise blocks in the new districts.[25,26]

R.L. Zielhuis[27] argues that health is in part the resultant of the interaction between man (the size of the burden he can bear) and environment (the burden). A functionally unstable equilibrium exists between these two elements. The environment contains stimuli vital to man: the primarily system-bound factors. These are man's essential requirements from the environment. They include the scope for physical and mental activity, food, oxygen, water, sound and human contact. In addition, the environment contains non-essential, primarily system-alien factors, such as chemical additives to food and pollution of air, water and soil. The essential factors are indispensable to health. However, they must be carefully portioned out. Non-essential factors, on the other hand, may harm health; the best portion here is therefore nil. As regards the essential factors, technological development leads to underloading with respect to physical activity, causing hypokinesis (motor retardation), cardiac infarctions, obesity and disorders of the motor system as manifested in backache. Technological development leads to mental overloading caused by too much (superfluous) information through traffic and noise in the form of undesirable sound, and to mental underloading caused by a lack of varying stimuli from the environment due to the extreme replacement of a diversified natural environment by the dull sameness of the modern city and as a result of increasingly monotonous work. Technological development also leads to a medically acceptable level of non-essential factors often being exceeded by air and water pollutants, while dangers threaten from food additives. Zielhuis advocates that, as an increasing number of individuals fail to adapt to technology, technology should adapt to man. Genetic adjustment to an 'unnatural' environment along the lines of the survival of the fittest is unacceptable to the medical profession. Consequently, public health policy should be directed towards adapting the environment to human beings, particularly to the most vulnerable members of the species.

2.6. *The Biologists*

A deep impression has been made by the warnings given by biologists and conservationists. Their concern relates to the dangers that man may run by acting in a way that makes no allowance for his dependence on the natural environment that surrounds him.

The anxiety of biologists and conservationists about the adverse effects of growth of production and population met with a clear response from society around 1960. That is not to say that before then there had been no disquiet among some biologists and conservationists about the negative effects of the growth of production. The opposite is the case. However, the concern was before then felt by individuals, related to specific natural areas and did not meet with a universal social response.

As early as the end of the last century biologists were devoting attention to the problems of water pollution, especially in research for water supply and fisheries. This work was greatly encouraged by the publications of R. Kolkwicz and M. Marsson, in which a system was devised for indicating the degree of pollution of the water by means of biological indicators.[28,29]

In his *Fundamentals of Ecology*, E.P. Odum mentions a number of works that may be regarded as building blocks for the creation of ecology as an independent branch of science.[30] As the pressure exerted by biology grew above all through the advent of ecology – the study of the interaction of organisms and their environment – the works listed below may be viewed as early warnings against the adverse effects of disturbing natural equilibria through human activities. With his *Deserts on the March* (1935), Paul Sears ushered in a series of publications stressing the need for conservation of nature.[31] Two other important publications describing the evil influence of man's activities on his environment are *The Road to Survival* by W. Vogt[32] and *Our Plundered Planet* by F. Osborn,[33] both published in 1948. Also of great influence has been A. Leopold's *The Land Ethic* (1949),[34] and the essay *The Ecology of Man* published in 1957 by P.B. Sears.[35] The latter makes a distinction between cultural patterns that are properly adapted to the environment and those that are not. Sears concludes that many 'natural disasters' do not deserve that description, since they are in fact consequences of man's lack of comprehension in his dealings with nature.

With the work of Rachel Carson, the objections of biologists and conservationists to the way in which man effectuates his increase of production really register for the first time on a large scale. Rachel Carson's *Silent Spring*,[36] published in 1962, is universally regarded as a milestone in thought on the effects of man's productive activities on his environment.[37] Before her book appeared in print, Rachel Carson published a few chapters in the *New Yorker*. These articles led President Kennedy to have the Science Advisory Committee perform an investigation, resulting in the report *Use of Pesticides*, published in 1963. This report contained recommendations for a change in policy in the use of these chemicals. In the Netherlands, Rachel Carson's work induced the Biological Council of the Royal Academy of Sciences to devote a symposium in 1964 to the control of insect pests under the title *Life or Death*.[38] This symposium placed much less emphasis than Rachel Carson did on the adverse side-effects of pesticides, but stressed much more the possibilities of other means of control of pests, such as biological control. Rachel Carson points above all to the great dangers of the mass spraying of agricultural crops with persistent pesticides. The increase in scale in farming, together with the introduction of mechanization and the use of artifical fertilizers and pesticides, has tremendously enhanced the productivity of primary production.* Monocultures form an artificially optimized feeding ground for those parasites (like insects and moulds) that use the selected crop as food. The resultant rapid expansion of these parasites is from the ecological point of view a normal reaction to restoration of the natural diversity, but is regarded as 'harmful' by farmers. As a result of increasing resistance of species of insects to common insecticides, agents of ever-greater strength or different effect are necessary. The poisons may be absorbed via the food chain in the fatty tissue of animals species higher up the chain in steadily growing concentrations. There they accumulate because they cannot be broken down. This process occurs not only in land animals and birds, but also in aquatic animals, because the poisons are washed out into brooks, rivers and oceans. The process has already led to mass mortality of fish and birds. Man is at the end of the food chain – when he kills nature, he threatens his own continued existence.

The Dutch biologist D.J. Kuenen also emphasizes man's dependence on his environment.[39] Biotic communities are a very complex whole which man must treat with caution. All biological processes have a built-in feedback mechanism. Man wrongly thinks that he can switch this mechanism off; by artificial interference with nature he merely postpones the feedback. The blow will be the harder in the measure that the environmental burden is further increased by man. In Kuenen's opinion, Malthus is being proved correct; it has merely taken a little longer than he himself thought.[40] Man would do well to slow the growth of population and production himself and not wait for disasters to strike.

*It is striking in this respect that about 1800 approx. 80% of the working population in Western Europe was employed in agriculture, as against some 10% in 1960; moreover, in the same period the quality and diversity of the food package have increased greatly.

2.7. Three Economists

In the next chapter recent economic literature is discussed. However, it is useful to recall here that some economists joined the ranks of the critics of growth, though more on the strength of moral and psychological considerations than on the grounds of an economic analysis. In this section we shall mention only three highly authoritative writers, viz. J.S. Mill, J.M. Keynes and J.K. Galbraith. Their works contain a number of pronouncements which may not give pride of place to the effect of the growth of production on the environment but nevertheless very clearly and outspokenly doubt the utility or the possibility of unlimited growth.

Not quite rightly, economists have today acquired rather an image of champions of indiscriminate maximization of production. This stems from the fact that most practising economists are employed on the one hand to defend the interests of firms which, as a result of the occurrence of external effects, only partly coincide with the public interest, and on the other hand for attainment of the objectives of economic policy. Among these objects, economic growth has acquired considerable priority since the Second World War; as has been described above and will be further explained in Chapter 5, the concept of economic growth is misused in this connection.

Of course, during its development economic theory has mainly concerned itself with the problems around the production and distribution of goods and services. After all, until recently production was the most important way of providing the scarce goods and services that are necessary to meet man's existing wants. However, some of the great thinkers in the field of economic theory had an interest in society extending beyond the economic problems of their time, and demonstrated in their writings that they were able to relativize the utility of the growth of production and consumption. Thus John Stuart Mill proves to be an avowed opponent of the endless pursuit of growth. The echo of his remarks in the chapter 'Of the Stationary State' in his *Principles of Political Economy*, published in 1862, still resounds in our day.[41] Here Mill rejects the state of progress advocated by many of his predecessors and contemporaries and makes a well-argued plea for a stationary state of society. According to Mill, the economist who studies the movement of growth cannot be satisfied with merely tracing the laws of that movement, since growth is not in its nature unlimited. One cannot escape the question: Towards what goal are we tending? Economists will most probably nevertheless always have realized that the increase of wealth is not boundless and that therefore at the end of what they term the progressive state lies the stationary state. Mill is of the opinion that this ultimate goal – the stationary state – has long been in view. The reason it was not reached long ago is that the goal itself flies before us as the result of our constant thirst for improvement. Mill believes that the stationary state cannot be avoided in the long run. He taxes the economists of his day with identifying everything that is economically desirable with the progressive state; in that case prosperity does not mean high production and a good distribution of wealth, but merely a rapid increase thereof. Next Mill quotes Malthus' ideas on population growth, and concludes from them that even in a growth situation prudential restraint on population is indispensable, to prevent population growth from outstripping the increase of capital, and the lowest classes of society from reaching the lowest possible standard of living. Mill believes that the struggle to progress in material terms which people wage together and against one another is not the natural and most desirable lot of mankind; he prefers by far a situation in which, while no one is poor, no one desires to be richer, nor has any reason to fear being thrust back by the efforts of others to push themselves forward. He thus states that he is indifferent to the kind of economic progress which excites the congratulations of ordinary politicians, namely the mere increase of production and accumulation. Only in less developed countries is growth a necessity. In industrially advanced countries there is only economic need for a better distribution of wealth. For the latter, a stricter restraint of population growth is an indispensable means. Embroidering on the theme of population growth, Mill makes the following comments. Assume, he says, that the increase in productivity can in fact keep up with population growth. Even then there is no reason to consider such growth desirable, for the population density necessary for enjoying the advantages of co-operation and of social intercourse has already been attained. Greater density will have an adverse effect on the development of people's characters, even if they are adequately clothed and fed. Neither the individual nor society can manage without a certain degree of solitude and without contact with nature. What satisfaction can be derived from a world from which the spontaneous activity of nature has vanished, in which every rood of land capable of growing food for human beings is brought into cultivation, in which every flowery waste or natural pasture is ploughed up, all quadrupeds or birds which are not domesticated for man's use are exterminated as his rivals for food, every hedgerow or superfluous tree is rooted out and in which there is scarcely a place left where a wild shrub or flower could grow without being eradicated as a weed in the name of improved agriculture? 'If the earth must lose that great portion of its pleasantness which it owes to things that the unlimited increase of wealth and population would extirpate from it, for the mere purpose of enabling it to support a larger, but not a better or a happier population, I sincerely hope, for the sake of posterity, that they will be content to be stationary, long before necessity compels them to it.'

There are two reasons why I have reproduced at such length John Stuart Mill's view of the undesirability and impossibility of unlimited (gross) growth of production. Firstly, to show that the great thinkers of economic theory were already wondering at an early stage of the Industrial Revolution – the starting point of the growth of production as we know it now – where growth should finally lead. Secondly, to remind the reader that for the 'classical economists' population growth was not a given fact as it was for the economic schools that came later. It seems that the reason for this remarkable difference must be sought in the fact that since around 1900 the growth of productivity in the industrialized countries has increasingly outstripped population growth. Or, in other words, population growth in these countries did not form so great a social problem in the first half of this century as in the days of Malthus, Ricardo and Mill.

This situation has now drastically changed. The fear voiced by John Stuart Mill a century ago has become a reality: the dense masses of people jammed into the urban agglomerations of the world mean a new form of poverty. Population growth and production growth together have ensured that the limits of the capacity of our environment have been exceeded in a qualitative, quantitative and physical sense. This manifests itself as a new scarcity, and that is how people feel it. The increase in this new scarcity goes on outside the market, making measurements of the problem very difficult. But, in my opinion, population policies should play an important part in tackling these problems.

In the foreword to his *Essays in Persuasion*, J.M. Keynes writes that he is profoundly convinced that the economic problem, the problem of want and poverty and the economic struggle between classes and nations, is nothing but a frightful, transistory and unnecessary muddle. According to Keynes, writing in 1931, the Western world now has the resources and the technique – if we could create the organization to use them – capable of reducing the economic problem which now absorbs our moral and material energies, to a position of secondary importance. 'Thus the author . . . hopes and believes that the day is not far off when the Economic Problem will take the back seat where it belongs, and that the arena of the heart and head will be occupied, or re-occupied, by our real problems – the problems of life and of human relations, of creation and behaviour and religion'.[42]

Although economic theory recognized the adverse effects in the production and consumption of goods and services at quite an early stage, it cannot be said that economic literature before the 1960's gave vigorous impulses towards awareness of the serious nature of these effects for human environment. The authors who did in fact do so will be discussed in Chapter 3. In the context of this chapter only one more name should be mentioned, viz. that of J.K. Galbraith.

Galbraith's *The Affluent Society*[43] is without doubt a remarkable book, which has also had considerable effect outside the circle of economists. However, the book does not deal directly with the undesirable effects of production and consumption on man's environment, and concepts like social costs and external diseconomies, doubtless known to Galbraith, are not mentioned. The book is more of an argued criticism of the primacy of private production and the consequent arrears in the most essential collective facilities. The quintessence of the ideas in *The Affluent Society* is the macro-economic application of the doctrine of diminishing marginal utility. With an increasing national income per head, the marginal utility of additional production falls. Conventional theory states that the pronounced expansion of the package of goods produced is not accompanied by any economic criterion in accordance with which it can be said which goods are more useful and which are less useful to man. This statement springs from the repudiation by economic theory of the possibility of comparison of interpersonal utility. According to Galbraith, two obvious facts are overlooked here. In the first place, some things are acquired before others. It is logical to assume that the more important things come first. In the second place, the individual's wants deserving of the epithet 'urgent' must originate within himself. If production is to increase, the wants must now be effectively contrived. In the absence of the contrivance, the increase would not occur. This means that, since the demand for this part of production would not exist were it not contrived, its utility or urgency, without contrivance, is zero. If we regard this production as marginal, we may say that the marginal utility of present aggregate output, without advertising and salesmanship, is zero. According to Galbraith, the economists who measure the gross national product wrongly make no allowance for the difference in utility of the component parts. The utility of collective services such as education, police, city cleansing and road-building, in which evident arrears have arisen, must be considered greater than the utility of a great deal of 'nonsensical consumption' furnished by private firms.

Although Galbraith does not deal directly with environmental deterioration, some of his arguments are close to the problem of social costs in our environment caused by the increasing production and consumption of goods and services. Thus, in particular, the remarks on the diminishing utility of the increasing production can appropriately be related to the question of the relative scarcity of and the relative preferences for produced goods on the one hand and the 'goods' of our environment, which are difficult or impossible to reproduce, on the other. However, in anticipation of Chapter 5, it may be remarked that, in my opinion, criticism of the fact that in compilation of the gross national product no allowance is made for the difference in utility of the various goods is not correct. The System of National Accounts does not in principle lend itself to measurement of factors like utility and consumer's surplus. Nevertheless, *The Affluent Society* has given an impulse to the criticism of growth that should not be underestimated.

2.8. Increasing Urgency of the Environmental Problem through Increase of Scale and Acceleration of Rate; Worldwide Effects

Recently the voices drawing attention to the ecological drawbacks of the growth of production have met with an increasingly wide response. People are becoming aware that the growth of the package of goods and services measured in national income is not in itself economic growth, since above all the sacrifices of the quality (and the quantity) of the environment not measured in national income are increasing hand over fist and assuming a form that is objectionable or even frightening to many. Such people consider that as a result the growth of production is an imperfect criterion of the growth of welfare. The latter is reflected in the public discussions in a strange but characteristic escalation of the concepts used in economic theory. Goods are called material welfare. The concept of welfare, used in the theory to designate the subjective satisfaction that we derive from the scarce goods and services, is given the name 'well-being'. The concept of well-being has come to take pride of place in the discussions on whether mankind is gaining or losing by the present development of production. These discussions are being conducted with growing vehemence. The opening of a malodorous factory close to a populated area is no longer applauded. There is a tendency now not to announce new industrial establishments proudly but rather to prepare them in silence. On the other hand, there is a growing urge on the part of the population to participate in decisions on the establishment of industry and road-building.

From the literature quoted in Section 2.4 it emerges that the occurrence of adverse effects in production is as old as our civilization and is perhaps inherent in it; the Dutch biologist M.J. Adriani may be right to speak of a tragic conflict between culture and nature.* These adverse effects did lead in the past to criticism of, for instance, working conditions and domestic hygiene, but – apart from a few exceptions – did not lead to doubt about the utility of further increasing production. In recent decades, such doubt has in my opinion taken root among large sections of the populations of industrialized countries.

There are two reasons for this:

(1) the drastic change in the relative scarcity of the quantity and quality of the goods and services produced on the one hand and the quantity and quality of the 'environmental goods' (the environmental functions) on the other; and

(2) the increase in scale of the adverse secondary effects of production and consumption on our environment and the acceleration of the speed at which they are happening.

The first point will be further considered in the following chapters.

The second point – the increase in scale – plays a part that must not be underrated in the public's view of the environmental question. The pollution of soil, water and air as a result of production and consumption in the industrialized world has assumed alarming proportions. It is general knowledge that the number of particles introduced into the atmosphere by industry, aircraft, and other factors, is increasing greatly, which may endanger the earth's heat economy. Natural biotic communities are being destroyed on a large scale. This is a result of deforestation and reclamation of land and the removal of oxygen from and the poisoning of water. The latter manifests itself in the disappearance of life from the rivers, big lakes and estuaries. A similar development is in danger of occurring in the oceans. These are threatened by oil, the dumping of chemical waste, persistent pesticides and heavy metals. Many plant and animal species (e.g. the whale) have died out in recent years or face annihilation. The increase in population and urbanization leads to dense and extensive conglomerations of human beings. Noise in our communities is increasing rapidly so that more and more people are being exposed to an objectionable and often even harmful noise level.

In comparison with earlier times there are three obvious differences with respect to the undesirable secondary effects of production activities: the increase in scale, the omnipresence and the speed with which

*In a lecture on 12 June 1970 in The Hague.

impairment of the environment proceeds. Formerly, side-effects like air and water pollution and noise nuisance had only local influence, while effects threatening cultivation, such as erosion, developed slowly. As a result of the rapid increase in pollution and the tremendous increase in its scale, this phenomenon has now acquired another dimension and the term 'environmental crisis' has come to be used. Many people have become scared of disasters.

The worldwide nature of environmental pollution outlined above will play a part in the determination of a point of view within international agreements. Further, it may play a role in the valuation of environmental goods by the authorities, when they are fixing shadow prices (discussed in Chapter 4). The next pages, therefore, discuss some of the possible worldwide effects and their possible consequences.

To get a better understanding of the likelihood and possible magnitude of disasters occurring on a world scale, the Massachusetts Institute of Technology organized a symposium in July 1970 attended by some fifty 'environmental specialists'. The results of this Study of Critical Environmental Problems (SCEP) are recorded in the report *Man's Impact on the Global Environment*.[44] The principal conclusions of the report are outlined below, with an occasional reference to other literature.

This report states two possible ways in which life on earth may be seriously endangered as a result of environmental pollution: by changes in the climate and by the disturbance of ecosystems. The disturbance of ecosystems may relate to the ecology of the oceanic environment and to changes in the great terrestrial systems. The authors of the report are very cautious about drawing conclusions and making definite pronouncements. As the report expressly states, the necessary data were fragmentary or contradictory and in some cases completely unavailable, despite the fact that the conference had been preceded by a year of extensive preparation of background material, most relevant data being freely accessible. The report thus gives probabilities, not certainties. The problems of radioactive waste were left out of consideration.

The atmosphere is a relatively stable system, in which a nearly perfect equilibrium exists between the solar radiation absorbed by the planet and the heat emitted by the earth. A reduction of the available energy of only 2% could lower the mean surface temperature by 2°C and produce an ice age. The fact that no wider fluctuations occur in our climate is the best evidence that the complex system of ocean and air currents, evaporation and precipitation, surface and cloud reflection and absorption form a complex feedback system for keeping the global energy balance nearly constant. As minor a disturbance as a thunderstorm releases the energy equivalent to many hydrogen bombs. Man cannot possibly hope to intervene in such a gigantic arena. However, in reality man does intervene, because he can – without intending to do so – reach some leverage points in the system.[45]

All combustion of fossil fuel produces carbon dioxide (CO_2). Since 1958 the content of CO_2 in the atmosphere has been steadily increasing at 0.2% per year. Half of the CO_2 produced by man stays in the atmosphere and causes the above increase in concentration; the other half goes into the biosphere and the oceans. Around the year 2000, if the present development continues, the concentration of CO_2 will have increased by 18% (from 320 ppm to 379 ppm). This might result in an additional increase in the earth's surface temperature by 0.5°C. A doubling of the CO_2 might increase mean annual surface temperatures by 2°C. Such a future climatic change would have incalculable consequences.

From natural sources, such as sea spray, windblown dust and volcanoes, large amounts of small particles enter the troposphere. Man adds to this a – provisionally – smaller quantity of particles. However, he does introduce significant quantities of sulphates, nitrates and hydrocarbons. The residence time of particles in the troposphere ranges from six days to two weeks, but in the lower stratosphere micron-size particles may remain from one to three years. Particles influence the heat balance of the earth both by absorption and by reflection of the radiation of the sun and the earth. The extent of the effect of particles introduced into the atmosphere by man is not known. It is not even possible to determine whether the changes brought about by particles will result in a warming or cooling of the earth's surface.

Just as little is known about the influence of aircraft contrails. In view of the greater sensitivity of the stratosphere (longer residence time of particles and photochemical processes) the report expresses genuine concern about the stratospheric flights of supersonic aircraft.*

Since the amount of carbon dioxide in the atmosphere is partly dependent on the biomass of forest lands, which serve as a reservoir, widespread destruction of forests could have serious climatic effects. Finally, an increase in arid and desert areas as a result of population growth or overgrazing may introduce dust particles into the atmosphere and thus influence the climate.

In discussing the possible ecological effects on a world scale, the

*As the reader will know, the American project for a supersonic transport (SST) was stopped, since it could not be demonstrated that this would not have any effects on the stratosphere. The Franco–British Concorde is now in scheduled operation. The Russian 'Concordski' is in limited operation.

SCEP report begins by stating the following facts. Man produces more than a million different kinds of products that eventually end up as waste. We are mobilizing many materials at rates greater than the global rates of geological erosion and deposition, great enough to change their global distributions. We are using now more than 40% of the total land surface and have reduced the total amount of organic matter in land vegetation by about one third. What we now need is an estimate of the ecological demand, a summation of all of man's demands upon the environment, such as the extraction of resources and the return of wastes. Only in this way can man's impact on the biosphere be assessed. The activities that produce ecological demand – agriculture, mining and industry – have now an estimated integrated rate of increase between 5% and 6% per year; the annual rate of population increase is 2%.

We must realize that almost all potential plant pests are controlled naturally, that most vegetables, fruits, berries and flowers are pollinated by insects, that commercial fish are still almost entirely produced in natural ecosystems, that vegetation reduces floods, prevents erosion and air-conditions and beautifies the landscape. In addition, fungi and minute soil animals work jointly on plant debris and weathered rock to produce soil. Natural ecosystems cycle matter via green plants, animals and decomposers, thus eliminating waste. Organisms regulate the amounts of nitrates, ammonia and methane in the environment. On a geological time scale, life regulates the amount of carbon dioxide, oxygen and nitrogen in the atmosphere. Finally, natural ecosystems also serve important recreational and aesthetic needs of man.

Some of these services will cease only when life is virtually annihilated; many others are easily impaired. However, these losses are gradual and progressive without discrete steps of change. The gradual attrition of natural systems results from most types of environmental pollution and thus measures the overall impact of man upon this environment. The health and vigour of ecological systems are easily reduced if: (1) general and widespread damage occurs to the predators,* (2) substantial numbers of species are lost, or (3) general biological activity is depressed. Most pollutants that attack life influence each of these three processes. Of these substances, special mention may be made of DDT and related persistent pesticides, mercury and other toxic heavy metals, oil and nutrients.

The use of pesticides creates new pests as a result of the destruction of the predators that kept the original 'pests' under control. DDT is not

*A predator is any animal organism that feeds on other live animal organisms. Predators form the crux in the feedback mechanism that maintains the natural equilibrium.

easily soluble in water, but adheres fairly well to particles of dust. In this way it is distributed all over the earth by the wind. By way of rain and rivers some of the DDT and other chlorinated hydrocarbons enters the oceans, where it accumulates in marine organisms.[46] No data are available on the concentration and the effects of DDT in the oceans. It is, however, known that DDT residues in mackerel caught off California often exceed the permissible tolerance levels for human consumption and that the reproduction of some game fish is threatened.

Mercury and many other heavy metals are highly toxic to specific life stages of a variety of organisms, especially shellfish. Most are concentrated in terrestrial and marine organisms by factors ranging from a few hundred to several hundred thousand times the concentration in the surrounding environment.

According to a very approximate estimate, 2 million tons of oil are introduced into the oceans every year. Very little is known about the effects of oil on marine life; the present research results are conflicting. Potential effects include direct kill of organisms through coating, asphyxiation or poisoning, plus destruction of food sources of organisms and the incorporation of sub-lethal quantities of oil products into organisms, resulting in reduced resistance to infection or in reproductive failures.

Eutrophication means over-fertilization of the water, principally with phosphorus and nitrogen. Eutrophication leads to an excess of organic matter that decomposes, removing oxygen and killing fish. According to the SCEP report, particularly the estuaries and the coastal waters are being increasingly eutrophied. This forms a serious threat to the marine environment, since many fish species have their nursery grounds here.

The above shows that the possibility of disasters threatens. These may assume a more than local character; it is even not impossible that they will be felt all over the world. It is with this catastrophic possibility that the study made by D.L. Meadows' team for the Club of Rome concerns itself. The relevant publication, *The Limits to Growth* (1972), is considered in Chapter 3.

2.9. Action Groups against Loss of Natural Species and against Pollution

It is evident from the preceding survey that warning voices against the continued growth of production are gaining in strength. There is no doubt that these warnings are being increasingly heeded, and that many people are firmly of the opinion that growth summons up serious objections and dangers. At the same time, however, most people want a higher real income, and there are indications that these desires are located precisely in highly polluting sectors like that of the motor car and holiday air travel. Weighing the growth of production against preservation of the environment's functions is in part an allocation problem. As the reader will be aware, according to welfare theory the optimum situation is obtained when the weighing process is performed in conformity with the preferences of the individuals. However, in the case of the environment, the difficulty occurs that these preferences are not evident from their market behaviour. As a kind of substitute for the revelation of preferences on the market one could take the manifestation of these preferences by action groups. The phenomenon of the environmental action group has acquired considerable proportions.

As an example, the advent of action groups in the Netherlands is very briefly outlined below, followed by a short sketch of the appearance of action groups as a possible substitute for the expression of preferences where these cannot be expressed via the market. Developments in the Netherlands do not differ from those in other industrialized countries. Initially a number of groups, operating independently of one another, come into being. After a few years these groups are combined or coordinated, and recognition by the authorities follows. As a result of this, influence on policy grows, but incapsulation also takes place. The latter leads to a second generation of action groups, which adopt a more fundamental approach to the environmental problem. In addition, the more lasting solutions of the environmental problem are emphasized, calling for recycling, durable consumer goods geared to repair, less mobility of persons, smaller distances for goods transport, smaller-scale, less intensive agriculture for a better possibility of survival of plant and animal species in the cultivated countryside, energy conservation and the spread of solar energy. The latter elements are above all brought strongly to the fore in the opposition to the commercial application of nuclear energy, which is dealt with separately in Section 2.10. There, after a survey of the problems involved in nuclear energy, a short sketch is given of the course of events in a number of highly industrialized countries.

The phenomenon of the action groups for the protection of nature and the environment arose in practically all industrialized countries in the sixties and seventies, the period in which alarm at the effects of continuing growth of production penetrated to large sections of the population. However, long before then there had been people in various parts of the world who gathered together to distribute information on and counteract the decline of plant and animal species and the pollution of water, soil and air that were already occurring even then. Thus the impairment of nature by reclamation and other activities led in 1906 to the founding of the Association for the Preservation of Places of Natural Interest in the Netherlands. This association was able to save a number of nature areas mainly by buying them up. In 1909, the Netherlands Association against the Pollution of Water, Soil and Air was set up, followed in 1937 by the Liaison Committee for Protection of Nature and Countryside. It was above all the latter committee which, after the Second World War, by its struggle against land consolidation, road-building, military training grounds and the expansion of industrial estates, shifted the emphasis from the securing of individual sites to the preservation of a differentiated natural environment for the whole of the Netherlands and to the initiation of well-considered physical planning. In hindsight such associations may be designated as 'action groups *avant la lettre*'.

One of the first groups in the Netherlands to oppose directly the external effects of industry was the Association against Air Pollution in and around the New Waterway Area, founded in 1960. (The New Waterway Area is the largest industrial region of the Netherlands; it contains the port of Rotterdam, which is one of the biggest in the world.) In 1971 it changed its name into the Association against Environmental Deterioration. One of the achievements of this association was to have firms shut down in situations of severe smog and noise nuisance. For instance, the ethylene plant of Gulf, built in 1970, was closed for several months in 1971.

The Provo movement in Amsterdam in the period from 1964 to 1967 attracted international attention. Part of this provocative protest clearly related to the impairment of the environment – notably the urban environment – as a result of the rising production and consumption of private goods. The white bicycles plan, presented as an alternative form of transport to stop private cars from ruining inner cities, has become famous. The agitation against the establishment of petrochemical industry in the area of the North Sea Canal, especially Mobil Oil, partly on account of the anticipated air pollution, was one of the first of its kind inside and outside the Netherlands. The Provo protests were further directed against the siting of big office buildings in the centre of Amsterdam, with the resultant depopulation of that centre, and against compulsive consumption.[47]

In 1965 the National Association for Preservation of the Wadden Sea was founded. It opposed the reclamation of this shallow sea between the Dutch mainland and the Frisian islands, the construction of dams extending to those islands and the laying of pipelines for the discharge of polluted water. Feelings have run particularly high both nationally and internationally with respect to the problem of discharging waste water from the potato flour and strawboard factories in that part of the country. Admittedly, construction of what is popularly known as the 'filth pipe' will eliminate the stench that has been plaguing the population of East Groningen for almost a century,* but in turn it will impair the quality of the water in the Wadden Sea. There is good reason to fear that as a result the birthplace of many species of fish and crustaceans will be irreparably harmed.

Today some 400 action groups[48] are operating in the Netherlands on a permanent basis; that is to say, this number does not include those action groups that have been set up for one specific project. There is regional and national coordination. A survey held by the *Rotterdamsch Nieuwsblad* in January 1971 among the inhabitants of the Rotterdam region revealed that 1% of the population were active members of an action group, 12% showed their dissatisfaction in some manner or the other (e.g. by signing a petition or taking part in a demonstration) and 85% were entirely or usually in agreement with the protests of action groups against dirty and dangerous firms.

Internationally, too, collaboration is taking place between action groups. For instance, the opposition of the action groups in Switzerland, Germany, France and the Netherlands is coordinated against the heating of the Rhine and its far-reaching pollution with salts (which harm agriculture), with biodegradable organic substances (which lower the oxygen content) and with persistent organic substances, heavy metals and PCBs (which accumulate via food chains and, inter alia, are the cause of the impending destruction of the seal population in the Wadden Sea area). There is serious concern about the quality of drinking water. Some 20 million people depend on the Rhine for their water supply. In the summer of 1977 the action groups of the Rhine riparian states organized a demonstration consisting of a cycle ride down the Rhine. In various towns along the route press conferences were held, at which information was furnished on the consequences of pollution of the Rhine which, despite the construction of treatment plants and discussions between the governments of the riparian states, continues to increase.

Another example is the collaboration between the action groups of Denmark, Germany and the Netherlands in the protection of the Wadden Sea area. The Wadden are threatened among other things by

*See p. 25.

impoldering, drilling for oil, pollution with persistent substances from the Rhine that penetrate the Wadden Sea by way of a coastal current, the establishment of petrochemical and other industry, discharge of untreated waste water and recreation. The Wadden Sea, which is regarded as one of the most important estuaries in the world, derives its importance above all from its function as a birthplace for fish and a foraging ground for birds of passage.

Of particular international importance is the World Wildlife Fund, whose aim is to protect threatened species of animals from becoming extinct throughout the world. In this endeavour the emphasis has increasingly come to fall on preservation of the natural environment – the habitat – of animals and plants, since realization has grown that only in this way can the survival of the species be guaranteed. The question of how the functions which wildlife performs for man can be quantified in economic terms or evaluated in some other way is also receiving the particular attention of the Dutch branch of the World Wildlife Fund (the Netherlands National Appeal).[49]

The activities of these action groups bring in their train a number of specific theoretical problems. Some of these relate to the functioning of a democratic system, for instance the question of the extent to which extraparliamentary actions are permissible and fruitful, and the degree to which the authorities must or may make allowance for such activities. We are not concerned with such matters. Our problem, to which we shall return in the course of this study, is how people's preferences are expressed. In the case of goods and services going via the market, this occurs 'automatically'. For the subjects spend their income in a manner that is deemed to correspond to their preferences. In that sense market prices reflect actual wants. But in the case of the environment this mechanism is inoperative. Nature is not traded via the market. The preferences are expressed in a political process in which nature is sacrificed or spared (as a rule the former is more frequent than the latter). This political process is of course the resultant of opposed interests, views and preferences, and for this reason it is difficult to derive from the decision-making anything about the individual preferences. Now the point is that the action groups express something of these preferences.

However, having said this, it has to be admitted that it is rather meaningless. After all, there are no scientific methods for measuring the intensity of these preferences. In actual fact they are not weighed against other desiderata, such as a higher real income in the traditional sense of the word. Surveys on the subject are not necessarily decisive, since the actual optional behaviour of people may differ from that which would be consistent with the way in which they complete questionnaires. Further, it is justified to assume that different people have different preferences; weighing these preferences between individuals presents a particularly tricky problem which cannot be solved by 'scientific' points of departure.

The matter is further complicated by the fact that sometimes we are concerned not only with simple preferences of the individual but also with political judgments of a much wider scope. In a number of cases action groups are not only motivated by concern for the environment but also reflect ideological preferences. In such cases the protests are directed not only against the establishment of a factory which will form a burden on the environment, but also against capitalism, or against a government whose composition and policy leave much to be desired in the view of the protester. In these actions a call for radical social reform sometimes resounds, and with it strong ideas about other people's wants.

The latter is very clearly the case with the actions under ideological direction, as with student protests, for example. These protests occasionally invoke the ideas of Marcuse,[50] who argues that man has lost his freedom through industrial capitalism; he has become the slave of the consumer goods imposed upon him. In this reasoning only revolutionary action can break the chains of slavery and restore the real needs. In other words, a distinction is made between the actual wants and the deeper, real needs of man. Marcuse is rather vague about these real needs, but they certainly include fewer consumer goods and more nature, peace and quiet, fresh air, and so on. We are concerned here with a normative judgment of a political nature, closely bound up with religious and spiritual criticism of growth (see Section 2.3). Marcuse is no hedonist; he does not proceed from what people actually want, but from what they would want if they were free in the special meaning that Marcuse attaches to that word. Whether this reasoning is true or not, it is, in my opinion, clear that those who adhere to it form a complication in an empirical attempt to establish people's wants. For their opinions as might emerge from surveys do not concern the environment as such but the whole social context. For this reason it also becomes more difficult to draw conclusions from the actual operations of some action groups.

Although in my opinion it is certain that the behaviour of the action groups demonstrates a change in valuation by the public – more preference for the preservation of nature and less preference for an increasing real income in the traditional sense of the word – the quantification of this shift in values encounters the theoretical difficulties mentioned above and discussed in greater detail in the chapters that follow. In fact, this is one of the crucial problems of this study.

2.10. Opposition to Nuclear Energy

The opposition to the commercial application of nuclear energy developed a good deal later than that to other activities threatening the environment. For, although nuclear energy has already been in commercial use – albeit on a small scale – since the beginning of the sixties, the protests against it did not start until the plans for considerable expansion of nuclear power plant construction became known. In the United States that was around 1970, in Western Europe and Japan about 1973.

Within a short time the protests assumed more violent forms than had been customary in actions against the construction of certain roads or the establishment of industrial concerns. There are various reasons for this. The main one seems to me to be the rigid attitude of those authorities and industrialists who are well aware of the relationship that everyone senses between energy supply and the level of production and consumption. Now that the long-predicted depletion of oil and natural gas has come within the time horizon of larger groups of people, it is realized with a shock that something has to be done, and done quickly, if production is not to stagnate in the near future as a result of a deficient energy supply. Many people are of the opinion that the expected gap can be filled in coming decades only by nuclear energy and that the latter must be got going quickly to obviate social chaos as a result of stagnating production.

In this argument an inadequate distinction is made, according to me, between level of production and growth of production, whether consciously or unconsciously. Many advocates of nuclear energy do not seem to realize that by stabilization of production in respect of a growth situation a considerable breather is created that can be used for carrying out programmes of energy conservation and research into less controversial forms of energy. Many opponents of nuclear energy create the impression of being unaware that unless production growth is checked the introduction of fast breeder reactors is difficult to avoid. In my opinion this point receives insufficient attention in the discussions. It will be further explained in Section 2.11.

Other reasons can be given for the escalation of campaigns against nuclear energy. For instance, the various governments do not seem very keen on a broad discussion inside and outside parliament. The decisions on the construction of nuclear power stations and regeneration and enrichment plants and on the storage of radioactive waste are not taken on the basis of parliamentary discussion, unless great pressure has been exerted. This brings nuclear energy within the discussion about the quality of the decision-making on the direction that technological development is to take; decisions on this subject have far-reaching social consequences. In this discussion the following questions play a part. Do the decisions on the introduction of complex technologies in fact fall into the hands of technocrats because members of governments and parliaments with insufficient technical knowledge allow themselves to be guided too much by the judgment of technical advisers who are often at the same time the leaders of the new projects? Are drawbacks played down and alternatives not seriously considered (including a zero alternative)? Does democracy as a result default in one of the most important social decisions: the choice of alternative technologies, and is that the reason for the increasingly hard attitude of action groups? Some make mention of a general dissatisfaction with the largeness of scale and complexity of the production structure; this dissatisfaction is said to come to a head with nuclear technology. According to this view many people have the feeling of living in a world dominated by technocracy, with a size of scale which is beyond one's powers of comprehension and which summons up feelings of impotence, fear and alienation.

The special nature of the threat to the human environment by nuclear energy also plays a part. True, the chance of accidents is probably a small one, but the consequences may be very great. The multiplication of very small by very big is regarded as an impossible task, but nevertheless we are obliged to form an idea of the result of this calculation in order to appraise our circumstances of life. Further, radioactivity is regarded by many people as a mysterious, stealthy evil. There is invisible radiation to which one *might* have been exposed. The consequences manifest themselves years later in the form of diseases from which one can die in great agony, or in harm to the health of children or grandchildren whom the victims of today will not even know. The uncertainty and the ethical problems which this calls forth are probably the reason why the churches have also come to participate in the discussion on the commercial use of nuclear energy.

Nuclear energy is a capital-intensive technology. The question is whether its introduction is all that favourable in the light of present-day unemployment, which has a structural component. Would it not be better to opt for the introduction of more labour-intensive but less controversial methods for solving the energy problem, such as energy-saving and solar energy? In my opinion it is already justifiable to ask this question for the industrialized part of the world, but it is even more cogent for the developing countries, with their big surpluses of relatively cheap labour. Through these considerations unions and Third-World groups also become involved in the discussion on nuclear energy.

Nuclear power stations have to stand somewhere, but nobody wants them as his neighbour. This leads to the question whether a risk for a few people is ethically more acceptable than a risk for a large number of people (decisions are taken by a majority!) and brings up the discussion on nuclear energy at regional political level as well. Some regions reject the establishment of nuclear power plants on the strength of their inhibiting effect on other activities that are irreconcilable with the safety standards that have to be observed in the vicinity of these plants.

Furthermore, there is the link with nuclear weapons that peace movements bring into the discussion on the use of nuclear energy for power generation. Beyond this lies the fear of the rise of authoritarian forms of government. Nuclear power stations call for a large-scale set-up, and energy is an essential good. These factors, combined with the possibility of causing considerable accidents, make nuclear power stations an extremely vulnerable element in society. Fear of terrorism may lead to drastic screening, to people being banned from certain jobs, as in the German *Berufsverbot*, and bypassing of parliament as regards access to the technical details of the various plants.

Finally, the fact that both provision of energy requirements by nuclear energy and other solutions to the energy problem call for very high capital investment has led to an either–or situation. In other words, as a result of the limited nature of the resources, a choice in one direction excludes a choice in another direction. The latter point is above all of great practical importance. Large sums of money were invested in research into and implementation of nuclear technology at a time when this was hardly objected to. This acts like a flywheel: by far the greater part of research funds for the development of new sources of energy still goes to the development of the application of nuclear energy; the sums voted for the encouragement of energy-saving and the use of solar energy are insignificant by comparison. A change may now be observed in this. However, it is to be doubted whether this will occur quickly enough to give the development of solar energy and its introduction into our society a real chance.

All the facts have probably led to the involvement of many, often very different groups in the discussion on nuclear energy and to the escalation of the protests to the violent street-fighting that took place in 1977 in Brokdorf, West Germany, and Creys-Malville, France.

2.11. The Energy Problem and Growth of Production

I shall try, below, to place the arguments for and against the commercial application of nuclear energy against the background of continuing cumulative growth of production and stabilized production respectively. The consequences of continuing growth will be extended *ad extremum* in this. For, although there are proponents of growth who say that production will have to be stabilized in the long run, the moment at which that ought to happen is moved further into the future all the time by these same proponents. A striking example is presented by the course of events in the North Sea fishing industry. It has been known for many decades that the increase in engine capacity of fishing vessels and the refinement of catching techniques cannot continue indefinitely, since this will ultimately lead to depletion of the fish stock. However, the moment at which a halt had to be called to growth was repeatedly put off. And even now that the powers of reproduction of the herring population have been reduced to 20% of the original level,[51] governments and the fishing industry seem unwilling or unable to give the fish stock a chance to recover, with all the predictable consequences of this failure to act. The effects of the point of view presented below on continued growth of production are here carried to extremes, because the present author doubts the realism of those who argue that growth should be checked, but only in ten, twenty, or thirty years' time.

Some people are of the opinion that it is not possible to halt growth as long as there are still possibilities of improving productivity. This is a very sombre view. It would mean that, if a majority of the population were to opt for a set of measures (energy-saving, environmentally acceptable, smaller-scale) that would lead to stabilized production, on the strength of the conviction that in this way undesirable risks of nuclear energy would be avoided (or the survival of plant and animal species and of man would be secured), this wish cannot be granted. In other words, our society would be totally uncontrollable on the point of regulation of the level of production. This view seems to be the basis of the energy scenarios prepared by official bodies. These all proceed from the production growth of 3 to 4% per year now desired by governments. As a result, information is withheld from the community regarding the possibilities of supplying energy in a situation of stabilized production, while that very information is required to test the assumption that the population is not in favour of stabilization of production.

The preferences for various sets of produced consumer goods and environmental goods (including safety) cannot be measured.* But if we are to arrive at a reasonable decision on important matters like the introduction or not of nuclear energy by feeling our way, then, at the very least, alternatives will have to be worked out with regard to the

*Cf. Chapter 4.

most important factors determining the need for introducing nuclear energy. These include, in any case, the level of production and consumption.

Practically all advocates of nuclear energy fail to take into consideration a programme that could lead to stabilized production. They base themselves on the growth rate of 3 to 4% per year desired by governments and business. It is expected in this assumption that the demand for oil and gas will exceed the supply within the foreseeable future (of the order of fifteen to twenty years). If no measures are taken now this will lead to a stagnation of production, with all its dreaded consequences.

In this reasoning it is rightly assumed that a positive relation exists between the growth of production and an increase in the consumption of energy.*[52] Through differences in production structure and consumer habits this may differ from country to country, but in any country the differences in the relation over time are small; until now, as a rough average, 1% production growth has been accompanied by 1 to 1.8% growth of energy consumption. This ratio can be improved in two ways: firstly by more efficient use of energy, and secondly by a change in the pattern of consumption and production in the direction of energy conservation. This second way amounts to checking economic growth, as we shall see below, and therefore does not fit into the pattern advocated by proponents of nuclear energy, who base the need for this form of energy on a continued growth of production.

Technical energy-saving measures may include better insulation of homes, the introduction of total energy systems, linking urban heating and electricity generation and developing more economical cars and domestic appliances. As a result of this the ratio is permanently improved, but owing to the cumulative nature of growth it gives only temporary relief, as the following numerical example may show.

At an energy-production elasticity of 1.5, 4% growth of production is accompanied by 6% growth of energy consumption; if the elasticity declines by 33% as a result of a vigorous energy-saving programme, energy consumption increases by 4%, other things being equal. In the first case the doubling period of energy consumption is twelve years, in the second eighteen years. In a cumulative growth process, more is consumed in each last doubling period than in all preceding periods

*A discussion is going on about the form of this relation. The form of the relation in time is, of course, important. However, all that matters here is that the relation is positive: an increase in production leads to an increase in energy consumption. This point is not disputed in the discussion.

together. This considerably accelerates the depletion. This acceleration is mitigated by conservation of energy, but not eliminated. At 6% growth of energy consumption, oil and gas reserves will be depleted within thirty to fifty years.[53] If we put this at exactly forty years, we postpone depletion by only ten years if we lower the rate of growth to 4%. (If production were stabilized this postponement would be one hundred and twenty-five years.) In a period of rapid introduction of energy-saving programmes an increase in production can even be temporarily accompanied by a reduction in energy consumption. But this situation can only be of short duration. There is a limit to the energy-saving possibilities,* and as soon as this is reached (or even before) continuing growth of production pulls energy consumption up along with itself again.

As stated, the relation can also be improved by changes in the pattern of consumption and consequently in the pattern of production geared to this. This comes down, among other things, to more cycling, less driving, less heating of rooms, more wearing of sweaters, eating fewer summer vegetables in winter, using fewer single-trip plastic goods and applying less artificial fertilizer and pesticides, with as probable pendant, for instance, a small petrochemical industry, smaller-scale farming and more repair and maintenance work. Measures taken in these directions have recently been designated as 'selective growth policy', because activities are selected which require little energy, which are environmentally acceptable, and which, on balance, almost always require permanent use of more labour. But in fact this means checking growth, also in the traditional sense, for growth is always obtaining more of the goods that one wishes to have,** and – to judge by human behaviour – these goods doubtless include energy-swallowing desires such as holiday flights, high room temperatures, heated hallways and unrestricted use of the private car. 'Selective growth' evidently amounts to a reduction of the supply of goods and services which the consumer holds in high esteem and is therefore a misleading term (the gain made in environmental goods and safety does not enter into consideration in growth rates and in the traditional appraisal of the result of growth). In all probability substantial use of this policy will lead to a considerable check on

*There is a highly theoretical possibility in which growth of production is not accompanied by increase in energy consumption. This would be the case if a contest between discoveries of new energy-saving technologies (plus sufficiently swift application of the latter) and growth of production were constantly won by the first factor. It seems highly improbable to the present author that this situation will ever occur continuously. Moreover, it seems more sensible first to bring about this situation than to anticipate it.

**Cf. Chapter 5.

production as traditionally measured in a country's national income. Improvement of the relation by this kind of change in behaviour therefore does not fit into the growth pattern which forms the point of departure for advocates of nuclear energy.

Switching to coal also has great drawbacks. At the growth of production desired by governments coal reserves are adequate for about one hundred years.[53] The enormous quantities that will then have to be burnt (the amount required doubles every ten to fifteen years) may have disastrous climatic effects. As the reader may know, approximately half of the CO_2 emission is buffered in the chlorophyll of the vegetation on land and the phytoplankton of the oceans, while the other half enters the atmosphere.[54] The latter half is the possible cause of the feared effects. The chance of this will increase when the buffer becomes saturated, since at that moment the increase in the CO_2 content in the atmosphere is accelerated. Furthermore, strip mining will severely impair the landscape. The efficiency of treatment of the sulphur dioxide content, depending on the kind of coal, lies between about 75 and 90%. Despite expensive and often energy-intensive techniques, the SO_2 content in the air will therefore exceed the critical values if growth continues. In addition, dust emission will increase, very large quantities of coal will have to be transported and large quantities of waste will result.

The alternative energy sources (chiefly solar energy) will with continuing growth only be able to supply a small part of the energy requirement, and then not before the year 2000. It is uncertain whether energy via nuclear fusion will ever be operationally feasible.

In view of the above, in a situation of continuing growth it is considered wise to expand the number of nuclear power stations as quickly as possible. In addition, most proponents of nuclear energy regard the introduction of fast breeder reactors as necessary at the earliest possible date, because these are expected to produce from a given amount of uranium over 40 to 50 times as much energy as the conventional reactors.[55] Estimates of the ultimately extractable amounts of uranium (and thorium) are much more uncertain than those for fossil fuels, but the economically extractable reserves of uranium – provided that they are used in breeder reactors – are in all probability much greater with an increasing energy price. The advocates of nuclear energy generally assume that, if fast breeder reactors are used, the reserves are sufficient to supply the energy requirement in a growth situation for several hundred years, but for only a few decades if conventional nuclear reactors are used. According to them it is not necessary to start worrying at this stage about the situation after the year 2200.

Advocates of nuclear energy strongly emphasize the clean nature of this form of energy, since no air pollution occurs as it does in the combustion of fossil fuels. Further, according to them nuclear energy is sufficiently safe. The chance of a serious accident in a power plant in which a large quantity of radioactivity is released as a result of the reactor core melting (loss of coolant accident) is estimated at once per million reactor years.*[56]

In my opinion doubt can rightly be cast on many of the arguments of proponents of the commercial application of nuclear energy. The increased probability of proliferation of nuclear weapons and the occurrence of an authoritarian form of government, the increase in the existing dissatisfaction with the largeness of scale, complexity and vulnerability of the production structure, and the greater risks for this and coming generations, are objections which in my opinion cannot be removed. The former aspects will not be considered further here. They seem more a matter of the extent of someone's belief in the ability of society to play with fire without accidents, and in the adaptability of people, than a problem regarding which more or less verifiable arguments can be weighed against one another. The latter aspect – the risks associated with the fissile material cycle – will be considered below.

As on the previous pages, the point of departure will be a growth

*The best-known study of risks of such a serious accident is the Rasmussen Report WASH 1400 of the U.S. Nuclear Regulatory Commission (the draft report was published in August 1974, the final report in October 1975). In this report the chances and consequences have been calculated for a major accident with a light water reactor without signs of ageing. The draft of the Rasmussen Report contains a graph from which the chance of fatalities in a serious reactor accident can be read off. Because it was desired to compare the risk with the risk of road accidents etc. only the numbers of immediate deaths were plotted in the graph. To illustrate the increase in the chance of an accident in a growth situation a point in the graph at which there are 100 or more deaths has been proceeded from below. According to the Rasmussen Report this occurrence has a chance of once per million light water reactor years. The consequences depend on the weather, the wind direction, population density and evacuation facilities. In the worst case, with a calculated chance of one in a thousand million light water reactor years, according to the final Rasmussen Report for the American situation the short-term consequences would be 3300 deaths and 45,000 cases of illness. The long-term consequences are stated as follows. In a period of 10 to 40 years after the reactor accident: 1500 fatal cases of cancer and 8000 cases of thyroid diseases per year. The calculated genetic effects in the first generation after the accident are 170 per year. In following generations this number slowly decreases.

For a nuclear reactor in a densely populated area like the western part of the Netherlands, G. van Dijk and W. Smit arrive at higher figures. In the worst case a million casualties are to be expected there, of whom 140,000 to 350,000 killed at once, depending on the evacuation and shielding facilities. The most characteristic aspect of a major reactor accident is the long-term effects as a result of contamination of the ground. Irrespective of weather conditions, existing norms mean that a stretch of land 20 kilometres wide and several hundred kilometres long becomes unusable for human occupation and industrial and agricultural purposes for years.

situation, since otherwise the arguments pro and con are placed in a different context and as a result can no longer be compared with one another. One argument from the preceding section is thus not answered: the need for rapid introduction of nuclear energy in order to fill the gap to be expected between supply and demand in a growth situation within the foreseeable future. However, insofar as the forecasts of the supply of fossil fuels are correct, this argument seems irrefutable. I know of no estimates from the literature that satisfactorily prove that, with the expected shortage of fossil fuels, sufficient other means become available (for instance a combination of permanent sources of energy and energy-saving) at a price that makes continuing growth of production on a world scale possible. But for greater certainty about this more research may be needed. A suggestion is made for this below.

The opponents of nuclear energy argue that nuclear energy is not clean and is above all unsafe. Nuclear power plants also discharge heat, and even more per unit of energy supplied than conventional ones. The calculations of the chances of accidents published so far relate exclusively to the functioning of the reactor and even then are highly theoretical in nature in the sense that in the absence of sufficient historical data they have been built up from calculations for parts of the reactor. In this approach the human error that may occur with a reactor in full operation can never be exactly determined.*[57] The advocates of nuclear energy generally assume that there is roughly one chance of a serious accident per million light water reactor years. Assuming that this is correct, with the 200 power plants now in operation one accident per 5,000 years somewhere in the world may be expected. In the event of nuclear energy making a substantial, say 50%, contribution to energy supply, 5,000 power stations will be needed on a rough estimate, which therefore means that an accident per 200 years may be expected (assuming that the 200 power plants in operation now supply 2% of the world energy requirement). At the growth rate now advocated, 15 years later a nuclear accident must be expected every 100 years, and 15 years after that every 50 years, and so on.** It should be added that the chance of accidents in breeder reactors is considered to be greater, that the conse-

*Attention is drawn to this point, inter alia, in a publication by the Union of Concerned Scientists, in which a large number of points of criticism of the draft and final Rasmussen Report are listed, such as errors, limitations and incorrect assumptions in the calculations of both the chances and the consequences.

**Of course, the development described above is only hypothetical. Reserves of uranium are too limited to allow of such growth for the system of light water reactors. Continuing with nuclear energy calls for a switch to the fast breeder reactor. For this type such detailed estimates of the chance of accidents have not been made. There are, however, theoretical indications that the chance of accidents and the consequences thereof are considerably greater. Cf., inter alia, D. Hayes, op. cit.

quences of an accident with such a reactor are more serious, and that – in the view of the objections to the use of coal in continuing growth – nuclear energy will quite soon have to meet more than 50% of the energy requirement.

A second objection (in addition to the partial disregarding of human error in the power station) which also weighs much more heavily in the case of the breeder reactor, is the failure to include in the calculation of chance the potential dangers of the rest of the fissile material cycle: enrichment, transport, regeneration and above all storage of the radioactive products of fission. Depending on the radioactive isotope, the latter have to be stored from hundreds to hundreds of thousands of years in a turbulent world full of incalculable people. No solution has been found as yet to this problem. Thought has been given for instance to storage underground, say in salt domes. But according to some geologists, in view of the inadequate knowledge of geological mechanisms, the stability of an area in the past is not enough of a basis to make it possible to establish the future stability of that area.[58] Making shafts and galleries and depositing heat-emitting radioactive material may have unexpected effects.

The third and most fundamental objection is the impossibility in principle of overall risk calculations, because risks are also caused by societal events such as blackmail by terrorists. Calculations of the chances of future events are based on an extrapolation of the past, on the assumption that past events will repeat themselves in the same way in the future. Firstly, with the rapid introduction of nuclear energy that is necessary if growth is to continue, insufficient reliable experience can be acquired with the various parts of the fissile material cycle in order to use the past as a 'sample' by means of which pronouncements on the future can be made. Secondly, extrapolation of the past to a distant future is impossible as regards societal events since the future of society is anything but an identical repetition of the past. It is therefore out of the question on theoretical grounds to make overall risk calculations for the use of nuclear energy.

Finally, in the presentation of the results to a public often untrained in calculation of chance one sometimes forgets to add that, when chance calculations indicate that an accident may be expected once per so many years, that accident may occur tomorrow. However, most people seem to be anything but reassured by the presentation of very small chances of accidents, probably because they feel intuitively what the true facts of the case are. In view of the possibly serious consequences of reactor accidents and the irreversibility of their effects, large groups of the population will have to live in constant fear if nuclear energy is applied on a substantial scale. This fear has already been found among the population in areas with a sizeable chemical industry (such as the Netherlands' Rijnmond).

On the strength of the above arguments, some opponents of nuclear energy conclude that a safe policy with regard to energy supply must start with stabilization of the level of production in the northern countries, where the greater part of the depletion of energy reserves occurs and where the volume of production is more than enough to supply the population with an acceptable package of consumer goods. With stabilized production, the period of depletion of oil, gas and coal is extended by a factor of five to twenty (at a given growth rate and level of consumption the factor increases according as the remaining reserves are greater and thus is much higher for coal than for oil and gas).[53] This factor can be raised to at least seven to twenty-eight by investing in energy-saving measures; these will also pay for themselves in business terms (quite apart from environmental considerations), if the prices of fossil fuels continue to increase as expected. Such investment would create a breathing space of several hundred years without the dangers of nuclear energy and with a considerable reduction of the environmental risks entailed by burning up fossil fuels at full speed. This breather can then be used for the development of applications of solar energy. Although the theoretical possibilities of the latter are known, practical application has only just begun, its spread into society will take several decades at least and the sums that have to be invested in it are of the order of 5% of national incomes for several decades.[59] Assuming that the use of nuclear fusion is undesirable on account of the objections to radioactive waste (which also apply in this case), or impossible by reason of technical difficulties that are too great, we shall sooner or later have to change from a stock quantity to a flow quantity. On account of the long development and lead times, it seems better not to delay this change until the moment when the stocks are depleted: if the time then remaining should prove to be too short, disintegration of society may be the result. Finally, there is also the familiar argument that it is a pity to burn up hydrocarbons, having regard to their many other possible uses.

Every choice that is made with regard to energy supply affects every member of the public. We are therefore confronted with a collective (and thus political) problem for which a collective decision must be taken. This means that as many people and groups as possible must share in that decision. For that purpose, all available choices must be given maximum publicity. This entails working out the various possible solutions to the expected energy shortage, with an approximation of the probabilities of the results and with a complete list of their specific advantages and disadvantages. In my opinion it is only in this way that deliberate and well-considered decisions can be taken with regard to the energy problem.

The above amounts to preparing various scenarios, from which a choice can then be made in a political weighing process. Making such scenarios considerably increases society's degrees of freedom, for by this means society will acquire an instrument for appraisal in precisely those decisions that will affect its own living conditions for a long period ahead.

However, making scenarios is not without its problems. The difficulties start with the choice of points of departure. These will not have to tie in with the political feasibility of this moment, at least not exclusively. For many are of the opinion that this feasibility is determined by the limited room for manoeuvring of governments with their short time in office. By adjusting the scenarios to such narrow margins, continuation of the existing course of events is in fact already opted for *a priori*. Such a restriction implies, fundamentally, a very low degree of controllability of our society. What it boils down to is that one says in advance: 'Other points of departure may perhaps lead to something better or even much better, but they're out of the question.' In my opinion the energy scenarios prepared so far by official bodies all have this unspoken restriction. In effect, therefore, the ability of citizens to choose, in these circumstances, is likewise restricted.

Two factors mainly determine the volume of energy consumption: the volume and nature of production and consumption, and the efficiency of energy use. It is therefore self-evident, first of all to make scenarios for various growth rates of production and for various possibilities of conservation.

The desire of governments to have production increase in the coming period by some 3% a year – apart from the adverse effects which this has on the environment and energy supply – in all probability reflects the preference of the population. The first scenario should therefore start from a cumulative growth of production of 3% per year. The following questions must be answered in this context:

(1) What production structure and what pattern of consumption are expected in the coming period?
(2) What kinds of energy sources now current are required for that?
(3) What price developments are expected for these sources of energy, and when are shortages in the supply expected to occur?
(4) What conservation measures can anticipate these shortages?

(5) If conservation is not enough, what quantities of other sources of energy are then required (coal, nuclear energy, solar energy)?
(6) What are the environmental and risk elements of these?
(7) How will employment develop?

In view of the arguments adduced above, it is not impossible that in this scenario considerable shifts in sources of energy will occur with risk elements (nuclear energy) and environmental effects (coal). These effects cannot be viewed in detachment from other effects that the growth of production and consumption entails. For instance, on the strength of existing literature it may be expected that growth of production will bring in its train an inevitable increase in pollution and – as a result of an enormous expansion in the use of space and a highly intensified use of land in agriculture which are inherent in growth – disastrous effects on plant and animal species.[60] It is therefore a good idea to include in the growth scenario the expected effects on the quality of water, soil and air, on use of space and on plant and animal species. This should be done in two stages: firstly, the gross effect, and secondly, the net effect that remains after application of the elimination measures possible at acceptable cost, with an estimate of the required expenditure. Finally, the above questions may be asked *mutatis mutandis* for the natural resources required for 3% growth of production, or at least the most important of these.

If the feared effects do in fact prove to occur in the scenario, the same exercise should be repeated for a production assumed to be stable.

Such a scenario has been produced in broad outline, with the aid of data now known, in the report *Energiebeleid met minder risico* by Th. Potma.[59] The report is also known under the name 'Het vergeten scenario' (The forgotten scenario). This study presumes the maintenance of the present level of production and investigates what energy-saving measures are possible in the coming twenty-five years and what utilization of factors of production is required for this (the costs). The measures are, moreover, tested on their environmental acceptability; the use of nuclear energy proves unnecessary. On the one hand, the measures encroach only to a small extent on comfort now available (less use of private cars, a less rapid spread of some new domestic appliances, such as freezers and electric clothes driers), while on the other an increase in comfort is planned (more houses, more central heating, more water heaters), so that on balance the existing comfort remains more or less the same. Attention is drawn to long-term solutions for the energy problem, such as production of new types of fuel by electrolysis of water with the aid of solar collectors in regions of the earth which are not (or are no longer) suitable for other purposes, such as the deserts. The intention of the report is to investigate to what extent possibilities now known can be used to create time for the development of permanent solutions and their entry into society. For the year 2000, Potma arrives at 70% of the energy consumption in 1975 if all available possibilities are utilized; 8% is covered by permanent sources of energy (above all, sun and wind), so that in 2000 the use of fossil fuel is 62% of that in 1975. He estimates, very broadly, that if the package of measures is introduced, production remains about the same and employment increases.

The latter conclusion need occasion no surprise. Energy (like environment and natural resources) is a scarce good, replacing labour. Anticipation of expected future scarcity of these elementary goods calls for the use of factors of production, including labour and inventivity (just as obtaining any scarce good does). The present author has already drawn attention to this before.[61]

Potma gives a preliminary approach, which can certainly be worked out further, deepened and thus improved (notably as regards the quantification of those aspects concerning the environment and natural resources) in the way broadly indicated above, but it is one of the very few studies that opens the way to a safer future on the point of energy supply. It could be elaborated by institutions equipped for that purpose under the direction of a number of people involved in the problem without institutional ties who must be enabled to control the research in complete freedom. This independence seems of importance in order to give a better chance to solutions or lines of thought which might possibly come into conflict with points of departure now generally accepted. The sacrifice that is made here consists in not adhering *a priori* to the increase in the package of produced goods and services. For those who have followed the literature on energy, environment and natural resources during the last decade this sacrifice cannot come as lightning out of a clear blue sky.

2.12. Opposition to Nuclear Energy in Several Countries

In the *United States* public opposition became significant only as more orders were placed for nuclear plants in the late sixties. The first attack came when the question of routine radioactive emissions was raised. In 1971, emergency core cooling emerged as a focal point for opposition. By 1973, a variety of grounds – from safety to economics and waste disposal – formed the main areas for opposition.

The Rasmussen Report mentioned above gave rise to a long and extended discussion. There is considerable disagreement among scientists and engineers on both the estimated probabilities and the potential effects of an accident.

The risks inherent in the rest of the fuel cycle also came under attack. The prospects of a plutonium economy with annual inventories of 30,000 to 200,000 kilograms make it plausible that someone can lay hands illegally on a critical mass (5 kg is sufficient for an atomic bomb). In 1977, President Carter decided to postpone this extensive use of plutonium, but other countries just embarking on breeder reactors (and a plutonium economy) were not enthusiastic about that.

The disposal of radioactive waste is another point of discussion. Most fuel is now stored at reactor sites. The delay in the construction of reprocessing plants in connection with the dangers of plutonium makes a different approach to the storage problem desirable. Solidification in glass and ceramic material and storage in underground salt caverns has provisionally been abandoned in the USA. Interim storage in above-ground tanks was also dropped after serious leakage in 1974. Now the solution is being sought again in underground storage in former salt mines.

Although a number of initiatives to place a moratorium on nuclear plants failed in seven states, there is still a fair opposition which has a considerable influence on the growth of nuclear power in the USA. In 1976, only three plants were ordered, whereas three to four years before the number ranged between fifteen and twenty-five.

In 1973, the Government of the *Federal Republic of Germany*, with only 2,190 MW of nuclear plant in operation, published a programme with 50,000 MW for 1985. Mainly owing to strong opposition in 1975–77, this projection had to be changed into 30,000 MW. The first effective opposition occurred in May 1972, when the Supreme Court withheld the operating licence for a plant until various legal issues had been clarified. Much greater opposition arose in 1973 and 1974 to two other proposed plants. This led not only to various petitions and the formation of many local action groups, but also to two occupations of the site of the dual plant.

The result was that the construction licence was withdrawn and in January 1976 the court ruled that construction work should not start until the following November. By the summer of 1977 the work had not been initiated. In the meantime the court had ruled that the containment of reactors had to be strengthened before a licence could be given.

In 1976 similar actions, like site occupation and barricades, took place at sites in the north of Germany. This likewise led to a halt in the construction of two plants. The Government decided that approval for the building of further nuclear power plants would be withheld until a final decision had been reached on the disposal of waste.

In the *United Kingdom*, compared with other countries, there was little opposition to nuclear power for a long time. Nuclear plants were already built there in the fifties and sixties. The British types of reactors were not criticized like the American light water reactor.

However, in 1976 and 1977 opposition developed to an extension of the reprocessing plant at Windscale and the plan to accept spent fuel from other countries for treatment there. In 1976, a report was also published by the Royal Commission on Environmental Pollution which advocated postponement of a plutonium economy and the commercial application of fast breeders.[62] One of the Royal Commission's principal recommendations was that 'there should be no commitment to a large programme of nuclear fission power until it has been demonstrated beyond reasonable doubt that a method exists to ensure the safe containment of long-lived, highly radioactive waste for the indefinite future'.

In a White Paper[63] published in May 1977 as the Government's answer to the Commission's report, it is stated that the latter's proposition 'is bound to be the dominant factor in any process preceding decisions about further large-scale programmes, including any programme of fast reactors'. The Secretary of State for the Environment, Peter Shore, said that there would be some sort of public debate held before final decisions were taken on the proposed commercial fast breeder reactor.

In March 1977, British Nuclear Fuels Ltd sought permission to expand the reprocessing plant for irradiated fissile material at Windscale. The Government ordered a public inquiry, which was held between 14 June and 4 November 1977. Mr Justice Parker, seconded by Sir Edward Pochin and Professor Warner, heard the arguments for and against for 100 days. Together these constituted some 4 million words, making this the most extensive public inquiry ever to have been held on nuclear energy.

In February 1978, Parker ruled that the reprocessing of oxide fuel from British reactors is desirable, since otherwise the stocks that have to be stored with a growing number of nuclear reactors would become unjustifiably large. Expansion of the nuclear industry is considered necessary to meet the increasing demand for energy and to reduce dependence on imported energy. According to Parker the risks of an accident are likely to be containable within tolerable levels. Justice Parker considers that reprocessing must take place at Windscale on account of the existing plants and know-how. Reprocessing elsewhere would require additional transport of plutonium. He also considers the reprocessing of fissile material from other countries to be favourable, since this would relieve the pressure on countries without nuclear weapons to develop their own facilities. Absence of facilities in Britain would encourage proliferation. Parker further takes the view that the total amount of highly active waste from reprocessing UK and foreign fuel combined will contain only a fraction of the plutonium which would be contained in UK fuel alone if such fuel were disposed of without reprocessing.

In his considerations Justice Parker explicitly assumes that the demand for energy will increase, and apparently regards that as implicitly desirable, or at least does not see it as a factor for which the pros and cons must be weighed first and foremost when examining Windscale. The considerations proceed from the *a priori* assumption of continuing growth of energy consumption. The most fundamental question on the introduction of nuclear energy, namely, whether that growth is necessary and desirable, is not discussed but is implicitly answered in the affirmative. In this Parker makes not a legal but a political pronouncement of the first order. This seems to me to be a mixture of law and politics which harms both. Justice Parker's ruling was incidentally followed by a political pronouncement. On 29 March 1978, the House of Commons voted by 186 to 56 to extend Windscale so that 1,200 tons of fissile material per year can be dealt with. On 29 April, a demonstration took place on Trafalgar Square.

Between 1970 and 1975, opposition escalated in *France*, with demonstrations being held, a moratorium being urged in parliament and the media beginning to play an important part. In 1975, 2,200 scientists, including employees of nuclear establishments, signed an appeal against nuclear power. This had a powerful impact and strengthened the opposition. Incidents (bombs at a construction site, and a number of explosions at other plants) highlighted the risk of sabotage. Three referenda produced large majorities against construction in certain areas where plants were to be built. Owing to the demand for electricity in recent years being lower than had been anticipated, fewer plants will probably be necessary than the Government envisaged in 1973.

None of the early nuclear plants in *Sweden* aroused significant opposition. The nuclear programme received overwhelming support in parliament, and expansion of the number of reactors was recommended in 1972. However, opposition began to develop because of the debate in the USA and the views of the Swedish Nobel prizewinner Professor H. Alfvén. Environmental groups later opposed nuclear plants. A nationwide discussion was initiated by the Government and reports were published on such matters as future energy requirements, underground reactors and reactor safety.

Opinion polls showed a large majority of the population to be against any expansion of the nuclear programme. Many were in favour of energy conservation at the same time. An energy bill in 1975 included only two reactors at existing sites and was adopted in Parliament.

During the 1976 elections, the Social Democrats (in favour of nuclear power) were defeated by a coalition of the Centre Party and others. The Centre Party had been campaigning for years against nuclear power, and this issue seems to have tipped the balance in the elections.

Under the new government the plants under construction will be completed, but for new plants it will have to be demonstrated that a solution has been found for the disposal of waste and reprocessing. Sweden hopes to be able to generate electricity by utilizing wind power.

In the *Netherlands*, opposition grew in particular after the Government's Energy Memorandum in 1974, which mentioned the construction of three nuclear power plants before 1985. Environmentalists, scientists and politicians were active in this. In January 1976, the Government decided to postpone the final decision to build the three power plants mentioned above.

After the discussion on the power plants, the Government and Parliament were involved in the controversies about the sale of reactor vessels produced by a Dutch firm to South Africa and the extension of the ultracentrifuge project for the enrichment of uranium. The Government several times escaped a crisis on nuclear matters, which formed part of the election campaign in May 1977. In June 1977, the largest Protestant church in the country asked for two years' postponement of nuclear power and for a public debate. The discussion on the expansion of the ultracentrifuge project and on the terms on which enriched uranium could perhaps be supplied to Brazil continued into the spring of 1978 with even more heat.

In a report by the Club of Rome, 'Goals for Mankind',[64] published in March 1977, the gaps between desirable national and global goals were analysed. The Netherlands was mentioned as one of the most world-conscious countries, where the massive opposition to nuclear is considered as a positive point 'because it shows the concern for the environment and safety'.

2.13. References

[1]Central Bureau of Statistics, *Nationale Rekeningen, 1971*. The Hague, 1972.

[2]*Yearbook of National Accounts Statistics, 1969*. Volume II. New York, 1970, Table 7; *idem, 1971*. Volume III. New York, 1973, Table 7.

[3]*Miljoenennota 1970*. Bijlage 15: Nota over de inkomensverdeling, p. 8.

[4]Cf. J. Pen. *Harmonie en Conflict*. Amsterdam, 1970.

[5]Cf. W.W. Rostow. *The Stages of Economic Growth. A Non-Communist Manifesto*. London, 1960, p. 102, where, with GNP as the criterion, it is asked what the political consequences will be if the Soviet Union, through its higher growth rate, takes over first place in the world, economically speaking, from the United States.
[6]M. Miller-Sweeny and J.L. Miller. *Bible Dictionary*. New York, 1952.
[7]Cf. W.H. van Dobben. Het vegetatiedek van de aarde en de invloed van de mens daarop. In: *De Groene Aarde*. Utrecht, 1966.
[8]Quoted from W.H. van Dobben. Loc. cit.
[9]W.H. van Dobben. Loc. cit.
[10]T.Y. Kingma Boltjes. Stuurloos varen. *Water, Bodem, Lucht* 44, 1959, No. 3/4, p. 114.
[11]R. Arvill. *Man and Environment*. Harmondsworth, 1967, p. 28; B.A. Kwast and J.A. Mulder. *Beknopt Leerboek der Economische Aardrijkskunde*. Groningen, 1950, p. 162; and D.J. Kuenen. *Mens en Milieu*. Leiden, 1965, p. 11.
[12]V. Westhoff. Bodemerosie als bedreiging van de menselijke samenleving. In: *Natuurkundige Voordrachten*. Nieuwe Reeks No. 45, 1967.
[13]D.J. Juvenal. *Saturarum Libri*. Book III, verse 232 et seq.
[14]Martial. Book XII, poem 57.
[15]D. Erasmus. *Betoog over de Lof der Geneeskunde*. Translation by L. Elout. Antwerp, 1950, p. 23.
[16]T.Y. Kingma Boltjes. Stuurloos varen. *Water, Bodem, Lucht* 44, 1959, No. 3/4, p. 114.
[17]T.Y. Kingma Boltjes. Loc. cit., p. 115. Further see the above quotation from Erasmus.
[18]G.M. Trevelyan. *English Social History*. London, 1945, pp. 337, 492, 563, 579. Idem: *Illustrated English Social History*. Volume IV. London, 1952, pp. 13, 118.
[19]Cf. J.H. Clapham. *An Economic History of Modern Britain, Free Trade and Steel, 1850–1886*. London, 1932, p. 105.
[20]G. Diggle. *A History of Widnes*. Widnes, 1961. Quotation from W.J. Reader. *Imperial Chemical Industries, a History*. London, 1970.
[21]F.V. Raspail. *Histoire Naturelle de la Santé et de la Maladie*. Third Edition. Paris/Brussels, 1860, Part I (First Edition, 1857).
[22]S.E. Pronk and C.M. de Reu. De wet verontreiniging oppervlaktewateren en zijn betekenis voor het milieubeheer in Nederland. *Benelux Economisch en Statistisch Kwartaalbericht*, No. 1, 1972, pp. 25–37.
[23]L. Herber. *Crisis in our Cities*. New Jersey, 1965.
[24]A. Mitscherlich. *Die Unwirtlichkeit unserer Städte*. Frankfurt am Main, 1965.
[25]W.J. Bladergroen. Kinderspel. In: *De Wereld van de Kleuter*. Groningen, 1963.
[26]Ph.H. Fiedeldij Dop. Psychohygiënische factoren. In: *Criteria voor Milieubeheer*. Amsterdam, 1970.
[27]Cf. among others, R.L. Zielhuis. Manipuleren binnen een ecosysteem. *Wetenschap en Samenleving*, No. 21, 1967; and R.L. Zielhuis. Potentiële en reële ziekmakende factoren in het milieu. In: *Het Milieu van onze Samenleving*. Bussum, 1970.
[28]R. Kolkwicz and M. Marsson. Oecologie der pflanzlichen Saprobien. *Berichte der Deutschen Botanischen Gesellschaft* 26, 1908, p. 505 et seq.
[29]R. Kolkwicz and M. Marsson. Oecologie der tierischen Saprobien. *Internationale Revue der gesamten Hydrobiologie und Hydrografie* 2, 1909, No. 2, p. 126 et seq.
[30]E.P. Odum. *Fundamentals of Ecology*. Third Edition. Philadelphia/London/Toronto, 1971.
[31]P.B. Sears. *Deserts on the March*. Oklahoma, 1935.
[32]W. Vogt. *The Road to Survival*. New York, 1948.
[33]F. Osborn. *Our Plundered Planet*. Boston, 1948.
[34]A. Leopold. The land ethic. In: *A Sand Country Almanac*. New York, 1949.
[35]P.B Sears. *The Ecology of Man*. Oregon, 1957.
[36]Rachel Carson. *Silent Spring*. Cambridge (Mass.), 1962.
[37]Cf. also E.P. Odum. Loc. cit., p. 513.
[38]J.W. Tesch et al. *Op Leven en Dood, Problemen rondom de Chemische en Biologische Bestrijding van Plagen*. Wageningen, 1964.
[39]Cf. among others, D.J. Kuenen. Het recht van de mens op leefruimte. In: *De Rechten*

van de Mens. Leiden, 1968; and: Milieubehoud is zelfbehoud. In: *Mens contra Milieu*. Baarn, 1970.

[40]Cf. also E.P. Odum. Loc. cit., p. 514.

[41]J.S. Mill. *Principles of Political Economy*. London, 1876, p. 452 et seq. (First Edition 1862).

[42]J.M. Keynes. *Essays in Persuasion*. London, 1931, p. VII.

[43]J.K. Galbraith. *The Affluent Society*. London, 1958.

[44]C.L. Wilson et al. *Man's Impact on the Global Environment, Assessment and Recommendations for Action*. Cambridge (Mass.), 1970.

[45]Cf. also R.A. Bryson and W.M. Wendland. *Climatic Effects of Atmospheric Pollution*; and J.M. Mitchell Jr. A preliminary revaluation of atmospheric pollution as a cause of the global temperature fluctuation of the past century. In: *Global Effects of Environmental Pollution*. Dordrecht, 1970.

[46]See also G.M. Woodwell. Changes in the chemistry of the oceans: the pattern of effects; and B. Lundholm. Interactions between oceans and terrestrial ecosystems. In: *The Global Effects of Environmental Pollution*. Dordrecht, 1970.

[47]Cf. Provo, No. 2, August 1965, and No. 6, January 1966; and H. Mulisch. *Bericht aan de Rattenkoning*. Amsterdam, 1967.

[48]Figure stated by the Stichting Centrum Milieuzorg, Amsterdam, May 1973.

[49]R. Hueting. Moet de natuur worden gekwantificeerd? *Economisch-Statistische Berichten*, 21 January 1970; and W. van Dieren and M.G. Wagenaar Hummelinck. *The Capital of Nature*. (In preparation).

[50]R. Marcuse. *One Dimensional Man, the Ideology of Industrial Society*. London, 1964.

[51]A.A.H.M. Corten. Beschermingsmaatregelen voor de Noordzeeharing: te weinig en te laat. *Visserij*, June/July 1977.

[52]See, among others, V. Smil and T. Kuz. European energy elasticities. *Energy Policy*, June 1976, p. 171 et seq. A critique of this by L.G. Brooks with a reply by V. Smil and T. Kuz may be found in *Energy Policy*, June 1977, p. 162 et seq.

[53]W.M. de Jong and G.W. Rathenau. *The Future Availability of Energy to the Netherlands*. Working paper for the Wetenschappelijke Raad voor het Regeringsbeleid. December 1976. A survey and evaluation are given of the estimates of depletion periods of oil, gas, coal and uranium.

[54]Minze Stuiver. Atmospheric carbon dioxide and carbon reservoir changes. *Science* 199, 1978, p. 253 et seq.

[55]S.S. Penner and L. Icerman. *Energy. Volume I: Demands, Resources, Impact, Technology and Policy*. Reading (Mass.), 1974.

[56]A discussion of the Rasmussen Report may be found, inter alia, in: G.G. Eichholz. *Environmental Aspects of Nuclear Power*. Ann Arbor (Mich.), 1976, p. 646 et seq.; D. Hayes. Nuclear power: the fifth horseman. *World Watch Paper 6*. Washington (D.C.), 1976; R. Gillette. Nuclear safety: calculating the odds of disaster. *Science* 185, 1974, p. 838. See also G. van Dijk and W. Smit. *Kleine Kansen, Grote Gevolgen*. Boerderijcahier 7601. T.H. Twente, Enschede, 1976.

[57]Union of Concerned Scientists. *The Risks of Nuclear Power Reactors*. Cambridge (Mass.), 1977. A concise version and a discussion of this may be found in: Hugh Nash. Rasmussen Report is demolished by Union of Concerned Scientists. In: *Not Man Apart*. San Francisco (Cal.), February 1978.

[58]G. de Marsily, E. Ledoux, A. Barbreau and J. Margat. Nuclear waste disposal: can the geologist guarantee isolation? *Science* 197, 1977, No. 4303, p. 519 et seq.

[59]Th. Potma. *Energiebeleid met Minder Risico*. Report published by the Vereniging Milieudefensie, September 1977.

[60]See for this, for instance, *De Komende Vijfentwintig Jaar. Een Toekomstverkenning voor Nederland*. Wetenschappelijke Raad voor het Regeringsbeleid. Rapporten aan de Regering No. 15. The Hague, 1977.

[61]R. Hueting. Milieu en werkgelegenheid. *Economisch-Statistische Berichten*, 5 March 1975.

[62]Royal Commission on Environmental Pollution. *Sixth Report, Nuclear Power and the Environment*. London, 1976.
[63]White Paper from the Secretary of State for the Environment (Cmnd. 6820). Derived from *Nature* 267, No. 5610, 2 June 1977.
[64]E. Lasslo et al. *Goals for Mankind*. New York, 1977.

Further:

A System of National Accounts and Supporting Tables. New York, 1953.
The *Bible*
Plato. *Critias*.
Use of Pesticides. Science Advisory Committee. Washington, 1963.

Chapter 3

SOME PIONEER WORKS ON ENVIRONMENTAL DETERIORATION AND ECONOMIC GROWTH

3.1. A. Marshall and A.C. Pigou

The first approach to economic analysis of the environmental problem may be found in A. Marshall, who introduced the concept of external economies.[1] Admittedly, Marshall had in mind only the advantages that accrue to the individual firm through general industrial development, such as inventions and improvements in machinery, in processes and the general organization of the business, but nevertheless this concept contains the key to the economic analysis of environmental deterioration. The advantages referred to by Marshall are enjoyed by the entrepreneur without payment and outside the market. Thus in principle the step has been taken that in the production of goods and services effects may occur outside the market that can influence the conditions of production for others.

A.C. Pigou comes much closer to the concept of loss of function introduced in this study. He makes a distinction between social net product and private net product of a national economy.[2] These two net products diverge because costs and benefits originating from market relations outside the market fall to persons not directly involved in production. As an example of a negative divergence Pigou mentions the uncompensated damage done to surrounding woods by sparks from railway engines. In Pigou's theory not only can the production conditions of third parties be influenced outside the market but the welfare of private persons can also be affected directly in both the positive and negative sense.

We shall return to this in Section 4.2, where the concept of loss of function is compared with the concepts of collective good and external effect.

3.2. K.W. Kapp

It was remarked in Section 2.7 that economic literature before the 1960's gave no vigorous impulses towards awareness of the serious nature of the adverse effects that occur in the production and consumption of goods and services. This was in spite of the fact that at least one pioneering work presented the external effects of production as *the* central theme of economic development since the industrial revolution. However, this book, *The Social Costs of Private Enterprise*, by K.W. Kapp,[3] published as early as 1950, did not receive the attention that it indubitably deserves. The considerably revised and partly rewritten second edition, published in 1963 under the title *Social Costs of Business Enterprise*,[4] also met with little response. It was not until 1967, the year of publication of E.J. Mishan's *The Costs of Economic Growth*,[5] that the economic implications of environmental deterioration became a subject of interest inside and outside the circle of economists.

Kapp's work is remarkable in two respects: firstly because it anticipated by some twenty years the incipient discussion of the far-reaching consequences of environmental deterioration and the exhaustion of natural resources, and secondly through its frontal attack on the bases of economic theory.

The main theme of Kapp's book is the central place which, according to him, social costs occupy in the social system. Kapp defines the term 'social costs' as all direct and indirect losses sustained by third persons or the general public as a result of unrestrained economic activities.[6] He has explicitly in mind here all burdens emanating from productive processes that are passed on to third parties and for which private entrepreneurs are not held accountable. This differs from the more usual definition, in which business expenditure and the effects passed on to third parties are together taken to be social costs. It emerges from the book that Kapp's definition of social costs has to be interpreted very broadly, namely, as all the adverse effects – avoidable or not – of the organization of production. In addition to the consequences for environmental deterioration these include a number of other adverse effects of private enterprise that are listed below.

In his book, Kapp gives an extensive description of environmental deterioration and of the exhaustion of non-renewable and the destruction of renewable natural resources. He starts by listing the well-known effects of air and water pollution, such as harm to health, reduced yields in agriculture, effects on flora and fauna, accelerated corrosion of materials, difficulties in the preparation of drinking water and dangers to aquatic life through, inter alia, oxygen deficiency, poisoning and heating.

Next Kapp deals with the destruction of what he calls renewable resources as a result of uncontrolled competition in the utilization of these resources. Over-hunting, over-fishing, excessive timber-felling and exhaustion of the soil have led and still lead to the extinction of species and erosion of fertile land. The irreversible destruction of renewable resources is leading to an impoverishment of the world for coming generations. In this way, man is himself limiting his possibilities of further economic growth. Kapp rightly believes that the only possibility of protecting human beings as a whole against this disastrous destruction of their own possibilities of life is to keep exploitation of these resources within close limits, which are to be formed by generous minimum numbers of individuals per population of animal species per area and by minimum replanting of trees. Kapp does not go into the many other conditions that must be satisfied to maintain a stable ecosystem. These also include, for instance, abiotic conditions such as the quantity of nutrient salts, soil structure, ground-water level, degree of acidity and of humidity; these factors too may be disturbed by man, for instance, as the result of pollution.

Kapp further deals with the problems of non-renewable resources like oil and coal. As a result of cut-throat competition, great waste occurs in production, and here too no allowance is made for the consequences for future generations.

Mention is also made of the worldwide problem of the dangers of radioactive waste.

Finally, Kapp emphasizes the increasingly severe consequences that the phenomena of congestion have for the human environment in urban agglomerations. These are caused in part by the over-concentration of industry. In commercial decisions account is taken only of the financial advantages to the business in question, and the adverse effects are shifted to others.

Kapp mentions certain adverse effects of production under conditions of free business enterprise that are not part of environmental deterioration and exhaustion of natural resources. These include harm to health, such as industrial accidents and occupational diseases; the consequences of technological change in production, such as the drop in the value of capital goods, firm closures and the obsolescence of knowledge and skills; unemployment caused by this technological change and by the economic cycle; duplication of capital goods in the production of raw materials (for instance, in drilling for oil), duplication in transportation of goods and persons, in distribution systems for goods and in research by competitive firms, the government and scientific institutions, the result being the occurrence of considerable overcapacities and – as regards research – retardation of the progress of science; planned obsolescence in consumer goods and the promotion of styles and fashions, thus reducing the utility that could be derived from the use of scarce resources; the waste in advertising directed only against the competitor's product instead of towards information on one's own product; the psycho-cultural harm done to the public by aggressive selling that exposes them to constant pressure to buy new articles and impairs their pattern of cultural values; finally, the waste as a result of a multiplicity of brands and lack of standardization.

This list clearly shows that Kapp's definition of social costs is not only broader than the concept of loss of function but also broader than the concept of external effects.* Not only the effects of economic activities on the environment (losses of function) or on third persons who are neither buyers nor sellers (external effects) are considered, but in addition all the supposed defects – unavoidable or not – of the structure of private-enterprise production.

In my opinion, the particular merit of Kapp's list of the adverse effects on our society of economic activities is that here, for the first time in economic literature, the effects of our methods of production on the environment are brought forward for discussion extensively and thoroughly. On the other drawbacks of the production structure of private enterprise and the operation of the market mechanism put forward by Kapp an extensive literature, which Kapp largely disregards, already existed even in 1950. Thus, for instance, the analysis of non-full employment developed in the literature and the instruments used to deal with this are not mentioned. However, the latter drawbacks are largely outside the scope of the present study. It will merely be remarked here that these drawbacks would have been more serious if an attempt had been made to demonstrate that a different system works better. However, Kapp makes no such attempt.

Kapp argues that social costs have increased so greatly in volume and weight that the bases of economic theory are no longer applicable to social reality. I believe this conclusion to be wrong. For the subject matter of economic theory relates to the problem of choice that arises with the utilization of scarce, alternatively applicable means of satisfying classifiable wants. Environmental deterioration, for instance, means the advent of a new category of scarce goods, requiring that important choices be made. It is the community that has to make these choices. In the final instance the institutional framework will determine what the result will be in the fundamental conflict between on the one hand the quantity and quality of the goods and services produced and on the other the quantity and quality of our environment and the other natural resources.

*Cf. Section 4.2.

As regards the bases of economic theory, it is of no importance whether the choice of scarce resources for competing ends is achieved by individual subjects via the market mechanism or by the government by means of the budget mechanism. The subject matter of economic theory – the problem of choice with regard to scarce means – is universal and certainly not bound to a specific economic order, in this case private enterprise, in which supply and demand come about largely via the market. In particular, Kapp's attack on the work of L. Robbins is therefore, to my way of thinking, tilting at windmills.

It would have been better if Kapp had merely stressed that the relevance of the market mechanism decreases with the growing importance of such phenomena as advanced environmental deterioration and exhaustion of stocks of raw materials and energy. Kapp overlooks the fact that the market mechanism too always operates within a legal framework and that changes in that framework also form economic decisions, since they have consequences for the extent to which the functions of the environment on the one hand, and the goods purchased by business for the market on the other, become available to the public.

Kapp himself also underlines the necessity of what he calls social choice.[7] However, he sees a theory of social choice as something entirely new and as a replacement for a theory in which values, value judgments and individual valuations are beyond scientific enquiry and have to be accepted as given.[8] But this is not so. After all, the literature on public finance concerns itself in detail with the satisfaction of collective desires and with the causes of the constant increase in the extent of those desires. In this respect, the environmental problem too does not contain anything new. As regards the problem of choice, protecting the quality of water or of a nature area is not different in principle from maintaining a city orchestra, a public art gallery or a police force. In all these cases one has to choose to do without other goods.

The system of collective decisions advocated by Kapp already exists. Thus we repeatedly opt via our various authorities for, among other things, the qualitative level of our environment. The preceding chapters of this study have already emphasized the conflict that then occurs between the quality and quantity of our environment, on the one hand, and the quality and quantity of the goods and services produced which are now becoming available to us, on the other. Kapp does not discuss this fundamental conflict. The reason is probably that Kapp concentrates too much on the imperfections of production by private enterprise. In so doing, he overlooks two important matters. In the first place, the government can also cause losses of function in the environment, and indeed does so (road-building, damming of estuaries). In the second place, in the consumption of the goods also, environmental deterioration is caused on a large scale. Kapp fails to see that consumption is an extension of production, and that in the choice between, for instance, environmental goods and produced goods the consumer also plays an unmistakable part. There is an interaction of producers' and consumers' behaviour. Apart from the undeniable fact of the existence of industrial lobbies, of the pressure exerted by advertising on the public to keep up production, incorrect arguments regarding employment, etc., the fundamental conflict does not, in my opinion, lie between consumer and producer, as Kapp suggests, but in the contradictory desires of the consumer himself. That makes solution of the environmental problem more difficult than in Kapp's simplistic representation, in which the business firm acts as a kind of exploiter, loading the burdens of environmental deterioration on the shoulders of its employees, the consumer and society as a whole. In my opinion it is inconceivable in the social order of today that each of these categories would passively accept these burdens unless there were for those groups compensatory advantages in the form of products at a price considerably lower than if the external effects were to be included in that price. However, the fact that a cultural lag may exist between the public and governmental bodies with regard to measures of environmental protection will be discussed in Section 4.6.

Kapp proves to be an advocate of the institution of objective standards for human health. In itself this idea is a valid one. However, two comments should be made on it. In the first place, health is now no longer defined as the absence of disease and disablement, but as the presence of physical, mental and social well-being. It is not easy to base objective standards on this definition of health without bringing in the preferences with regard to the environment and other factors influencing well-being (good housing, for instance). In the second place standards exclusively directed towards health need not be ecologically sound standards.* Despite these drawbacks, standards will nevertheless have to be laid down for the increasing number of substances that threaten health and the environment and also for the quantitative and spatial aspects of environmental deterioration.

Kapp rightly points to the need for information on environmental deterioration. According to him the economist should embark on thorough research in close cooperation with scientific disciplines. Perhaps the present study may be regarded as a modest instance of what Kapp had in mind.

*See Section 4.7, pp. 144 et seq.

3.3. K.E. Boulding

In three articles,[9] K.E. Boulding comes to the conclusion that in the future the concepts of economic growth and national income will no longer have the slightest importance. The economy of yesterday and today, says Boulding, is to be interpreted as an open system. Input in the form of natural resources passes from a reservoir (the earth), regarded as inexhaustible and therefore non-economic, into the sphere of production and consumption (the throughput) and then vanishes as output in the reservoir. Of this flow only the middle part – the throughput – has so far received attention from economics. The volume of this throughput is roughly measured by gross national product.

The result of the whole process of input, throughput and output is that raw materials stored in concentrated form in the earth, after production and use, are diffused in disorderly fashion over the earth's surface; the energy stored mainly in fossil fuels and fissionable material (insofar as it is not contained in the product) disappears into space. Use of both natural resources and energy may therefore be interpreted as an increase in entropy. This process will not be able to continue indefinitely, because the reservoir earth is not inexhaustible. Supplies of natural resources and energy are being depleted, while the carrying capacity of the environment is being exceeded, which is reflected in increasing environmental pollution. As a result, man will be obliged to switch from an open to a closed system. In the latter, the output is again used as input, so that a cyclical process comes into being. The economic system of the earth may then be compared to that of a spaceship.

According to Boulding, the crucial element in the spaceship economy will be energy. For the cyclical process can relate only to raw materials, since energy that has passed into space cannot be recirculated. In other words, the energy stored in fossil fuels and fissionable material is irrevocably lost after use. On the other hand, the recycling of the used materials means reconcentration, the reduction of entropy; this calls for an additional input of energy.

Thus the spaceship economy depends on those sources of energy which, by human criteria, are inexhaustible and do not pollute to such an extent that the carrying capacity of the environment is exceeded. These are wind power, tidal power, geophysical energy, water power and, above all, solar energy. Boulding considers the possibility of producing energy by means of nuclear fusion – for which the base material is available in abundance – very slight. It follows from the above that the degree of utilization of these forms of energy is one of the most important factors determining the possible level of activities in a spaceship economy.

In the cyclical economy of spaceship earth the concepts of gross national product and economic growth fall entirely apart. The level of the throughput is no longer important, but rather maintenance of capital stock, interpreted as the state or condition of society and the people living in it. The fewer means required to maintain this capital stock, the better the economy is. This implies that the success of the economy must no longer be measured by as high a national income as possible but by the lowest possible national income. It is therefore better to speak of gross national costs, not gross national income. Gross national costs must logically be minimized.

In my opinion, Boulding's analysis is correct in principle. It seems irrefutable that, once the carrying capacity of the environment and the stock of natural resources are exhausted, the input of clean energy into a cyclical economy will be one of the most important factors determining the possible level of activities. It is highly probable that this level of activities will of necessity lie much lower than the current one. This means that, the further population and production continue to grow, the greater the drop will eventually have to be. Boulding's analysis in fact arrives at the same conclusions as the model approach by Forrester and Meadows to be discussed below.

3.4. E.J. Mishan

There are three reasons why Mishan's *The Costs of Economic Growth*[10] has been the first work by an economist to meet with a great response from both economists and the public. The first is because the unpleasant effects of the overburdening of the environment, against which biologists, among others, had already been warning for a long time, became increasingly obvious at the end of the sixties; in other words, the time was ripe for such a work. The second is because Mishan aimed with literary force of conviction at the direct consequences of technological development for the daily life of the man in the street. The third is because Mishan makes a highly personal attack on the spirit of the present time, an attack which incidentally is concerned only in part with the environmental problem.

Mishan deals with a large number of adverse effects of economic growth in a highly industrialized society, economic growth being simply interpreted as the percentage increase in real national income. Unlike the approach followed in the present study, he does not attempt to start from the subject matter of economists so as to arrive at a further analysis of the concepts of economic growth and national income. Mishan in fact describes the costs of the growth of production of goods and services. The costs that Mishan has in mind relate to the external effects, i.e. to the sacrifices of the production and use of goods for which no allowance is made in the decisions of producers and consumers.

As in the case of Kapp – who, strangely enough is not mentioned, any more than Boulding is – the effects on the environment form only a part of the adverse effects of the growth of production discussed. However, Mishan launches no attack on the bases of economic theory or on the system of private enterprise. While according to him the large-scale occurrence of external effects is the result of an unrestrained commercial attitude of society, he points out – in my opinion rightly – that the activities of both producers and consumers are conducted within a legal framework that determines the extent to which the external effects occur; this legal framework is ultimately determined by the public. Like Galbraith – who *is* mentioned – Mishan criticizes the emphasis that Western society lays on stepping up production, of which an increasing part can be achieved only by creating wants for new articles and the simultaneous encouragement of dissatisfaction with products in use. Among the disadvantages created by this state of affairs Mishan includes not only environmental deterioration but also the influence on our cultural pattern. The latter facet, where, in my opinion, he arrives at a number of highly disputable conclusions, will not be discussed here.

Mishan begins his book with the statement that all matters that can be measured statistically receive disproportionate emphasis in economic policy. Imports, exports, the state of the balance of payments, the degree of employment, monetary reserves, the price level and production can be expressed in figures. Their indices are closely followed, and fluctuations in these indices form front-page news in the financial press. Of all the indices, the production index occupies the most important place. Things are well with the economy when production increases. In addition, exports are regarded as crucial, especially on account of the state of the balance of payments and the position of Britain in the world.

According to Mishan, all this concern about the current economic quantities is highly exaggerated. Thus the need to export is evoked by the desire to import. And imports consist largely of luxury goods that are anything but vital and are also caused to some extent by the fact that the British population has become too large for the country to supply it with the necessities of life. The need to export can be largely eliminated in the short term by restricting imports of all kinds of goods that are not strictly necessary. Although Mishan does not say as much, it follows from his reasoning that in the long term the urgency of importing and exporting can be done away with by population control.*

Of much more essential importance to the happiness of ordinary people than the trend of the above indices are the external effects brought into being by production aimed purely at the pursuit of profit. These are increasing hand over fist and are not expressed in figures. Of the effects occurring in the environment, Mishan lays great stress on the congestion of the cities by traffic, suburban sprawl rendered possible by the private car, the noise nuisance caused by airports and the reduced quality of beautiful historic towns and of unique landscapes as a result of mass tourism. In addition Mishan makes more incidental mention of the pollution of beaches by oil and sewage, air pollution and the eradication of wild fauna by uncontrolled use of pesticides. Numerous things once freely available to the population have become scarce, according to Mishan. The rich heritage of natural beauty is being systematically destroyed for ourselves and for posterity. To halt this state of affairs strict legislation is necessary, and economic policy must be directed towards transferring resources from private production to the restoration of a good environment. This will succeed only if there is a new view of the purpose of life. Awareness of the changes occurring in the environment is a prerequisite for that. Mishan regards his book above all as a contribution to that process of awareness.

When external effects occur, the market price of a good is no longer a reliable indicator of its marginal value to society. The social value, i.e. the value remaining after subtracting from the market price the estimated value of the damage inflicted on others by producing and consuming the good, may not only be well below the market price, it may even be negative. As is known, in optimal allocation of the factors of production the marginal costs are always equal to the price of the product. When negative effects occur, for an optimal situation production must therefore be contracted until the social value of the good is raised sufficiently to become equal to its marginal costs. The same result can be arrived at by raising the production costs by means of paying compensation to the victims or by making eliminatory provisions. In this way the private marginal-cost pricing rule is transformed into the social marginal-cost pricing rule, whereby in all sectors production is required to be such that prices are equal to social marginal cost.

Application of this rule requires the external effects to be valued in

*This reasoning is already moving in the direction of smaller autonomous production units, the solution to the environment problem advocated by the group of scientists that compiled *Blueprint for Survival*, to be discussed below.

terms of money. Mishan rightly says that this is mostly difficult or even impossible. Demonstrable financial damage is usually diffuse and hard to identify statistically. The immediate unpleasant effects must be measured in money by the victims themselves, with the drawbacks mentioned in Chapter 4 of the present study.* But, Mishan shows, even if the external effects can in fact be expressed in money, this does not in itself lead to an unambiguous optimum. The optimum that comes into being in a scheme in which the originator compensates the victims may differ from the optimum that comes about when the victims pay the originator. Economics cannot say who must compensate whom, for that is a distribution problem. It is a matter of what society as a whole and the law think fair.

Consequently, so as to arrive at a better environment, Mishan is of the opinion that amenity rights should be instituted. Just as the rights of private land may not be infringed, these amenity rights would have to be protected by the courts. No man could be forced against his will to absorb the noxious by-products of the activity of others. In a number of cases, says Mishan, compensation is not necessary and a higher level of welfare can be attained for all the parties concerned by the institution of separate facilities. As an example Mishan mentions dividing a beach into parts where transistor radios could and could not be used. Mishan's separate facilities are apparently reducible to good physical planning.

Mishan approaches environmental deterioration mainly as a problem of allocation and of fairness. But the problems of environmental deterioration go further. In the first place, in addition to the conflict between individuals and groups (on which Mishan mainly concentrates), there is the conflict among the individuals themselves, in other words, among the whole community. In the second place, there is the conflict between the present and future generations. The choice between the use of our environment for production and consumption on the one hand and the availability of the environmental functions impaired as a result on the other goes much further than the traditional allocation problem.** Accordingly, as we come closer to the limits of the environment and the other natural resources – which, incidentally, are not mentioned by Mishan – the conflict between groups becomes less important and the problem narrows down to the fundamental question of how far we are now prepared to go with the growth of production (and population) at the expense, perhaps, of irreparable loss of environmental goods and of possibilities of life for the future. The problems of choice bound up with

*Cf. Section 4.5.

**Cf. p. 9.

this can be solved only by changes in the legal framework; in those changes the preferences of the community are reflected. In the latter two conflicts it is no longer a matter of fairness between groups but of preferences by the community with regard to collective goods.

3.5. W. Isard

Along with a number of other research scientists, W. Isard linked the regional activity–analysis format (which is broadly of the form of the input–output table used in economics) of the Plymouth Bay region, in New England, to an ecological input–output table for that bay.[11] The ecological system is described by means of the food chain of the organisms inhabiting the bay. The numerical relations between the various organisms have been determined empirically. The two tables have been linked together via mutual inputs and outputs. Thus outputs from the ecological to the social system are flounder and water. Outputs from the social to the ecological system include water pollution and road construction. By means of the empirically determined input–output coefficients the system makes it possible to quantify in physical units the consequences that alternative actions in the social system have for the ecological system. These consequences have, in turn, an effect on the social system. The latter effect, insofar as it exerts an influence on market prices or consumption, or data that can be derived from the market, can be valued in money.

According to the authors, this method can be of particular assistance in cost–benefit analyses for alternative policy plans. In my opinion, there is a danger that in this process data that can be derived from the market acquire too great an importance and data that cannot be so derived may be neglected. Thus estimates can be derived from the market for effects on recreation and (commercial) fishing, but not for the direct preferences for, say, a stable ecosystem with a wide variety of species, clean air or – when spawning grounds are dammed off – for the possibilities of catching fish in the future.

3.6. A.V. Kneese, R.U. Ayres and R.C. d'Arge

A.V. Kneese, R.U. Ayres and R.C. d'Arge argue in three articles[12] that recycling is the only means of preventing society in the long run from grinding to a halt against the increasing quantities of waste from production and consumption. With the aid of a model they attempt to calculate an optimal allocation of the factors of production, taking into account environmental pollution and recycling. The authors state that the model cannot be worked out because important numerical data and relations (including the preferences) cannot be determined in principle. Apart from this, in my opinion such an approach cannot offer a solution because in a situation of growth the environmental problem is more than just an allocation problem in the traditional sense.

3.7. W.W. Leontief

W.W. Leontief has devised a method for including in the accepted input–output model the environmental deterioration that results from the emission or discharge of pollutants[13].* He starts from an input–output table in physical quantities, to which a row for pollution has been added. To be able to take this step the pollution of each branch of industry must be known. Next he distinguishes a separate sector in which all anti-pollution activities are summarized. With the costs of anti-pollution measures as new datum he adds this sector as a column to the usual input–output system expressed in terms of money. The model thus extended creates the possibility of calculating for alternative standards of abatement the consequences of anti-pollution measures for all branches of industry.

In a model inspired by Leontief, the Dutch Central Planning Bureau has calculated the consequences of the technically greatest possible elimination of the quantifiable part of water pollution with biodegradable organic matter, of air pollution resulting from the combustion of fossil fuels and of solid waste.[14] Use has been made in this model of the calculations performed by the Department for Environmental Statistics of the Central Bureau of Statistics.[15]

3.8. J.W. Forrester and D.L. Meadows

J.W. Forrester and D.L. Meadows have tried to simulate the worldwide relations of a number of strategic quantities by a computer model.[16] The first model was devised by Forrester; the model set up later by Meadows is more extensive. The model contains levels, changes in these levels and auxiliary variables. These three kinds of quantities

*In the terminology of this study it is therefore a question of qualitative competition. Quantitative and spatial competition plays no part.

are linked by mathematical relations. The levels relate to population, capital, non-renewable resources, land and pollution. Land and capital are subdivided according to their applications, including agriculture, industry and services; population is subdivided into age groups. The extent of the changes in the levels is determined, on the one hand, by the height of the levels and, on the other, by the auxiliary variables. The latter comprise all factors which – apart from the levels – influence the changes. In addition, relations between the auxiliary variables themselves may also exist. The auxiliary variables are dissimilar in character. Examples of auxiliary variables are industrial production, food, lifetime multiplier from pollution (a factor giving the influence of pollution on life expectancy), pollution absorption time (at a high level of pollution the environment can neutralize pollution less quickly than at a low level) and fraction of capital allocated to obtaining resources (according as the resources are depleted, more capital is utilized to produce them). A broad impression of the working of the model may be obtained from Figure 3.1, in which the levels are shown by rectangles, the changes in the levels by valves and the auxiliary variables by circles. The solid arrows in Figure 3.1 represent the increases or decreases in the levels, and the broken arrows the remaining mathematical relations. The three planes represent successive points in time. The dashed lines demarcate periods. When all quantities of period 1 are known, all quantities from period 2 can be calculated by utilizing the arrows (the general relationships). By iteration of this procedure a long period of time can be described.

It emerges from Figure 3.1 that, starting from a certain quantity in period 1, it is always possible to arrive at that same quantity in a later period via a number of arrows. This then forms a feedback loop. The model consists of a network of a very large number of such feedback loops. The combination of all these feedbacks regulates the trend of the quantities in time. The feedbacks may be positive or negative. Thus there is a negative feedback that links the population via quantity of food per capita, mortality and number of deaths per year with the population again (in a later period), while on the other hand there is a positive feedback which, via the number of births and the auxiliary variables acting on this, causes the population to increase. In the same way, for instance, pollution is influenced on the one hand by the generation of pollution and on the other by the possibilities that the environment has of rendering that pollution harmless.

The relations assumed in the model are based in part on existing statistical material and in part on the insight of experts in each of the various fields. The model was validated and corrected in such a way that the

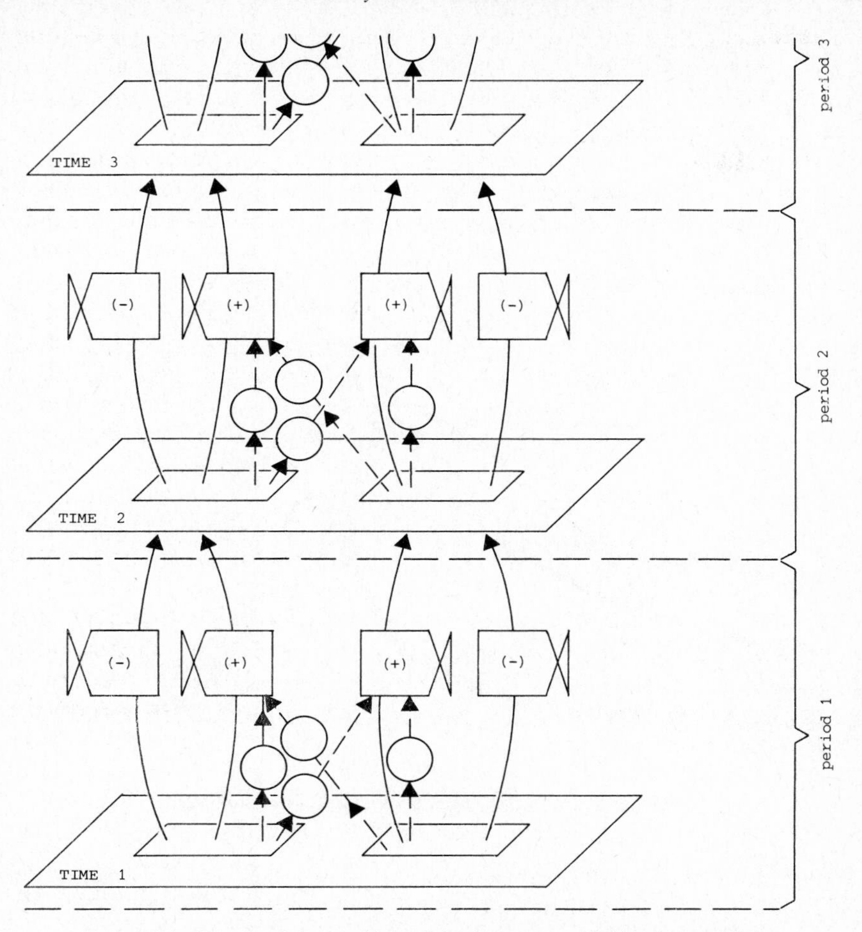

Figure 3.1. Sketch of the working of the Forrester and Meadows model.

1900–70 period is reasonably described. Then, with the relations unchanged, the calculation continued up to the year 2100. The results of this standard model appear in Figure 3.2, taken from Meadows' *The Limits to Growth*.

Figure 3.2 shows that the natural resources are being exhausted at an ever-increasing rate and that population, industrial output per capita, pollution and food per capita initially increase strongly, this being followed by a very abrupt decline. This movement is caused directly or indirectly by the reaching of the limits of the environment, as a result of which the negative feedbacks dominate the positive ones. The most

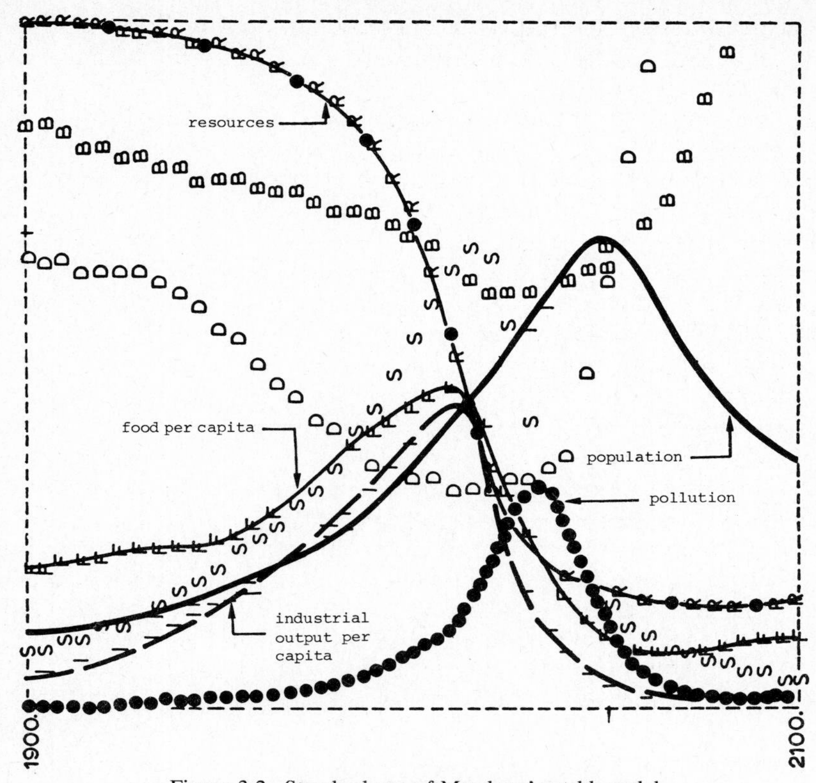

Figure 3.2. Standard run of Meadows' world model.

important factor is the exhaustion of resources. As a result, the possibilities of industrial output decrease. Together with the increasing pollution, this causes a decrease in food production. The violence of the change is intensified by the physical and social time delays occurring in the model. Thus the size of the population reacts with a considerable lag to the fall in the number of births. The influence of pollutants in the environment in many cases continues to make itself felt years after the emissions have been stopped. Capital cannot be transferred immediately from one sector to another.

Little imagination is required to see that the trend of the graphs as has been described above would mean a world disaster. Forrester and Meadows have therefore investigated with the aid of a number of model simulations how such a catastrophic development can be obviated. First of all, they investigated what the effect could be of new technologies. The technological developments considered are the availability of very large quantities of nuclear energy, considerable recycling of resources, strict pollution control, a considerable increase in food production and 'perfect' birth control.

The authors next compute a number of variants of the standard model by incorporating one or more of these technological changes. The results show that not a single combination of the technological changes considered is capable of averting the catastrophe, as will be illustrated below by means of a few examples.

In one of the simulations the reserves of resources that can be exploited are doubled by the use of 'unlimited' nuclear energy, which will also make extensive programmes of recycling and substitution possible. If these changes are made to the model, the growth of population, industrial output and food production is halted by the rapidly increasing pollution; a pollution crisis occurs. On the assumption of 'unlimited' energy, recycling and, moreover strict pollution control the growth of population and output is stopped by a drastic reduction in the area of arable land, the yield from which is finally no longer sufficient for the increased population, even if factors of production are switched in an effort to help; this crisis is accompanied by great strain as a result of high population densities. Increasing agricultural productivity still further by, for instance, new varieties and providing methods of birth control that cause all families to have exactly the number of children they want* also prove inadequate to prevent a crisis situation when industrial output and population continue to increase. Measured in time, all the measures considered are found to give little respite. Through the great growth of population and industrial output, the room created is soon used up.

The question arises why, in all these simulations, a disaster continues to happen. Broadly speaking, the explanation is as follows: the effect of technological measures is that they temporarily put negative feedbacks to growth of population and industrial output out of operation. The result is that in the course of time the limits of the environment are reached all the more violently. The conclusion that Forrester and Meadows draw is clear and not really surprising: in a finite world growth cannot continue indefinitely.

Since technological intervention in the negative feedback does not prove satisfactory, Forrester and Meadows next checked what effect weakening the positive feedback loops that cause the growth may have. Since the two most powerful positive feedbacks are population growth and capital growth, this would amount to voluntary restriction of

*In this assumption too the population continues to increase, though more slowly.

industrial output and population. Meadows, in particular, rightly stresses that this implies a complete change in the pattern of values now current. The simulations performed by the authors with stabilized population and stabilized capital therefore amount to entering value judgments in the model. These simulations show that only the combination of technological changes and changes in value can lead to a stable situation. True, there is still a slow decline in natural resources but, according to the authors, in this situation man will have enough time to seek solutions for this.

Meadows in particular emphasizes that the results given by the model are not predictions. Reality is so complex and the information so incomplete that it is hardly imaginable that the model has both the right structure and the right numerical values. The authors point out that the structure of the model – the quantities chosen and the relations assumed between them – is of decisive importance to the results; the influence of the numerical values entered in the relations is subordinate to this. A striking simplification in the model is the use of world averages, as a result of which a division of the world into rich and poor countries does not occur in the model. The numerical effect of this cannot be stated.

Consequently, there is no certainty about the results. However, in all the simulations that start from an unchanged pattern of behaviour there is one result that continues to appear with great persistence, namely the collision between population and production growth and the limits of the environment. The authors think it probable that this result will continue to apply both upon refinement of the structure and upon improvement of the numerical values of the model.

Finally, Meadows emphasizes the unpredictability of human behaviour. In the first series of models it was assumed that the pattern of behaviour from the 1900–1970 period (the period for which the model was verified) is maintained. The main characteristic of this behaviour is that the growth of population and production must be able to continue. According to the authors, this assumption is the principal cornerstone of the prevailing pattern of values of society. In the models that lead to equilibrium a changed behaviour, based on a totally different pattern of values, has been assumed. Both the assumption of unchanged behaviour and that of changed behaviour are speculations.

Criticism of the models of Forrester and Meadows has come from many quarters, and has largely narrowed down to the objections that the authors themselves also have and which have been given above. The sensitivity of the model to a number of variables has been underestimated by the authors. In addition, criticism has been voiced which is not entirely correct as regards content. For instance, it has been argued from various sides that the operation of the price mechanism has not been allowed for in the model.[17] The price mechanism – which after all is also a feedback mechanism – has been introduced into the model in a direct way. Thus allowance has been made for the fact that when raw materials become scarcer their winning requires increasing capital and when food becomes scarcer capital is transferred from the industrial and service sector to agriculture. In this way, the implications of the price mechanism are included. However, the model does not allow for possible substitutions of less scarce economic goods for scarce ones. It cannot be said, therefore, whether the price mechanism has sufficient weight in the model.

The criticism by the World Bank[18] has received considerable attention. The most fundamental objection relates to the structure of the model. To start with, it is argued that Meadows et al. sometimes interpret superficially observed correlations as causal connections, and that the mathematical form of those connections is determined by the unnecessarily stringent restrictions of the Dynamo computer language. The model as a whole is considered much too simple, inter alia in its treatment of pollution. It is further suggested that the model be extended by taking into account the division of the world into rich and poor countries. More detailed criticism of the model concerns the way in which the interest rate influences industrial investment, and the inadequate operation of the price mechanism. There is also criticism of the fact that no allowance has been made for new technological developments. As well as the structure, the input data used for the model are criticized. In particular, the estimates of resource reserves are considered too low in many cases.

In my opinion a number of these points could certainly lead to improvement of the model. However, one aspect of the World Bank report is disturbing. It is repeatedly suggested that Meadows is not aware of the general limitations of the model. This point often gives rise to fierce criticism, but Meadows himself emphasized its provisional nature.

As a conclusion to the criticism the World Bank gives the following reasoning.

The model is depicted as follows schematically (Figure 3.3): the carrying capacity of the globe is constant. The actual population develops in accordance with curve I or II, depending on the effectiveness of the feedback mechanisms. Starting from this representation of the model, the World Bank applies a modification: it is posited that the carrying capacity of the globe can in fact increase. The motivation for this assumption is that up to now new supplies of

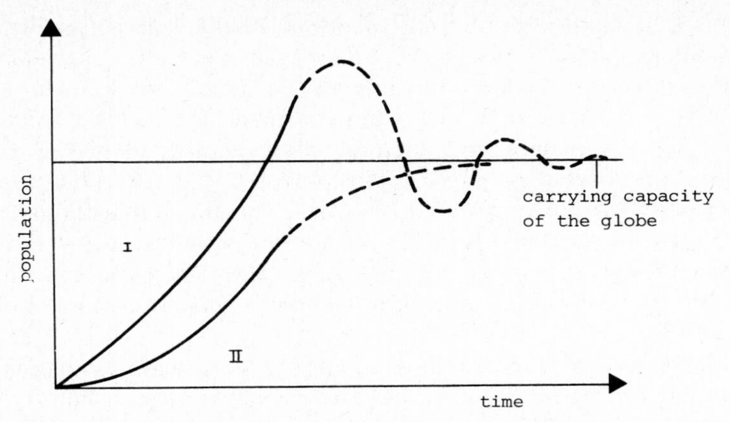

Figure 3.3. The Meadows model according to the World Bank in schematic form.

natural resources have always been discovered. According to this reasoning, a model changed in this way would be as illustrated in Figure 3.4. Continuing population growth would then be possible without a catastrophe.

The following may be adduced against this reasoning. Firstly, the simplified description of the model is not correct: Meadows et al. certainly do not assume that the human carrying capacity of the globe is constant. This capacity will vary in the course of time while the model is being worked through and will certainly decrease when a large part of

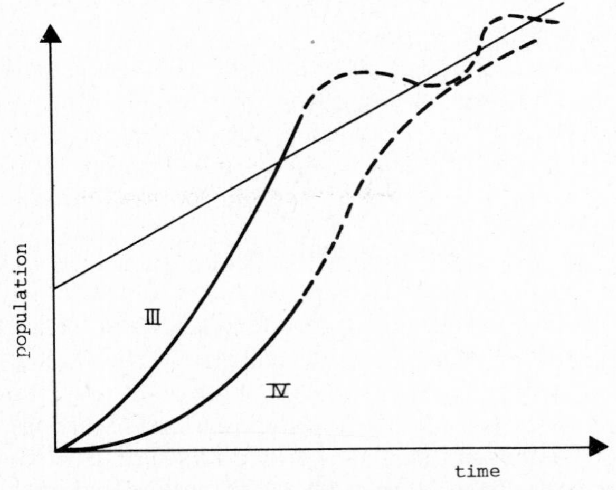

Figure 3.4. Schematically depicted amendment of the Meadows model according to the World Bank.

the resources has been exhausted. The only thing that Meadows et al. do interpret as constant is the initial stock of raw materials and auxiliaries.

Secondly, the following may be argued against the modification of the model. The straight line may be interpreted as a representation of the amount of raw materials originally present on earth or of the human carrying capacity of the globe. In the former case the line must in theory run horizontally. If the resource reserves have been estimated too low by Meadows et al., the straight line must move upwards, but definitely not increase in time. In the second case there would no longer be any question of a straight line but of a line with a relatively erratic trend; this will certainly also start to decrease when the limit is approached of the stock of raw materials in the globe, which is after all finite. In either explanation the proposed trend of the world population (curves III and IV) does not hold good.

A number of other critics also suggest supplementations to the models. In particular, P.M.E.M. van der Grinten and P.J. de Jong have supplied an elegant addition.[19] In those models, by means of which Forrester and Meadows ultimately arrived at a stable world, they used abrupt, non-recurring changes in the variables. Van der Grinten and de Jong replace this by a continuous adjustment that can change from moment to moment. This adjustment includes both purely technological changes and changes in the pattern of values. In this way, there are more possibilities of stabilizing the world model and the required changes are less drastic. So far, the procedure has been applied only to Forrester's model; for Meadows' model this adjustment is also possible in principle, but the mathematics is more complicated.

3.9. A Blueprint for Survival

In the January 1972 issue of *The Ecologist* a number of research scientists of various disciplines endeavoured to indicate how society could achieve a greatly reduced chance of collapse through environmental pollution and shortages of natural resources. They entitled their article 'A Blueprint for Survival'.[20] The importance of this contribution lies in the fact that an attempt has been made to indicate what steps must be taken to arrive at an integrated approach to the problem of pollution and exhaustion. On the basis mainly of the literature also discussed in the present study, it is concluded that a safe society must be founded on stability (not on growth) and on cycles within the potential of the ecosystems.

This can be achieved only when a local equilibrium is established between production and waste to be absorbed by the environment. The principal recommendation of the Blueprint is therefore to arrive at decentralized units in which the activities of the towns and the countryside can be integrated. This requires a tremendous intervention in the present pattern of human life; the latter can be brought about only if society deliberately abjures the drift to the metropolis.

3.10. B. Commoner

Commoner too points out that man, as part of the ecosphere, makes a big mistake by changing the ever-repeating cycles of nature into rectilinear events.[21] When components of ecosystems are withdrawn from them or large quantities of strange, non-biodegradable components are added to them, the productivity of these systems is lastingly impaired. The biological processes may be interpreted as our biological capital on which our whole productivity depends. If we destroy this capital, any technology will be worthless.

Commoner demonstrates by means of statistical material that the growth of national income in the United States in the period 1946–68 may be largely ascribed to replacement of production processes causing little pollution and consuming little energy by technologies causing great pollution and using large amounts of energy, in both agriculture and industry. Moreover, there was large-scale replacement of biodegradable products by non-biodegradable ones foreign to the environment. According to the author, environmental pollution is due not so much to population growth and increase in the quantity of production as to the above changes in particular. As support for this argument it is adduced that the increase in the pollution (measured in concentrations) is a multiple of the increase in population and production (measured by the gross national product).

Commoner's conclusion seems disputable to me. In the first place it disregards the fact that increase in the amount of production in all probability would not have been possible without the development described by Commoner. There is precisely a clear conflict between the environment and the amount of goods and services produced, as also between the environment and population growth. In the second place, in my opinion the increase in environmental deterioration cannot be placed under one denominator and expressed in a percentage.

Apart from the conclusion, Commoner's approach is highly illuminating for an insight into the causes of environmental deterioration.

The author rightly recommends calculating the energy and pollution component of each product. I believe that such calculations are indispensable to good environmental management.

3.11. Explanation of the Works Chosen

As the title of this chapter indicates, only a few pioneer works on environmental deterioration and economic growth were discussed above. This provides an opportunity to check the reasoning to be developed in Chapters 4 and 5 against the major works in this field. It is not the intention to give a survey of the literature. That would require a separate (and extensive) study.

In the selection the author allowed himself to be guided by two questions: by whom was a certain idea first published and is the book concerned with environmental deterioration *and* economic growth? In addition, subjective appreciation will doubtless have played a part. Perhaps not all readers would have arrived at the same choice.

By way of illustration a number of remarks follow on a study not discussed above, namely, the second report to the Club of Rome.[23] Mesarovic and Pestel seriously criticize the work of Meadows and Forrester, who according to them start from 'undifferentiated growth'. Against this they set 'organic growth'. Just as the organs of an organism grow in dependence on one another through the division of differentiated cells, so the ten regions into which the authors have divided the world and which are dependent on one another grow. The authors show how greatly the gap will increase between poor and rich regions without corrective measures, and calculate that reducing this difference by quick aid to poor regions by rich ones is considerably cheaper than doing so by slow aid.

In all computer runs the totalized national income of the world grows cumulatively by about 3% a year, which amounts to quadruplication within the period of fifty years considered (see, inter alia, Figures 5.1 and 5.2). True, the importance of national income to welfare is criticized, but the fact that this is a correct criterion of the volume of production is ignored. The authors do not explain how space can be found (for cars, roads, industry, agricultural land, houses, etc.) with this enormous growth of production and consumption, how sufficient energy can be generated at the – low – price that makes such enormous growth possible, how sufficient natural resources can be extracted at a low price (the authors convey the impression that they do not realize that increasing the price of energy and natural resources halts growth) and how treatment techniques can be developed with a treating efficiency high enough to keep the pollution and climatic effects occurring with this growth within safe limits.

Finally, with this growth disastrous effects on plant and animal species may be feared as a result of, among other things, the fragmentation of space and the intensification of agriculture. The authors do not indicate how these effects can be avoided. The carrying capacity of the ecosystems is mentioned in the text as a factor on which human life is completely dependent, but they do not state what assumptions are made about what is called in the study the ecological level and what the consequences are for the ecological system in the various computer runs. Evidently, the environmental factors mentioned above have not been integrated into the model and there are thus partial approaches, as also emerges from an analysis of the available material.[24,25] The reason why no section has been devoted above to studies like *Mankind at the Turning Point* (and *Mensen tellen* by Garbutt and Linnemann,[26] to give one last example) is that the connection between environmental deterioration and growth – the subject of this book – is not made.

3.12. Conclusions from the Literature

The main outlines of thoughts on the problems of the new scarcity and economic growth find their best expression in the works of Kapp, Mishan, Boulding, Forrester and Meadows. The other authors discussed in this chapter – and the authors to be considered in Chapter 5, who have concerned themselves especially with measuring national income – discuss important aspects or make (political) recommendations for arriving at a balanced situation, but to my way of thinking they add no new aspects to the main outlines of the problem.

Of the authors mentioned above, a clear division can be made between Kapp and Mishan, on the one hand, and Boulding, Forrester and Meadows, on the other.

Kapp and Mishan both start from the traditional definition of economic growth as the increase in the national (or worldwide) income which, as we have seen, amounts to the increase in the quantity of goods and services produced. Neither of the two explicitly puts forward the extent to which national income overestimates actual growth as a consequence of measures against environmental deterioration (the problem of duplication and the valuation of the losses of function, see Chapters 4 and 5). However, Kapp expressly states that the exhaustion of the carrying capacity of the environment and of the stock of natural resources will limit the possibilities of further economic growth –

interpreted as growth of production. Mishan emphasizes that economic growth – likewise interpreted as increase in production – brings in its train a large number of negative effects for the welfare of the subjects; these effects, though not (yet) expressed in money, are most probably of greater importance than the increase in production. It may be concluded from the work of both authors that national income as an indicator of welfare declines in importance according as the losses of function in the environment increase. This conclusion follows in the case of Mishan directly from his observation that the market price of many goods no longer represents the marginal value to the community. With Kapp, the conclusion follows more indirectly from his observation that the consequences of environmental deterioration and the exhaustion of stocks of raw materials and energy by the producers have to be borne by third parties or the community.

In addition, from the work of Kapp and Mishan the hopeful conclusion could still be drawn that further economic growth – in the sense of increase in the means of satisfying wants – is still possible. Allowing for the external effects, in other words, a drastic reallocation of the means of production, does not exclude the possibility of further growth of production. The authors evidently regard the problem of the new scarcity still as a cost and allocation problem in the traditional sense.

Hope of further growth may no longer be derived from the works of Boulding, Forrester and Meadows. These authors start from the finite nature of the world. Space, carrying capacity of the environment, food production and natural resources are finite quantities whose limits have already been reached or exceeded. In this way, a macro-economics is introduced which is of a different dimension from the instruments inspired by Keynes, which relate only to quantities derived from the sphere of production (national income, production, consumption and employment). This new macro-economics is much more comprehensive and, above all, much grimmer than the macro-economics of Keynesianism. There is no longer any question of the solution to the economic problem expected by Keynes.* Scarcity will dominate man's life more than ever.

The new macro-economics was given the name 'spaceship economics' by Boulding. Spaceship earth is characterized by the absolutely finite nature of all the resources required for human wants (in other words, there are no free goods). The activity level of man is determined in the spaceship economy by the possibilities of recycling and clean energy input.

In this situation, economic growth (in the interpretation defended

*Cf. p. 32.

here of increase in the satisfaction of wants) is no longer possible by an increase in the means for satisfying wants. As economic growth amounts to eliminating scarcity and scarcity relates to the strain between means and wants,* it follows that an increase in the satisfaction of wants from now on is possible only by change – i.e. reduction – in the wants.

Meadows, in particular, stresses that the principal characteristic of our pattern of values of recent decades is that the growth of production and population must be able to continue. The models show that continuation of this pattern leads to disasters. This means that avoiding catastrophes is possible only either by dictating from above what people may and may not do, or by a change in people's pattern of values. In the first case, we shall be faced with a considerable reduction of the satisfaction of wants – in other words, with a considerable 'negative economic growth' – which will doubtless create great tension and therefore may not be feasible. In the second case, the need for goods now rated highly (and for a large number of children) would become less, as a result of which a drop in production (and a decline in population) would not lead to a reduction of the satisfaction of wants – and thus would not result in 'negative growth'. The hope for a solution to the environmental problem must therefore be placed above all in a change in the pattern of values or, to put it in more popular terms, a change in mentality.

It may be illuminating to illustrate what is meant here by a concrete example. In 1970, the present author sent the action group against the construction of a road through the Kennemer dunes to the beach a list of advantages (+) and disadvantages (−) of both construction (A) and non-construction (B) of the road. This list is shown in Table 3.1.[22]

We are concerned here with a finite situation: whatever solution is chosen, one of the functions of the dune area is always sacrificed.* The extent of this sacrifice depends, inter alia, on the intensity of the preferences for driving or cycling to the beach. Now, the point at issue is that, with the present strong preferences for motoring, solutions such as that represented by B mean a considerable decline in the satisfaction of wants, whereas in the case of a change in the pattern of wants in the direction of a greater preference for cycling and a dislike of driving, no 'negative growth' occurs in solutions such as that of B. In the latter case, replacement of roads already constructed by cycle tracks also means an increase in economic growth.

The reader of the 'Blueprint' is, in fact, confronted with the same

*Cf. Chapters 1 and 5.

**Use of a stretch of dune for motoring is, of course, also a function of the area in question.

Table 3.1

(A) Road constructed	
1 – Costs of constructing and maintaining the road	9 + More comfortable access to the beach
2 – Car operating costs	
3 – Impoverishment of flora and fauna	
4 – Loss of a quiet area for walks	
5 – Danger factor for water extraction plus the provisions required	
6 – Allotment of part of the quantifiable and non-quantifiable costs of hypokinesis (cardiologist etc.) because of the exercise not taken when driving to the beach	
7 – Air pollution	
8 – (a) Costs of building car park, resulting in (b) Further impairment of the dune area	
(B) Road not constructed, existing cycle track left intact	
10 – Costs of maintaining cycle track	13 + Enjoyment during cycling
11 – Costs of (folding) bicycle kilometres	
12 – Costs of maintaining cycle storage racks	

choice on a large scale as has been shown here on a small scale. However, this micro-scale example is less of a strain on the imagination than an example in which the present patterns of man's production and consumption are compared with a totally different way of life.

Like the compilers of the Blueprint, Boulding makes a jump in time in his analysis: the economic system of today is compared with the system to be expected in the near future. However, the question central to this study is what the new scarcity means to the existing concept of economic growth. In Chapters 4 and 5 it is argued that this question cannot be answered because, on the one hand, the need for a livable world in the future cannot be measured, and, on the other, there is an absence of standards for a permissible level of activities. Forrester, Meadows and Boulding in fact come to the same conclusion. Meadows makes the comment that the model simulations show that the possibilities of choice decrease according as growth continues. Boulding concludes that the level of activities will depend on the possibility of clean energy input into the cyclical system. He therefore recommends that every effort be devoted to research into the use of inexhaustible and non-polluting sources of energy.

3.13. References

[1]A. Marshall. *Principles of Economics*. Eighth Edition. London, 1969, p. 221 et seq. (First Edition, 1890).
[2]A.C. Pigou. *The Economics of Welfare*. New York, 1962, pp. 131–135, pp. 183–196. (First Edition, 1920).
[3]K.W. Kapp. *The Social Costs of Private Enterprise*. Cambridge (Mass.), 1950.
[4]K.W. Kapp. *Social Costs of Business Enterprise*. London, 1963.
[5]E.J. Mishan. *The Costs of Economic Growth*. London, 1967.
[6]K.W. Kapp. *Social Costs of Business Enterprise*, p. 13.
[7]Especially in Chapters 14 and 15 of *Social Costs of Business Enterprise*; and more recently in: Social costs, neo-classical economics, environmental planning: a reply. In: *Political Economy of Environment*. Paris, 1972.
[8]Cf., among others, Social costs, neo-classical economics, p. 122.
[9]K.E. Boulding. The economics of the coming spaceship earth. In: *Environmental Quality in a Growing Economy*, Baltimore, 1966; Fun and games with the gross national product – the role of misleading indicators in social policy. In: *The Environmental Crisis*. London, 1970; Environment and economics. In: *Environment, Resources, Pollution and Society*. Stanford (Cal.), 1971.
[10]E.J. Mishan. *The Costs of Economic Growth*. London, 1967.
[11]W. Isard et al. On the linkage of socio-economic and ecological systems. *The Regional Science Association: Papers* 21, 1968; W. Isard. Some notes on the linkage of the ecologic and economic systems. *Regional Science Association: Papers* 22, 1969.
[12]A.V. Kneese and R.C. d'Arge, Pervasive external costs and the response of society. In: *The Analysis and Evaluation of Public Expenditures: The PPB System*. A compendium of papers submitted to the Subcommittee on Economy in Government of the Joint Economic Committee, 91 Congr., 1 sess., 1969; R.U. Ayres and A.V. Kneese. Production, consumption and externalities. *American Economic Review*, June 1969; A.V. Kneese. Economic responsibility for the by-products of production. *The Annals of the American Academy of Political and Social Science* 389, May 1970.
[13]W.W. Leontief. Environmental repercussions and the economic structure: an input–output approach. *The Review of Economics and Statistics*, August 1970.
[14]Central Planning Office. *Economische Gevolgen van Bestrijding van Milieuverontreiniging*. Monografie No. 20. The Hague, 1975.
[15]Central Bureau of Statistics. *Waterverontreiniging met Afbreekbaar Organisch en Eutrofiërend Materiaal*. The Hague, 1972; and *Luchtverontreiniging door Verbranding van Fossiele Brandstoffen 1960–1972*. The Hague, 1975.
[16]J.W. Forrester. *World Dynamics*. Cambridge (Mass.), 1971; D.H. Meadows et al. *The Limits to Growth*. New York, 1972.
[17]See, among others, L.H. Klaassen. Niettes–welleszijn. *Economische-Statistische Berichten*, 19 July 1972.
[18]*Report on the Limits to Growth, A Study by the World Bank*. Washington (D.C.), 1972.
[19]P.M.E.M. van der Grinten and P.J. de Jong. Werelddynamica gezien vanuit de systeem- en regeltechniek. *Chemisch Weekblad*, 10 December 1971. Idem. Werelddynamica, een uitgangspunt voor een wereldbeleid? *Chemisch Weekblad*, 10 March 1972.
[20]D. Arthur et al. A blueprint for survival. *The Ecologist* 2, 1972, No. 1.
[21]B. Commoner. *The Closing Circle*. London, 1972.
[22]See R. Hueting. *Wat is de Natuur ons Waard?* Baarn, 1970, p. 116 et seq.
[23]M. Mesarovic and E. Pestel. *Mankind at the Turning Point*. New York, 1974.
[24]C. de Beurs and R. Tweehuysen. *Tweede Rapport aan de Club van Rome Nader Bezien*. Commissie Maatschappij Modellen, T.N.O. Delft, 1975.
[25]M. Mesarovic and E. Pestel. *Multilevel Computer Model of the World Development System*. IIASA Report SP-74-1. Luxembourg, 1974.
[26]J. Garbutt, H. Linnemann et al. *Mensen Tellen*. Utrecht/Antwerp, 1976.

Chapter 4

NEW SCARCITY: LOSSES OF FUNCTION BY THE ENVIRONMENT

4.1. *Classification and Competition of Environmental Functions*

In order to introduce some system into the extremely complex whole of our environment, the classic division into the components water, soil and air has been utilized. The basis for a further breakdown on behalf of economic research lies in the fact that each of these components presents numerous possible uses for man. As a result of the development of society (population growth, increase in the quantity of goods and services produced per head of the population), the possible uses are becoming increasingly inadequate to meet the existing wants. Some of the possible uses are of course absolutely essential to human life; others are less important. Here we recognize the familiar basic pattern from the relationship between man and goods: goods are often scarce and are of varying importance to man; according as the available quantity is less, the marginal utility increases.

We intend to approach the human environment in the same way. In doing so, we call the possible uses of the environment for man *functions*. The latter correspond in part to the concept usefulness as it is employed in economics: the capacity of a good to be desired. Behind this usefulness there lies in turn the objective value in use: the ability of a good to bring about an effective result, whether that result is desired by man or not. (The satisfaction of wants that is ultimately evoked is called the utility.[1]) Now, one difficulty is that some vital functions of the environment are not appreciated by people because they do not know how important these functions are to life on earth (including human life). Consequently, the functions do not fully coincide with usefulness; in part they coincide with the objective value in use.

Insofar as people recognize the importance of the environment, we can start from their wants – the typical procedure followed by economists since 1870. This presents an anthropocentric starting point for quantifying the value. When the intensity of these wants can be derived from the market or from market behaviour, shadow prices of the environmental functions can be calculated in this way. This is discussed in Section 4.4.

However, it appears that people often do not realize what harm is done if the environment functions badly. A striking example is the discharge of mercury into the waters of Minamata Bay, Japan, by industrial plants, which led to paralysis and death for the mainly fish-eating local population; the connection could not be established until after the event. When chlorinated hydrocarbons like DDT, dieldrin and aldrin were first used, it was not realized that they accumulate in food chains. Only during the last few years have we become aware of the climatological consequences of CO_2 emission.*

It is probable that many forms of production and consumption will have consequences for the environment which are unknown or insufficiently known as yet.** This harm to the environment will probably bring about a reduced satisfaction of wants in the future, but this does not make its effect felt on the present valuations made by people. That is why usefulness gives nothing to go on and why the value of environmental functions cannot be based on the actual wants felt. This circumstance forms a serious methodological stumbling block in the path to quantification of the value of the environment. The problem is, of course, discussed again below.

The environment is not a homogeneous good. That is already evident from the first rough breakdown into the components water, soil and air. Nor can a component be used in the same way for different purposes. The classification into functions has been inspired by the idea that each use makes certain qualitative requirements of an environmental component that often differ greatly. Each function of an environmental component thus on the one hand satisfies specific human wants and on the other makes specific requirements of the quality of a component. The concept of function also reflects the fact that it is not a question of an isolated quantity of a good but of the capacity of the good as a kind to satisfy wants. Every loss of a good as a unique 'individual' is definitive. The function of a good is replaceable, as long as the good is not exhausted as a kind and as long as substitutes can be found for the good. Substitution of environmental functions takes place by the measures for compensation of loss of function to be discussed below.

*See p. 37 of this study.

**Cf. among others pp. 36–39 where the M.I.T. study *Man's Impact on the Global Environment* is discussed. Nothing can be said for certain about, in particular, adverse and possibly even catastrophic future ecological and climatological effects of human activities. Knowledge is very incomplete.

In this study only the components water and air have been systematized with the aid of the concept of function. As regards water, a distinction has been made between the following functions: water for drinking, water for cooling, water for flushing and transport, process water, water for agricultural purposes, water for recreation, water in the natural environment, navigable water, water as an element in the social environment, utilization of water for construction, and water as a dumping ground for waste. In the elaboration the functions have been further subdivided. Thus recreational water can be further broken down into water for swimming, fishing, boating, skating, and waterside recreation. Each of the further subdivided functions evidently again satisfies separate wants and makes its own specific qualitative requirements. Thus water for fishing makes quite different requirements of the quality of the water than does water for swimming; process water makes requirements that are different from and stricter than those of cooling water.

Of the functions in the component air, mention may be made of air as a factor in human life (loss of function manifests itself for instance in irritation of the respiratory organs upon inhalation of polluted air), as a factor in agriculture, and as a medium for storing matter (loss of function here may lead to accelerated corrosion).

As long as the space, the quantity and the quality of an environmental component are such that a claim laid to a function is not at the expense of availability of the other functions for the existing needs thereof, there is no question of an economic problem with regard to that environmental component. If, for instance, in a certain region the burden of biodegradable organic matter on the water can be handled by the water's capacity for self-purification, without invalidating its use as recreational water, drinking water, etc., this is not interpreted in this study as environmental deterioration. The recreational water can then meet the existing wants undisturbed and to the same extent as before; the supply of drinking water can proceed normally, the costs being confined, for instance, to distribution costs or simple filtering through a sand bed, depending on the local situation. But as soon as the claim to a function of an environmental component leads to reduced availability of another function, we may speak of environmental deterioration in the economic sense. For then there is a loss of usefulness and, consequently, a reduction in satisfaction of wants that was possible before.

In this economic study, *environmental deterioration* is defined as *decreased availability of functions of an environmental component*. Or, more briefly, as *loss of function*. Loss of function has apparently occurred because, as a consequence of the increasing burden on the environment, so great a claim is laid to the various functions of the environment that these functions have come to compete with one another. In other words, the claim laid by a human activity to a certain function is at the expense of another function. It is therefore self-evident to classify the losses of function occurring by investigating where *competition of functions* is to be found in an environmental component.

An environmental component always has three aspects, a quantitative one (the amount of matter), a qualitative one (the degree of pollution) and a spatial aspect. The decreased availability of a function may relate to each of these three aspects. The competitive use of functions is therefore divided into quantitative, qualitative and spatial competition.

A situation in which the quantity of a component is inadequate for its use or intended use may be described as *quantitative competition of functions*. Here the functions directly confront one another. Quantitative competition is absolute; withdrawal on behalf of a certain function entirely excludes use for other functions. With regard to water, this takes place by actual withdrawal of water from the environment. In the case of air, quantitative competition plays no part. Apart from the quality, the quantity of air is always adequately present for use to be made of it. In soil (which will not be dealt with in the present study), quantitative competition relates in any case to matters like sand excavations; at present it cannot be said whether using up raw materials must also be classified in this way.

When there is not enough space for the use or intended use of the functions, *spatial competition of functions* occurs. This occurs above all on soil.* Since the functions of soil have not yet been classified and because the spatial aspects of water and air in many cases overlap those of soil, it is the intention to consider the spatial aspects of soil, water and air together at a later stage. Instances of overlapping are the spatial competition between roads and waterways (components soil and water) and collisions of aircraft with buildings and of birds with high-tension cables (components air and soil).

At first sight, it may not seem obvious to include space and amount of matter in an environmental study. However, this study is concerned principally with the economic consequences of environmental deterioration. Now, the consequences of a shortage of space and matter caused by the increase in production and population prove comparable to those of environmental pollution in the usual sense. Both, therefore,

*Thus urban space is clearly not enough for the existing wants in the spheres of walking, driving, cycling, public transport and children at play. Further, in most countries there is severe competition with regard to the use of space for suburbanization, road-building, recreation, farming, and the natural environment.

come to the fore in the study as losses of function. Thus the availability of the recreational function of a piece of land may decrease as a result of noise nuisance but also by its being taken up by roads; the consequences of space being taken up by all kinds of activities are probably at least as serious for the natural environment function as the consequences of pollution. The losses of function occupy a central position.

In an environmental component qualitative changes may occur. These can be brought about in two ways. Firstly, as the result of direct introduction of waste into the soil, direct dumping or discharging of waste into the water, direct emission of substances or the causing of sound vibrations in the air. Secondly, they may be the result of an unintentional or 'unavoidable' side-effect in the utilization of other functions. In both cases the environment is used in its function of getting rid of waste. When, as a result of this use, a component of the environment becomes less suitable for other possible uses, we speak of *qualitative competition of functions*. In the case of the component water, this function is described as water used as a dumping ground for waste. As regards air, the term 'air as a medium into which to release waste matter' has been opted for; this includes not only the emission of injurious substances but also noise nuisance.

Utilization of this function therefore decreases the availability of the other functions. In other words, competition occurs between the function dumping ground for waste and the other functions. In this case, the competition between the functions is indirect. It occurs via the qualitative change, which is the vector of the competition. Qualitative competition is by degrees; loss of function depends on the degree of change. Both change and loss of function may be described in scientific or technical terms, as may also be measures of elimination and compensation* required for restoration or replacement of functions. In tracing the losses of function, it has been found that the use of water and air as media for accommodating the waste products of human activities now leads to decreased availability of all other functions.

In order to obtain a complete picture, the functions have been classified in tables in Appendix I. The method of this classification is explained below.** First of all, the separate functions of an environmental component have been arrayed against one another in a table with two identical accesses. Next it has been investigated where the use of a certain function of the environmental component leads to

*For a description of the concepts compensation and elimination, see p. 116.

**The reader who is not interested in the technical elaboration of the tablets can skip Appendix I and confine himself to the following text.

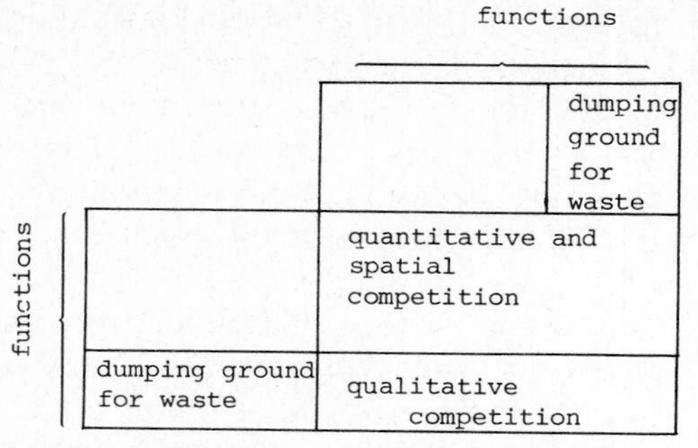

Figure 4.1. Competitive use of functions.

decreased availability of another function. This is shown in the cells of the table. The losses of function may be the result of quantitative, qualitative and spatial competition of functions. The losses of function as a result of quantitative and spatial competition follow directly from the confrontation of the functions. All cases of qualitative competition result from utilization of the function labelled dumping ground for waste, which appears on the last row and in the last column of a preliminary table. This has, in principle, the form shown in Figure 4.1, but has not been elaborated in Appendix I.

As the elaboration has been performed only for the quantitative and qualitative aspects of water and the qualitative aspects of air, the first tables for water and air acquire the form shown in Figures 4.2* and 4.3, respectively.

The differences between the three kinds of competition make it desirable to derive per component from the first table three sets of tables for quantitative, spatial and qualitative competition. However, because the soil and the losses of function as the result of spatial competition will be dealt with at a later stage and as air has no quantitative aspects, there only remain of these three sets per component:

– for water: quantitative and qualitative competition,
– for air: qualitative competition.

The losses of function as a result of quantitative competition in water have been classified in a table entitled 'Losses of function as a result of quantitative competition in water, by functions', which takes the form shown in Figure 4.4.

*The function described as dumping ground for waste has not been included in the head of the table because in practice in the case of water no appreciable forms of quantitative competition between this function and the other functions occur.

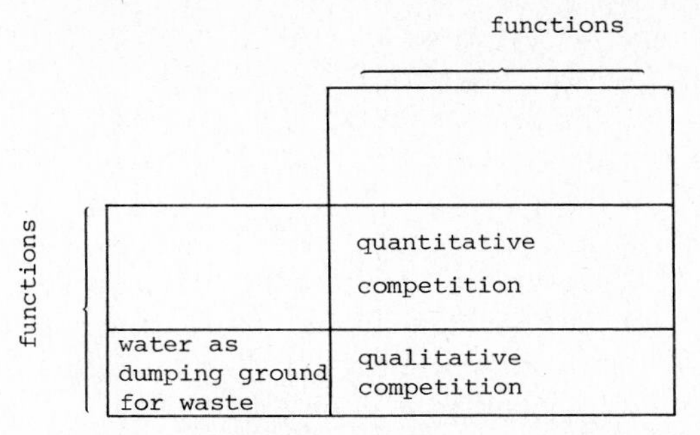

Figure 4.2. Competitive use of water by functions.

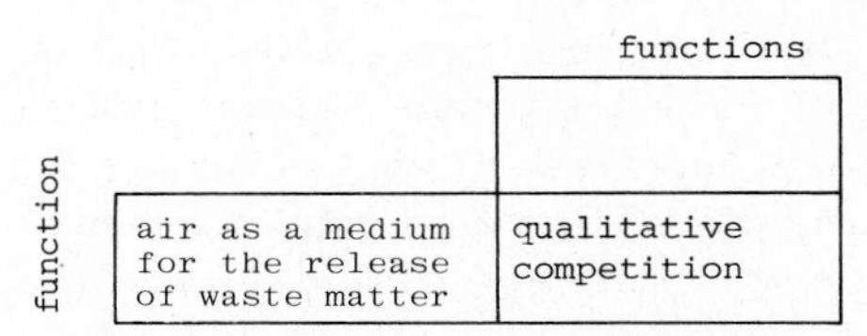

Figure 4.3. Competitive use of air by functions.

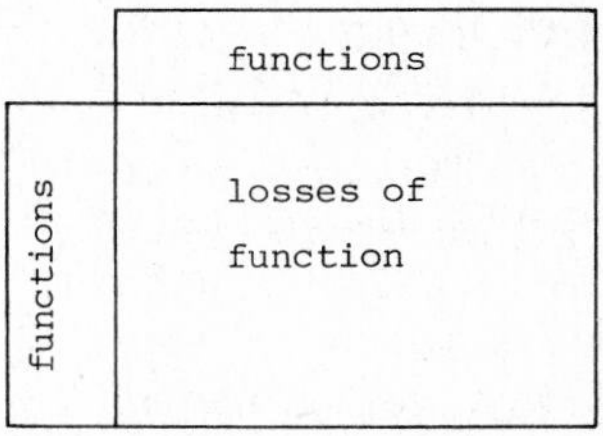

functions

functions

losses of
function

Figure 4.4. Losses of function as a result of quantitative competition in water, by functions.

In this table the functions are in direct competition with one another. It immediately follows from this which losses of function occur and which activities cause the losses. The next stage is to investigate what measures can compensate for these losses of function and what sums of money they involve. The losses of function have been brought together on a list entitled 'Description of the losses of function as a result of quantitative competition in water, by functions' (see Appendix I). In this list, the losses of function are concisely defined, and in addition it is briefly indicated what financial damage – to be derived in principle from the market – is caused by the loss of function and what measures can lead to compensation for the losses of function. To clarify this, let us take the example of the withdrawal of ground water for the supply of drinking and industrial water, which will reduce the ground water level. This in turn will reduce agricultural yields, which may be compensated for by irrigation, by the use of additional water, etc.[2]

At the present stage of our investigation it is not possible to quantify the losses of function caused by quantitative competition. In the elaboration, priority has been accorded to those forms of environmental deterioration whose elimination is the most urgent, with due observance of feasibility, which in turn depends on the data available. The choice fell on a few forms of environmental pollution, listed below, that are covered by the concept qualitative competition.

In the set of tables showing the losses of function due to qualitative competition, the functions do not compete directly. There is an intermediate stage: a human activity introduces an agent into the environment. By *agent*, in this context, is meant *a constituent or amount of energy (in whatsoever form) which may cause loss of function either by its addition to or by its withdrawal from the environment by man*. An agent could be a chemical, plant, animal, heat, radioactivity etc. The agent can trigger a change in the environment which is in fact responsible for the loss of function.*

In the tables, agents and changes are listed together, not separately. The nomenclature is based as much as possible on the agent. However, in cases where this would lead to a highly artificial nomenclature, the change has been stated in the table instead of the agent. Thus under the component water the very varied substances leading to a change in the acidity of the water are not listed, but the change in acidity itself.

The agents are subdivided into biological, chemical and physical. In water, for example, we find pathogenic organisms, animals and plants as biological agents. The terms 'animals' and 'plants' here refer to addition to or withdrawal from the environment of organisms. The chemical agents are subdivided among others into biodegradable organic matter, inorganic toxic substances, saline substances and eutrophicating matter. Physical agents include heat, radioactive substances and silt. In the component air, only pathogenic organisms have been listed as biological agents. Of greater importance here are the chemical agents, such as sulphur oxides and sulphuric acid, carbon monoxide, nitrogen oxides, inorganic fluorine compounds etc. Finally, there are the physical agents, of which sound is the most important.

*In this study a change in environment is defined as a case of an agent influencing one or more components of the environment. In the practical investigation, it will be examined in which cases this influence leads to loss of function and in which cases the environment quickly restores the original situation.

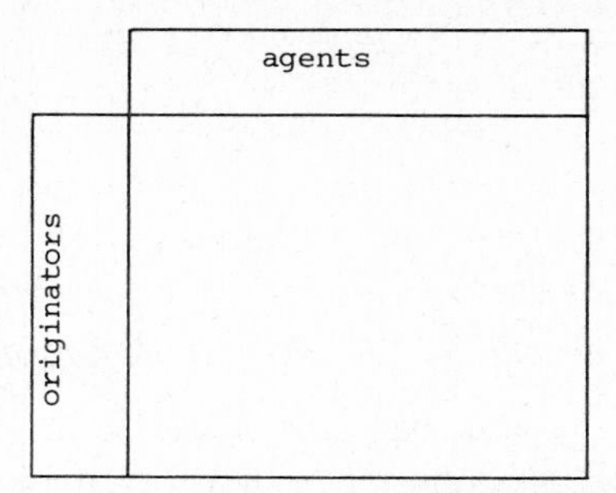

Figure 4.5. Qualitative competition in water (or air); agents by originators.

The subdivision into originating activities of these agents is broadly the same for the components water and air. A distinction is made between production, consumption (by households), exchange with other environmental components and import and export. The production processes have been subdivided into auxiliary processes and general processes, such as transport, heating, packaging, etc. on the one hand, and specific processes like agriculture and horticulture, industry, bioindustry on the other.

The various originating activities and changes are arrayed against each other in a table entitled 'Qualitative competition in water (or air); agents by originators', as shown in Figure 4.5. By means of this table it has been investigated which activities – insofar as this could be established – introduce a certain agent into the environment.

Next, the listed agents have been arrayed against the functions that the component possesses. This table is called 'Losses of function as a result of qualitative competition in water (or air); by agent and by function', and has the form shown in Figure 4.6. In the cells of this table the losses of function occurring as a result of the agents are classified. The losses of function found in the investigation were brought together

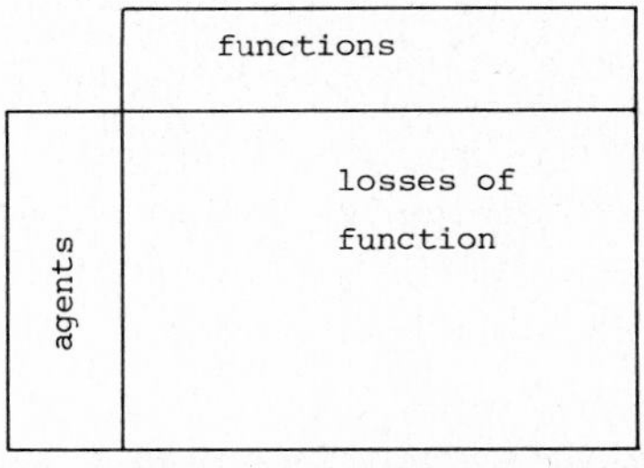

functions
losses of function
agents

Figure 4.6. Losses of function as a result of qualitative competition in water (or air); by agent and by function.

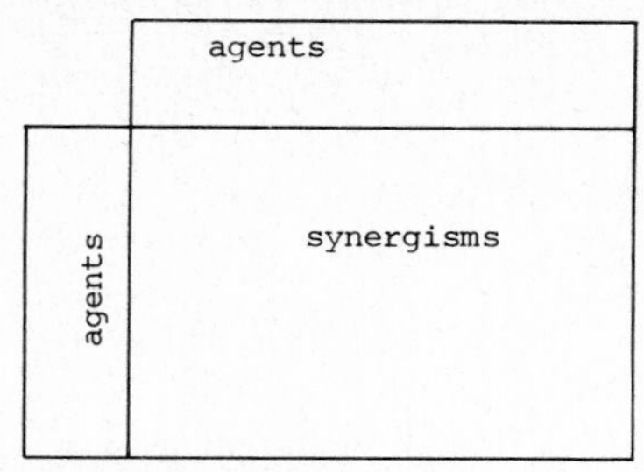

Figure 4.7. Qualitative competition; synergisms caused by the action of two or more agents.

functions
losses of
function
synergisms

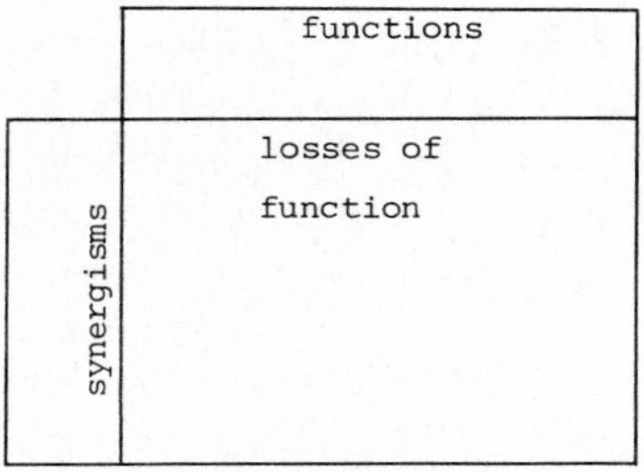

Figure 4.8. Losses of function as a result of qualitative competition in water (or air); by synergism and by function.

in the list entitled 'Description of losses of function as a result of qualitative competition in water (or air); by agent and by function'. In this list, the losses of function are concisely defined, and, moreover, it is briefly indicated what financial damage – to be derived in principle from the market – is caused by the loss of function and what measures can lead to restoration of function.

In both water and air a number of losses of function occur which are caused by the synergistic action of two or more agents.* These ought to be classified in two tables, namely 'Qualitative competition; synergisms caused by the action of two or more agents' and 'Losses of function as a result of qualitative competition in water (or air), by synergism and by function'. These should take the form of Figures 4.7** and 4.8.

As the quantitative information on the synergistic action of substances is as yet very limited, such a table with its corresponding list has not been elaborated in Appendix I.

*One speaks of synergistic action if the effect of two or more agents together is greater than the effect of each of the agents separately.

**The table of Figure 4.7 ought in fact to be multidimensional in form.

In the tables discussed above the connection between originators and agent and that between agent and loss of function are described. There will, above all, be a need for information that indicates the connection between the originating activity and the loss of function. When only one originator, one agent and one function are involved, it immediately follows that that particular originator brings about the whole loss of function. In practice the situation is seldom so simple. For it is possible that:

- one originator introduces several agents into the environment;
- one agent originates from several originating activities;
- one agent affects several functions;
- one function is affected by several agents.

Furthermore, the originators, the resultant environmental changes and the places where the loss of function occurs are distributed irregularly over the country. For these reasons, in order to be able to establish the connection between originating activity and loss of function, the following two conditions have to be fulfilled:

(1) It must be possible to calculate the losses of function caused by the agent from the environmental change caused by the agent (which usually amounts to a change in concentration of the agent).
(2) It must be possible to discover the contribution to the agent per originator.

In practice these conditions will seldom be fully complied with.

For a complete insight in the case of qualitative competition, in fact a third table is also required, in which the originating activities are arrayed against the losses of function. This table has not been compiled, on account of the difficulties described above. It is, however, implicitly present in the tables 'originators against agents' and 'agents against functions'. The three tables indicated here together form the three sides of a cube, owing to the fact that two tables always have one axis in common. The cube then consists of a large number of blocks, each representing a conceivable case of function-influencing, with originator and agent. Some blocks are empty: the originator does not introduce that agent into the environment, or the agent has no effect on that function. The axes are used to list originators, agents and functions (see Figure 4.9).

It will be clear that in this framework only those facets of influence on the environment that man recognizes as injurious find expression. Of course this also includes the effects which are expected to become injurious in the future. This anthropocentric approach – which is inherent in an economic viewpoint – means that the weight of an

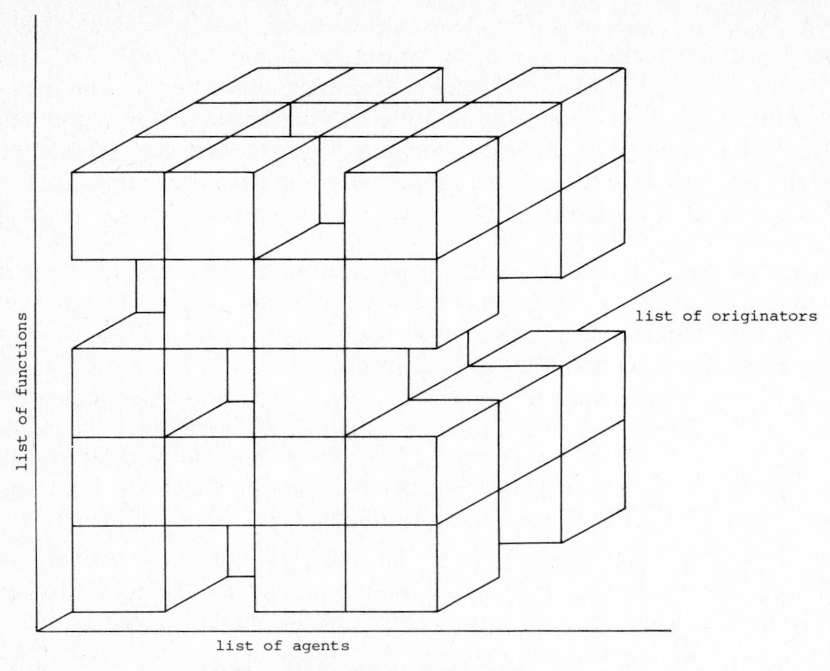

Figure 4.9. Cases of loss of function.

influence on the environment is made dependent on man's perception. Here lies the difference from an ecological approach, in which environmental changes are, in principle, studied independently of the weight that man attaches to them.

One final example of loss of function as a result of qualitative competition follows. Discharge of the agent 'biodegradable organic matter' into water (the originators being industry and population, among others) leads, via an increase in the concentration of this matter, to oxygen deficiency in the water. Losses of function as a result of this include increased fish mortality and, in very serious cases, putrefaction ('dead water').

4.2. Environmental Functions, Collective Goods, External Effects and Opportunity Costs

In the preceding section a system of analysis has been developed to permit consideration of the complex whole of the environment. In the sections that follow it will be explained what information is needed for taking decisions for the restoration of possible uses that have been lost as a result of qualitative competition of functions, to which our investigation has so far been confined. These decisions always amount to weighing costs and benefits bound up with reacquiring or preserving environmental functions. First, however, it will be investigated below whether or not environmental functions must be regarded as collective goods and whether or not the concept loss of function coincides with the concept external effect that is used in economic theory. This is important, for two reasons: firstly, for answering the question of who takes the decisions regarding the quality of the environment; secondly, so as to further demarcate the concept environmental function introduced in this study.

The following criteria for collective goods are stated in the literature:[3]

(1) A collective good is technically non-divisible into units that can be sold on a market (non-divisibility).
(2) Nobody can be excluded from using it by price determination (non-exclusivity). The use of a collective good cannot therefore be restricted by charging a price for it.
(3) Consumption of a collective good by one does not lead to reduction of the consumption by another (non-rivalry).
(4) A collective good is a case of '100% externality'. All the profits accrue to the community and therefore cannot be internalized via reflection of individual preferences in price determination.

In the preceding section environmental goods were defined as functions of an environmental component. If the functions of the components water and air are checked against the above criteria, it emerges that some functions do not comply with the existing criteria of a collective good and others do.

In the component water most functions cannot be called collective goods. Thus drinking water, the various forms of industrial and recreational water, agricultural water and water as a dumping ground for waste are not collective goods according to the criteria mentioned. In these functions, water can be divided into units that can be distributed by means of price determination. This is already quite clearly the case with drinking water. But when water is functioning as a dumping ground for waste, too, separation of quantities and price determination are possible. Price determination is directly possible by means of charges which, for instance, can be put so high that discharge of biodegradable organic matter does not exceed the self-purifying capacity of the water. One can then continue discharging for those activities of which there is the most urgent need, while the other activities are excluded from use of the function. Price determination for the function of water as a dumping ground for waste is also indirectly possible by setting standards for the effluent; attaining the standard requires taking treating measures (e.g. building plants), and this increases the price of the products of the activity.

The function 'water in the natural environment' in the component water is collective in nature. This function is not divisible, price determination is not possible, there is non-rivalry and 100% externality.

The above considerations again show in a different way that an environmental component is not a homogeneous good. For the component water as a whole no definite answer could be given to the question whether or not it is a collective good on the strength of the above criteria. A check against these criteria would show that, as regards divisibility, non-exclusivity and 100% externality, water sometimes is a collective good and sometimes is not. According to the non-rivalry criterion, water could never be interpreted as a collective good, since the various possible uses nearly all compete with one another.

In the medium air, all functions distinguished in this study must be interpreted as collective goods, with the exception of the function 'air as a medium into which to release waste matter'. Division into marketable units is not possible. Nor can anyone be excluded from use by means of price determination. The functions also satisfy the criteria of non-rivalry and of 100% externality.

The function 'air as a medium into which to release waste matter' cannot be interpreted as a collective good. True, division into units is not technically feasible, but price determination is quite definitely possible for this function, as in the case of the corresponding function of water. Use of this function can be regulated both directly and indirectly by means of price determination. Certain activities can be excluded from use of the function by both charges and setting standards. On the other hand, as in the case of water, the benefits from the use of the function 'air as a medium into which to release waste matter' accrue to certain subjects only and not to the community as a whole. For the production and consumption of certain goods causes air pollution or noise nuisance for the community, and if no charges or provisions are made for this, these goods become available with fewer sacrifices than in the case of charging or setting standards; the users and producers of these goods are the only ones who profit from this.

Evidently, environmental goods – defined as functions of an environmental component – can only partly be interpreted as collective goods according to the criteria used in the literature. It is particularly noteworthy that the important function 'dumping ground for waste' is not in fact a collective good.

Nevertheless, the subjects cannot influence the valuation of the environmental functions via the market mechanism. This is because the way in which they are used is determined by the government (i.e. by the community) in the case of all functions, including those whose use leads to qualitative changes in the environment (the function 'dumping ground for waste'). This important aspect will be reverted to in Section 4.7.

In view of the rapid qualitative decline of the environment, probably too high a value is assigned to the function 'dumping ground for waste' and too low a value to the other functions (see Section 4.7). Assigning higher values to the latter environmental functions leads to fewer goods and services being produced and to more environmental goods. Establishing the desired equilibrium between the two categories of goods is possible only by means of a joint decision, for, when a producer makes allowance in production for the environment without his competitors following suit, he prices himself out of the market. Production under free enterprise makes it obligatory to adhere to the lowest standard of producers' behaviour with respect to the environment applicable at any given moment. Consumers can express their preference for non-polluting products. Furthermore, by changing the pattern and behaviour of consumption, they can contribute to the regaining of a better environment. In practice, however, attempts in that direction prove to fail, for various reasons. The most important of these seems to me that many people, in the belief that 'most of the others' will not follow suit, see something quixotic in voluntary consumer campaigns.

The growing severity of the problem of environmental deterioration has caused the interest of economic literature in the concept of external effect greatly to increase. A study of the definitions used in the literature shows on the one hand that adverse effects on the environment as a result of human activities are only one part – though an important one – of the concept of external effect. On the other hand, the concept of loss of function, although closely related to the concept of external effect, does not seem wholly identical with it.

T. Scitovsky divides the external effects into two categories, namely 'pecuniary external economies' and 'technological external economies of direct interdependence'[4].*

By pecuniary external economies Scitovsky, in emulation of J. Viner, means the services (and disservices) rendered free (without

*It emerges from the context that 'external economies' means both positive and negative external effects.

compensation) by one producer to another via market relations. Scitovsky argues that this interdependence of firms through the market mechanisme is an 'all-pervading' phenomenon that is of great importance, above all in countries that are still in an initial stage of economic development.

By the technological, direct external effects, i.e. those not operating via market relations, Scitovsky means the following four phenomena:

(1) The interdependence of consumers' satisfaction. By this is meant the phenomenon that the satisfaction of the individuals' wants is partly dependent on the quantity and quality of the consumption of others;
(2) the direct influence of the producers on the satisfaction of the individual such as the consequences of factory smoke, noise nuisance from industrial plant, and so on;
(3) the productivity-increasing inventions becoming available without charge to the producers;
(4) the advantages and disadvantages accruing to a producer as a result of the activities of other producers.

Both the pecuniary external economies and the last two of the effects not occurring via the market are more or less identical with the external economies already deemed so important by Alfred Marshall.[5] They relate chiefly to the advantages that occur when firms are concentrated in a certain region, such as supplies of raw and auxiliary materials and of specialized semi-finished products at lower prices, the availability of well-trained labour, the stimulating effect of the occurrence of the right 'industrial climate', the quick onward flow of inventions of all kinds, and so on.

The direct external effects not operating via the market listed under points 1 and 2 above were probably first mentioned by A. C. Pigou.[6] He places these effects in the context of discussion of his concepts of private net product and social net product.

Pigou calls the 'envy effect'[7] psychical in character and he does not discuss it further; though it affects the welfare of individuals, it has no influence on the concept of social net product. The latter, like the private net product, consists of 'physical elements and objective services only', the value of which may be measured in terms of money on the market.[8]

According to Pigou, divergences between the private and social net product are largely insusceptible to a modification of the contractual relation of the contracting parties, since these differences are the result of services and disservices rendered to persons other than the contracting parties. Costs and benefits then accrue outside the market to persons not directly involved in production.[9] Apparently, therefore, we are concerned here with external effects. Pigou gives a fairly large number of examples. These include on the one hand items like uncompensated damage to a wood caused by sparks from a train and harm to property and health as a result of factory smoke, and on the other items like extra expenditure on prisons and police caused by the consequences of the production of intoxicants, extra spending on the army to protect investments abroad and, in addition, the advantages of scientific research not paid for by the producer.

The external effects mentioned by Pigou – apart from the benefits of scientific research, which of course come under point 3 – could more or less coincide with the technological external economies placed by Scitovsky under point 2. However, they are broader, since Pigou extends them to include effects leading to specific government expenditure, such as on the police and the army.

It will be clear from this concise survey[10] that the external effects cover a much wider field than the concept of loss of function used in this study. As regards its scope the latter concept coincides only with the technological external economies listed by Scitovsky under point 2, at least insofar as these relate to negative effects in the environment and also without the restriction solely to the effects of producers on consumers.

The following may be remarked about the content of the concepts of external effect and loss of function. The present author has the impression that in principle the concept of loss of function can be interpreted as a special category of the external effects. And yet the content of the two concepts does not seem entirely the same. Perhaps this is because, at the time that the concept of external effect made its way into economic literature, the finite character of our environment and thus the inevitability of the occurrence of competition between environmental functions were not yet as clearly manifest as they are now. In the case of losses of function one can hardly speak of 'side-effects' or 'unintentional side-effects' as one can with external effects. Losses of function are often deliberately allowed for in decisions by the government, the only body that can influence the degree of availability of competing functions (cf. Section 4.7). When competition occurs between environmental functions, the functions are always used at each other's expense; in this process it is not possible, in analogy with external effects, to make a distinction between 'main functions' and 'side-functions'.

P. Hennipman posits that in modern welfare theory the term external effects is often used in particular for 'the positive or negative influence operating outside the market which, as a side-effect of economic actions, is exerted on the conditions of production or the level of satisfaction of other households'.[11] It emerges from this definition that in modern welfare theory the pecuniary external economies operating via the market are usually no longer regarded as external effects. Another striking feature of this definition is that it does not confine itself (as Pigou does) to 'physical' damage that can be measured on the market; all effects that influence the satisfaction of wants are subsumed under it.

Hennipman's succinct definition of the concept of external effect is well suited for comparing this concept with that of loss of function. It seems to me that the content of both concepts is not entirely the same, for the following two reasons.

(1) Losses of function are caused by concrete, objectively ascertainable quantitative, spatial or qualitative changes in an environmental component, as a result of which one or more functions now partially or wholly lack the qualities that make the functions suitable for their specific use. The concept of loss of function is therefore connected on the one hand with the matter of the environmental component and determined on the other by the demand for the function. The loss of function is an objectification of the influence exerted on the satisfaction of wants or the conditions of production (see the above definition of the external effect). This objectification is necessary both for the statistical systematization of environmental deterioration and for the estimates to be made. For the influence on the level of satisfaction of wants itself cannot be measured. However, satisfaction of wants depends on the availability of scarce goods, in this case the functions of the environmental components. By means of the concept of function, environmental deterioration can be defined in the economic sense (namely as decreased availability of functions) and can further be classified in losses of function, while finally an economic quantification of environmental deterioration (though only a partial one) can be performed via estimates in terms of money of the measures needed for restoration of function and of the damage resulting from losses of function. In conclusion, it may be added that an external effect may in many cases be neutralized by settlement in money; for exclusion of loss of function elimination by concrete measures is always necessary.*

(2) A second substantial difference between the concepts of external effect and loss of function lies in the fact that, according to the

*For the concept of elimination, see p. 116.

definitions, the government cannot cause external effects but can cause losses of function. The definition of external effect as an influence operating outside the market implies that this effect can occur only if a market does in fact exist. These are evidently effects on 'outsiders' who do not belong to the parties constituting the market, the buyers and sellers of goods and services. Since government services are not performed by way of the market mechanism, one could argue on the strength of this that no external effect can thereby occur. However, of more fundamental importance than this formal distinction is the fact that the government is assumed to take into account the interests of all citizens when making its decisions. This implies that in principle all parties are represented in a government decision. Particularly for this reason there can be no question of influence on 'outsiders' for whom no allowance is made in the decision. However, losses of function can most certainly be caused by the government. Thus, when a road is built through a nature area or a sewer is laid to discharge into a river, sea or inland sea, important functions of the environment are impaired, however closely the government has weighed the various interests. Moreover, in such a case it does not matter whether others than the users of the road or the sewer suffer damage through the loss of function. Even if every citizen makes equal use of the road or sewer, a number of functions of the environment are nevertheless lost wholly or partially for the same citizens.

In somewhat different form the same thing occurs with goods and services produced by the market. For, as emphasized above, the government decides on the circumstances in which goods and services from industry are produced and consumed. In the final instance the statutory framework determines the degree of pollution of our environment. The conflict between the quantity of goods and services produced and the quality of the environment is therefore not confined to the 'market economy', but continues fully to apply if production is collectivized partially or even wholly. The heart of the conflict lies in the finite carrying capacity of the environment.

The alarming thing about this situation is that a series of decisions at all kinds of different levels, each of which is taken for the point in question in accordance with the preferences of the subjects and each of which has a limited effect on the environment, may lead in combination to an effect which is considerably more serious than the sum of the parts. This aspect was illustrated in Chapter 2 in the discussion of studies such as *Man's Impact on the Global Environment*. The situation can be summarized as an uncontrolled process in which the sum of the separate decisions leads to a result that nobody wants.

We are, of course, 100% dependent on our environment, which is finite. Man's level of activities has now increased so greatly that more and more activities are conflicting because the use of one environmental function is at the expense of availability of other functions. In this situation, the costs of use of an environmental function by an activity also include the loss of possible uses of our environment for other activities (needless to say, the term 'use' here also implies reservation of sufficient space and guarantee of adequate quality for the functioning of natural ecosystems, and 'activity' also includes the need to retain a sufficient degree of biological stability). Losses of function can therefore best be defined as opportunity costs.

4.3. Environmental Indicators

Our investigation is concerned with both the physical aspect and the value aspect of the environment. The value aspect is dealt with in the following sections. Data on the physical aspects that are discussed in this section can serve as indicators of the quality of the environment. Indicators are thus numerical data that illustrate certain aspects of the environment. Only the indicators relating to environmental deterioration as a consequence of qualitative competition will be discussed below.

In qualitative competition the weighing of costs and benefits connected with the functions of an environmental component will always have to be preceded by measurement of a few indicators (in any case emission). The indicators that designate the state and the trend of qualitative environmental deterioration are not only indispensable to the cost–benefit analysis to be discussed below, but also clearly possess an independent role. For the indicators to be dealt with below also give an impression of the state of the environment quite apart from the cost aspect. The independent role of the environmental indicators becomes more important according as more of the data required for drawing up a cost-benefit analysis are absent. Our investigation has shown that in general the costs of restoration of function can be estimated; in fact in theory this is always so, because cessation of an activity is also interpreted as elimination. Since much of the need for environmental functions cannot find expression on the market, the benefits of restoration of function can only very partly be expressed in terms of money. For this reason environmental indicators are also of great importance for a third purpose, namely for drawing up a cost–effectiveness analysis.*

The following indicators of qualitative environmental deterioration can be used:

1. emission during a given period;
2. concentration of pollution in the environment (immission);
3. the effects of pollution (e.g. greater mortality among fish, the disappearance of oxygen-loving water organisms).

Indicator No. 1

The statistical reflection of this indicator is the total emission per period. The level of emissions produced by man can be raised, for instance, by an increase in the activities of production and consumption or by less careful behaviour. Emission can be eliminated by all kinds of measures by which the agent is removed from the source (including reduction of the polluting activity).

Indicator No. 2

The substances emitted disperse in the environment, sometimes undergo changes there and attain a certain concentration. This can be measured or calculated.

In the first case the sum of the natural concentration of pollution and that caused by man is measured. The man-made part, with which this investigation is concerned, must then be estimated. Thus the total concentration in air of (among other factors) hydrogen sulphide, ozone and methane, and also the total concentration in water of such substances as salt, biodegradable organic matter and phosphates, is caused in part by natural processes. If no measurements are available, the man-made concentration can be calculated from emissions, using a rough model. The existing data on concentrations can be collected and reproduced in statistical form.

Indicator No. 3

The concentrations now disturb utilization of the environmental components; they cause loss of function. The level of the concentration is one of the variables that determines the extent to which this loss of function occurs; among other variables are temperature and humidity of the air. Partly because of this fact, the connection between concentration and loss of function is not automatically clear.** It is therefore desirable

*Cf. p. 137.

**Attack of plants by sulphur dioxide is highly dependent on the degree of humidity. In water containing a large amount of floating silt, algal bloom does not occur, despite a high concentration of nutrient salts.

to use a third indicator of environmental deterioration: the effects of the pollutants in an environmental component. This third indicator may be regarded as the finishing touch to the two preceding ones. It shows directly the quality of the environment and can also serve to trace emitted substances of which the adverse effects are not yet known.

We intend to continue to compile time series for the principal agents in water, air and soil in accordance with the pattern outlined above. This seems important because such information can act as a warning and at the same time record the effect of measures taken. Whether this arrangement will prove successful in the future depends mainly on the extent to which data on substances become available.

4.4. Cost Curves and Shadow Prices of Environmental Functions

In this section the concept of shadow price of environmental functions will be defined. However, this will be done only for functions whose availability has decreased as a result of qualitative competition. Use will be made of the concepts of elimination, compensation and financial damage, which will therefore have to be defined first. By comparing the cost curve of measures of elimination with the cost curve of measures of compensation and financial damage, a first approach to the shadow price is obtained.

Loss of function as a result of qualitative competition can be abolished by measures of elimination. These may consist in making all kinds of provisions or of reducing the polluting activity. In this study *elimination* is defined as *removal of the agent at source*, as a result of which the function is wholly or partly restored. In principle, the costs of elimination can be calculated for various degrees of purity or, in other words, for various degrees of restoration of function.

Against the costs of purification we naturally have the benefits of restoration of the function. In a number of cases the latter can be derived from market data. Where this is not possible, they will have to be approximated in another way. This is dealt with further in the following section.

The benefits to be established from market data include the reduction of the costs of compensatory measures taken as a consequence of the loss of function as well as the reduction of the financial damage resulting from the pollution. *Compensation* is defined here as *making alternative provisions* as whole or partial replacement for the affected function. Compensation is nearly always much less effective than elimination; it usually amounts to the creation of a substitute for the original function. *Financial damage* means *the decline in the income or wealth* of private households, business or the government *as a result of loss of function*.

By adopting measures consisting of elimination of the agent, compensatory measures already taken can become wholly or partly superfluous and financial damage as a result of loss of function can be reduced. Thus if noise nuisance by cars, mopeds and aircraft is eliminated (e.g. by prescribing engines with a lower sound level), compensatory measures such as fitting double glazing and taking sleeping pills become superfluous. By eliminating the agent silting restoration of productivity in a part of the agricultural sector (notably the Westland) occurs.

The expenditure on measures of compensation by private households, for instance the costs of travel to go swimming somewhere else when coastal or inland water in the vicinity is polluted, can in theory be estimated by means of budget surveys; however, in practice this proves to encounter great difficulties. Compensatory expenditure by the government and business can in principle by approximated from existing statistical material, national estimates, questionnaires and literature. Financial damage can in principle be estimated by means of questionnaires or theoretical calculations.

Both financial damage and compensation are interpreted here as revealed preferences for a given function. As regards compensation, this will be immediately clear: after all, provisions are made to replace the function originally present. However, amounts of damage can also be interpreted as revealed preferences, since they are losses suffered as a result of the disappearance of a function. In practice one can often choose between accepting damage and taking compensatory measures. Thus in the case of corrosion of steel by air pollution the choice exists between accepting the additional damage from corrosion and better protection of the material.

The most elegant solution would be to compare, per function, the costs and benefits of restoration of function with one another. However, this will seldom prove possible in practice. A cost–benefit analysis for an agent and a number of functions impaired by this agent has more chance of success. For the sake of simplicity it is assumed below that one given function is impaired by one agent. This function is not influenced by other agents, and the agent in question does not impair any other functions. Of course, this situation occurs rarely if ever in practice. The assumption is made solely to simplify the following theoretical explanation.

The costs of elimination and the costs of compensatory measures and financial damage can be presented graphically (Figure 4.10).[12] For this purpose, a scale is plotted on the abscissa giving the degree of purity of the environmental component. The degree of purity will increase as emission of the agent decreases. In the following reasoning it has been assumed that this increase is linear.*

On the ordinate both the total costs of elimination (the E curve) and the sum of the total costs of compensation and financial damage (the $C + D$ curve) are plotted. The following may be said about the shape of the two curves. According as the purity becomes greater and the total availability of the function is approached, in most cases the E curve will display a progressive rise. This is in line with the experience with cost curves in general (Figure 4.10(A)). The $(C + D)$ curve comes into being via a number of intermediate steps. Emission leads via a distribution pattern to a concentration. This concentration leads via dose–effect relations** to consequences for people, animals, plants and/or objects. These consequences are ultimately expressed in terms of money. The curves that reproduce dose–effect relations in general become increasingly steep according as the concentration becomes greater. This increase makes its effect felt in the shape of the $(C + D)$ curve. This will therefore in general become increasingly steep from right to left (Figure 4.10(A)).

On the extreme assumption – which will seldom hold in practice – that the $(C + D)$ curve reproduces the total preferences for the function, the minimum of the total costs $(C + D + E)$ lies at the point where the sum of the two curves (curve T) displays a minimum. With the shape described above of the E curve and the $(C + D)$ curve, curve T will be U-shaped, so that an obvious minimum occurs.*** This minimum represents the optimum of purification. The total social costs are minimum here, while the difference between benefits and costs is maximum.

The latter can be demonstrated as follows in curves (Figure 4.11). The total benefits equal $-(C + D)$. By subtracting the costs from this

*By the horizontal axis 'availability of the function' is stated in addition to 'degree of purity'. This addition might suggest that in this way a unit of measurement is defined, 'availability of the function', which likewise has a linear relation to emission. However, this is not so. The addition has been made because in an economic approach one is ultimately concerned with the function. For practical reasons the scale has been coupled to the agent. One can only say of the degree of availability that it increases along with purity.

**By a dose–effect relation is meant the functional relation between concentration of the agent introduced into the environment and the resultant effect. Strictly speaking one ought therefore to speak of a concentration–effect relation.

***Only in one exceptional case is there no minimum, viz. when the curve of the sum of the costs $(C + D + E)$ runs horizontally. This is the case, inter alia, when both curves are linear and moreover form the same angle to the abscissa.

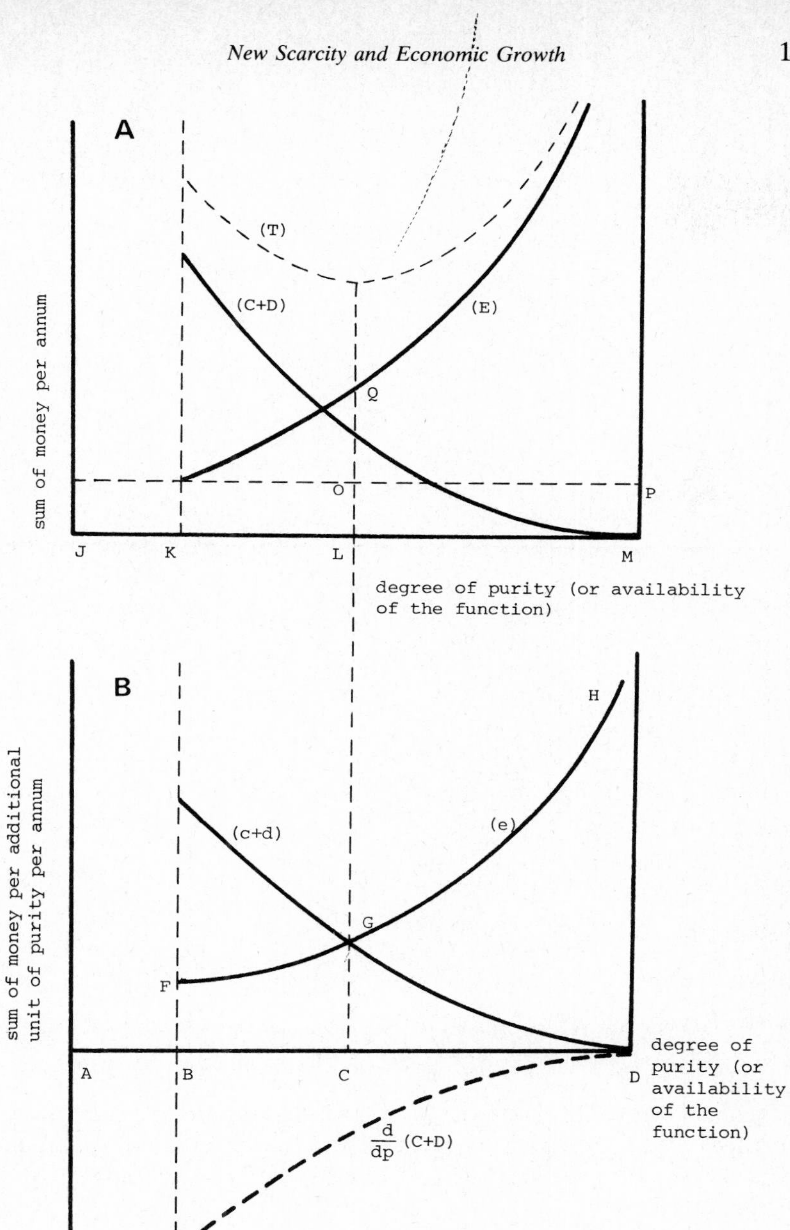

Figure 4.10. Costs of elimination and revealed preferences for an environmental function; (A) total curves, (B) marginal curves.

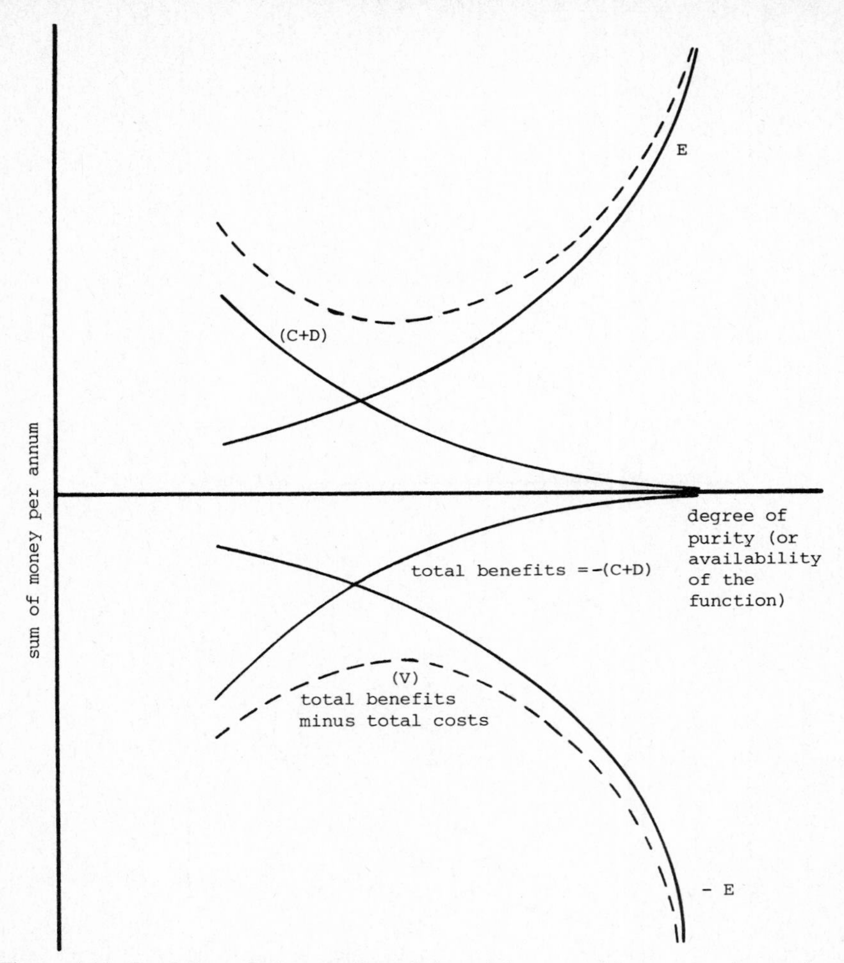

Figure 4.11. Depiction of the equality of the minimum social costs to the maximum benefits minus costs.

(or adding $-E$) one finds curve V, which reproduces total benefits minus total costs. The maximum of this corresponds to the minimum in Figure 4.10(A) (in fact the whole of Figure 4.10(A) is now in mirror image).

Of course, all this can be reproduced with marginal quantities too (Figure 4.10(B)). In that case, the annual sum of money per additional unit of purity appears on the vertical axis. The increase by one unit of purity corresponds to a given reduction in emission of the pollutant. As stated, to stress the cost–benefit aspect one can interpret the reduction in the costs of compensation and financial damage with increasing purity as benefits. In the graph the following then happens: the first derivative of the $(C + D)$ curve, which lies in the fourth quadrant, where it runs from bottom left to top right, is reflected to the first quadrant, where it runs from top left to bottom right (curve $c + d$). This operation may be notated as follows: $-(\mathrm{d}/\mathrm{d}p)\ (C + D) = +(c + d)$, where the symbol p represents purity. At the point where the mirrored curve intersects the marginal e curve the above–mentioned optimum is to be found.

Perhaps it may be useful to demonstrate in algebra that the minimum of the total costs and the point of intersection of the marginal curves tally. This proceeds as follows:

Total costs of elimination: E.

Marginal costs of elimination: $\mathrm{d}E/\mathrm{d}p = e$.

Total costs of compensation plus damage: $(C + D)$.

Marginal benefits: $-(\mathrm{d}/\mathrm{d}p)(C + D) = (c + d)$.

Condition for minimum social costs: $(C + D + E)$ minimal; as long as the U shape of this curve applies, this is equivalent to

$$\frac{\mathrm{d}}{\mathrm{d}p}(C + D + E) = 0,$$

$$\frac{\mathrm{d}}{\mathrm{d}p}E + \frac{\mathrm{d}}{\mathrm{d}p}(C + D) = 0,$$

$$e - (c + d) = 0,$$

$$e = (c + d);$$

and therefore, the point of intersection of $(c + d)$ and e corresponds to $(C + D + E)$ minimal.*

This defines the optimal degree of purification. The marginal costs of achieving optimal purification may be found on the e curve, and the marginal benefits of this on the $(c + d)$ curve. Starting from the adage that the price which reflects the social costs is equal to the marginal costs, the distance from the abscissa to the e curve at the optimum yields the shadow price of the environmental function. *The shadow price of*

*In theory it is possible that the minimum of the total costs is located at the extreme left or the extreme right of the figure. The first case occurs when the marginal elimination cost curve lies in its entirety above the $(c + d)$ curve (even the very beginning of purification requires a greater sum of money than the compensatory costs and financial damage thus saved). This situation will seldom occur. The second case (the minimum of the total costs is to the right of the figure) occurs when the entire marginal elimination cost curve is located under the $(c + d)$ curve. This could happen when the marginal costs of elimination are nil or even negative, a very improbable situation.

an environmental function is therefore equal to the marginal costs of elimination at optimal restoration of function.

The concept of shadow price is universally used in cost–benefit analyses. The expression indicates that the shadow price is not an amount that comes about on the market at which de facto goods are exchanged. The shadow price indicates the sum of the social opportunity costs that come into being in the use of factors of production for a certain purpose. The shadow price should therefore reflect the marginal social costs.[13] According to E. J. Mishan, it is the price that is more appropriate for the purpose of economic calculation than the existing price, or a price that is attributed to a good in the complete absence of a market price.[14]

Let us assume that no measures for restoration of function have been taken as yet and that *B* represents the degree of purity in the starting situation. If, as has been assumed here as the extreme case, all preferences are expressed in *C* and *D*, the shadow price is equal to *CG*. Here *G* is the point of intersection of the marginal *e* and $(c + d)$ curves. The total costs to be incurred at the optimal degree of restoration of function are reproduced by the area *BCGF*, corresponding to the line section *OQ* in Figure 4.10(A). When measures have already been taken in the starting situation, the costs of these can also be estimated in principle. Line *FB* then shifts to the left, so that the area *BCGF* becomes larger (the horizontal line *OP* shifts downwards in its entirety, so that *OQ* becomes greater). *A* (and *J*) is the point that indicates the degree of pollution at which the function has become entirely unusable. In most cases, as will be explained below, this point cannot be exactly established, any more than *D* (and *M*), which indicates the point at which the function is fully available.

Figure 4.10(B) again draws attention to the fact that (polluting) production* and environmental functions may be regarded as each other's opportunity costs. For purification from *B* to *C* is accompanied by the utilization of the means *BCGF*, which reproduce the sacrificed alternative on behalf of the restoration of function to *C*. The remaining loss of function *CD* forms the sacrificed alternative on behalf of the remaining polluting activities; the area *CDHG* indicates the sacrifices still remaining to make the function fully available.

In the figure the cost curves do not continue to the vertical axis. This is connected with the fact that the zero point of the elimination cost

*Elimination measures are of course production *costs*. They merely restore the adverse effects of production and consumption (of produced goods) and cause no addition to the quantity of goods and services becoming available. This point will be elaborated in Chapter 5, in which the concept of economic growth is again considered.

curve is difficult to determine. In the above reasoning it has been implicitly assumed that the costs of elimination are zero for the least expensive way of production, in which no allowance at all is made for the environment (and a way of consumption to which the same applies). Our investigation always proceeds from the situation at a given moment in time. At this moment in time the elimination costs are theoretically equal to the difference between the actual costs of production and the costs of the production process in which no allowance is made for the environment. Definition of the latter process is often rather arbitrary. For instance, it has to be investigated which measures have been taken on behalf of the environment and which on behalf of improvements in productivity, apart from consideration of the environment. In a number of cases the two will coincide. As a result, practically insoluble problems of appropriation occur. For these reasons, it is generally not feasible to place the zero point J of the purity scale exactly at the pollution caused by the process in question. The horizontal scale has therefore been chosen in such a way that point K, which indicates the degree of purity in the starting situation, always falls to the right of point J.

Defining the scale in this way leads to calculation of the costs of elimination with the exception of one constant amount (line section OL in Figure 4.10(A)). Fortunately, this presents no problem in determining the optimum: that continues to be at the same point on the horizontal axis. If one is working with marginal curves, this constant amount disappears upon differentiation. The level of the marginal e curve – and thus the shadow price – has therefore been unambiguously determined.

In the practice of the investigation the uncertainty about the zero point of the scale presents no particular problem. One is always concerned with a known starting situation, to be indicated as a point on the horizontal axis (in the figure the dotted ordinate has been drawn from this point). The investigation is concerned in the first place with the additional elimination costs that have to be incurred to attain the optimum from this point. Only in the second place are the costs calculated, as far as possible, of measures taken in the past on behalf of the environment; in the process problems of appropriation will in fact have to be solved arbitrarily.

Our investigation endeavours to find out data on both indicators (emissions, concentrations and ecological indicators) and costs. With regard to costs of elimination it is attempted to estimate both the (total) costs already incurred and the amounts required for full restoration of function, while as far as possible the costs of measures of compensation and the financial damage are also estimated.

The first calculations performed will be briefly summarized in

Appendix II. For the costs of elimination of the emissions of biodegradable organic matter and of chlorides it was possible to construct an E curve. For chlorides a $(C + D)$ curve could also be constructed.

As already mentioned, it will seldom be possible to consider one agent and one function separately. Elimination of an agent will usually also restore other functions than the one considered, wholly or partially; other agents too often impair the function under consideration; financial damage and measures of compensation often relate to more than one function. This entails problems of imputation. It will be clear that these can be better solved according as more data become available, with which the rows and columns of the table 'agents versus functions' can be completed.*

In the investigation, the method of estimation starting from the agent has been opted for. In this method the costs of elimination per agent are therefore compared in the first instance with the losses of function caused by this agent. Our investigation has resulted in the insight that in principle the emissions and the costs of elimination can be tracked down by theoretical calculations or by means of questionnaires.** The estimates of costs of compensation and financial damage entail much greater difficulties. However, the greatest difficulty of all lies in the establishment of the preferences, which cannot be directly approached from the market, as can costs of compensation and financial damage. Some brief comments will be made on this difficulty in the following sections.

To conclude this section, the following may be remarked. Qualitative competition is a matter of degree. The greater the concentration of the agent, the greater the loss of function. Here restoration of function is often possible not only through direct reduction of the level of activities (partial or complete cessation of the activity producing the agent) but also by taking certain measures (such as purification). The latter partly reopens the possibility of reallocation in the traditional sense. Quantitative and spatial competition is of an absolute nature. Here the functions are in direct competition with one another. Since one cannot make extra matter or space, withdrawal on behalf of a given function excludes the use of another function. This means that the loss of function as a result of quantitative and spatial competition can be eliminated only by reducing the level of activities. This entails reallocation via the level of activities. Since our investigation is not

*See pp. 199 and 212.

**For various reasons it has not yet proved possible to start with questionnaires. The first results of the investigation have been obtained by theoretical calculations.

concerned in the first instance with quantitative and spatial competition, this section has not examined the costs and benefits connected with restoration of quantitative and spatial loss of function. However, it follows from the preceding remarks that the costs of restoration of a certain function always amount here to abandoning the use of other functions of the environmental component in question. The benefits roughly tally with those discussed under qualitative competition.

4.5. *Estimating the Urgency of Wants from Behaviour or Questioning*

It is clear that the losses of possible uses of the environment are only very partially compensated for, while in addition they are not always reflected in financial damage. Often, too, the possibility of compensation does not exist. Thus double-glazing may reduce the nuisance of traffic noise inside the house, but not outside; it continues to be impossible to open windows in fine weather without being disturbed by noise. Stench is practically inescapable. A compensatory measure like moving to a clean area is feasible only for the happy few. Financial damage through noise nuisance and air pollution is very incompletely reflected in the fall in value of the house, as a result of the tightness on the housing market and the immobilization caused by ties to work and the neighbourhood.[15] Artificial swimming pools can hardly compensate for the loss of clean bathing beaches. The loss of flora, fauna and scenery and the poor prospects for the future cannot be measured in compensation or financial damage; yet there is obviously a great need for unvitiated nature and a safe future.

In addition to the difficulty that preferences are not reflected on the market, there is the problem of inadequate knowledge of the objective value in use of environmental functions referred to in the first section of this chapter. When individuals are not aware of the significance of environmental functions and the loss thereof, no urgency of wants can be measured.

This means that the shadow price of most environmental functions is higher, for some functions indeed much higher, than the point of intersection of the e curve and the $(c + d)$ curve (Figure 4.10(B)).

Part of this surplus value, to be indicated below by X, is equal to the urgency of the want for an environmental function valued in terms of money, insofar as this is not reflected in expenditure on compensatory measures and financial damage; X is therefore the amount that individuals would spend on the restoration of an environmental function of their own volition, if there were a market for this function. The level of X depends of course on the degree of availability of the function and will increase strongly, above all in the case of vital environmental functions, according as the availability decreases. We therefore have here a curve showing the relation between the degree of availability of the function and the level of X. The first derivative of this curve must be superimposed on the $(c + d)$ curve. The point of intersection of the e curve and the $(c + d + x)$ curve indicates the shadow price in which the preferences not reflected in compensatory costs and financial damage have also been allowed for. In this section it will be investigated what methods there are of approaching X by estimating the urgency of wants which cannot be reflected in costs of compensation or financial damage. It will prove that the possibilities presented by the existing methods are limited. The only possibility that then remains is for the government to estimate X on the strength of its insight into the preferences of individuals. This aspect will be dealt with in the next section.

In addition to X there may be a further surplus value present. This comes into being because people are not aware of the utility of the environmental functions. We must now fall back on the objective value in use of the environmental functions. For this the government will have to estimate the value by its own efforts, i.e. in detachment from its idea of the preferences of the present generation. Let us call this value Y. This aspect too is discussed in the following section.

In order to estimate X, the urgency of wants for environmental functions not reflected in costs of compensation and financial damage, the following methods are available, and will be briefly discussed below:

- attempts can be made to derive the urgency of the want for an environmental function from the pattern of behaviour with regard to an *unimpaired function* with the aid of market data;
- one can try to express this intensity in terms of money by asking individuals how much they would be prepared to pay for the restoration of loss of function, what it would be worth to them to suffer no loss of function or what amount they wish to receive as compensation for an existing loss of function.

For various reasons, the possibilities of valuing the want for an unimpaired function in terms of money from individual behaviour are very limited. For instance, there is no point to this approach for a number of functions essential to human life. Functions such as air for physiological functioning and water as raw material for drinking water are used up to the point of full satisfaction of the wants when they are freely available. Not the slightest subsidiary action needs to be performed to breathe in clean air; the effort to obtain drinking water is restricted to a fixed pattern of simple filtration and distribution. For the rest, the value of these functions consists of consumer's surplus. The level of this can safely be put at infinite. Furthermore, the preferences for a number of functions cannot be expressed in behaviour. This, for instance, is the case with functions serving as means of production. After all, the whole of production depends on the services of the environment. This well-known fact, which is again emphasized by Commoner (see Section 3.10), does not lead to special individual behaviour as long as the functions are available to a sufficient degree. Only when loss of function occurs can compensatory measures and financial damage be established.

It is therefore not surprising that the literature on the derivation of sums of money from behaviour as regards the environment relates mainly to recreation areas. For here the opportunity does arise to approximate in terms of money the value of an unimpaired recreational function from behaviour, such as travelling expenses consisting of kilometre costs and costs of travelling time, sums of money spent on recreation. Some of the suggestions made in the literature will be briefly outlined below.[16]

The United States National Park Service has proposed that the benefits of a recreation area be measured by means of the expenditure incurred during visits to such areas.[17] This has rightly met with the criticism that what is estimated by this method is not the benefits of the recreation area, but the secondary effect on ancillary concerns. Moreover, part of the expenditure (food) is not connected with the recreational visit.

There seems to be more point to the proposal by R. P. Marks and S. Myers to assign to one hour of recreation spent in the open air the value of the average expenditure per hour on analogous recreation.[18] In my opinion this suggestion rightly proceeds from the principle of opportunity costs, which in fact also forms the basis for the costs of compensatory measures mentioned in the preceding section. When a recreational possibility of the environment is taken away from us, we shall necessarily have to switch to other existing forms of relaxation. It has been argued against the method that the calculation wrongly assumes that the amount that people spend on market recreation indicates what free recreation is actually worth to them, that recreation for which one does not pay is usually very different from recreation for which one pays and that the price paid for market recreation can be depressed by the availability of free recreation.[19]

A. H. Trice and S. E. Wood, developing an idea by H. Hotelling, suggest constructing a collective demand curve from the costs of travel to a recreation site.[20] Around the latter a number of concentric circles are drawn, demarcating the residential areas around the recreation site. The average costs of travel from each of the zones to the recreation site are taken as points of the demand curve for that site. According to Trice and Wood, the costs of travel from the most distant zone then represent the market value of the recreation amenity. All visitors from nearer zones enjoy a consumer's surplus equal to the difference between the average costs of travel from their own zone and those from the most distant zone. The total benefits of the recreation site, according to Trice and Wood, are equal to the sum of the consumer's surpluses thus established.

The following objections can be made to this method.[21] In the first place, there seems to be no point in calculating the consumer's surplus of recreation sites. In my opinion calculations of the value of environmental goods derive their importance above all from the provision of an instrument by which weighting with produced goods and services can take place. Consumer's surplus relates to the difference between the integral utility of a good and the product of price (as indication of the marginal utility) and quantity. Consequently, the calculated consumer's surplus cannot be compared with the prices of market goods; in the case of some market goods the above-mentioned product is low in respect of the consumer's surplus (e.g. water, bread and some forms of medical aid), and in the case of others high (luxury goods which can be sold only with a great deal of advertising). In the second place, the calculation by Trice and Wood relates to a good that can be used for a zero price (visiting the site costs nothing, unlike a trip to a cinema or dolphinarium), but which is nevertheless scarce. It is therefore questionable whether the hatched part of Figure 4.12 can be interpreted in its entirety as consumer's surplus. In the third place, what Trice and Wood call market value is in fact used as the integral utility obtained by the recreationists, it being assumed that all recreationists assign the same utility to the site

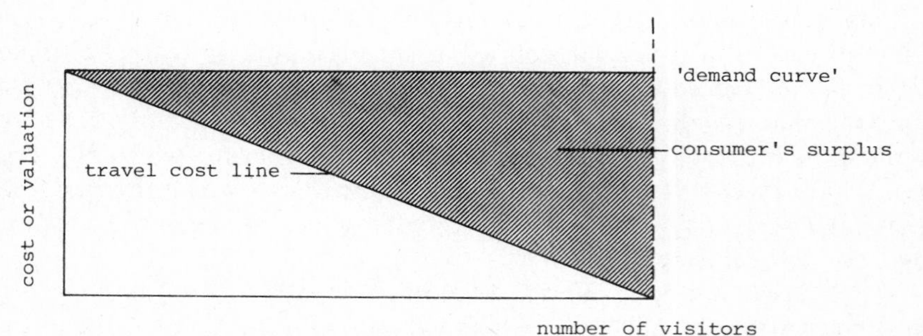

Figure 4.12. Demand curve for a recreation site (Trice and Wood).

as the visitors living furthest away. Trice and Wood therefore obviously proceed from a horizontal demand curve. As a result, both differences in income and differences in taste are ignored. In the fourth place, the travelling costs of the recreationists from the various zones are in fact used by Trice and Wood as a series of prices. This means that a monopolist applying price discrimination is taken as a basis. Perfect price discrimination rarely occurs with market goods. I therefore feel that the method of Trice and Wood greatly overestimates the size of the consumer's surplus. To make matters clearer, this has been illustrated in Figure 4.12.[22]

In my opinion, a more realistic approach to the benefits of a recreation site is given by M. Clawson.[23] He first constructs a demand curve that shows the relationship between the number of visits per 1,000 inhabitants (*V*) of the zones around the recreation site and the travel and hotel costs per visit (*C*). This curve appears in Figure 4.13 with the omission of the hotel costs to which the objections already listed above can be made and which in any case influence only the level of the curve.

Now Clawson assumes that the residents of each of the zones react as a group in the same way to an increase in costs and that it makes no difference to them whether the costs increase as a result of greater costs of travel or as the result of an admission charge. Investigation shows, for instance, that the residents of the outermost zone can reach the site at an average cost of $100 and the residents of the innermost zone for $10. At the same time, in the construction of the curve of Figure 4.13 it has been established that 10% of the population of the outermost zone visits the site. In that case, on the assumptions made, 10% of the population of the innermost zone will be prepared to pay an admission of $90 for a visit. The difference in costs of travel between, on the one hand, the outermost and the closest zone but one and, on the other hand, the

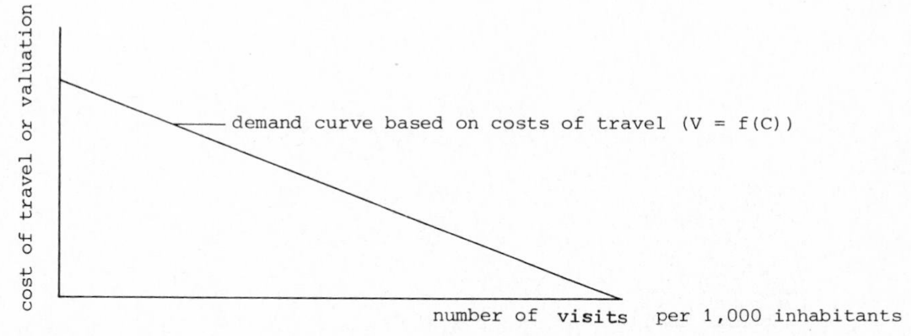

Figure 4.13. Demand curve for a recreation site on a basis of the costs of travel (Clawson).

most distant zone but one (25% of whose population visits the site) and the innermost zone proves to be \$80. In that case, 10% of the population of the closest zone but one and 25% of the innermost zone will be prepared to pay \$80 admission.

In this way Clawson derives from the first curve a second curve, which he calls the demand curve for the recreation site itself. Now, according to Clawson, the benefits of the site measured in terms of money are equal to the sum that a monopolist not applying price discrimination can collect as a maximum from the (imaginary) admissions. This maximum is reached at the point where the marginal revenues equal zero. This is illustrated in Figure 4.14.

The benefits of the recreational function of an environmental component (water or soil) calculated with the aid of Clawson's method are, in my opinion, reasonably comparable with the market price of produced goods. A drawback that is difficult to resolve is that the preferences for the future are not reflected. An advantage is that in Clawson's method the benefits increase according as the innermost zones are relatively more densely populated. The demand curve then becomes convex in shape and the hatched rectangle in Figure 4.14 becomes greater. However, the disadvantage of this is that the method leaves no scope for the influence of the numbers of visitors; as this number increases, the utility per recreationist decreases. Finally, Clawson makes no allowance for the travelling time factor, which may proceed to yield a considerable disutility, above all as congestion increases.

J. L. Knetsch[24] and J. B. Stevens[25] have refined Clawson's method by incorporating in equation $V = f(C)$, Figure 4.13, the influence of the income of the various zones (Y), the degree of congestion in the site (G), and the competition of alternative recreation sites (S). The equation then assumes the form $V = f(C,Y,S,G)$.

The last method that will be discussed here is that of F. Bouma.[26]

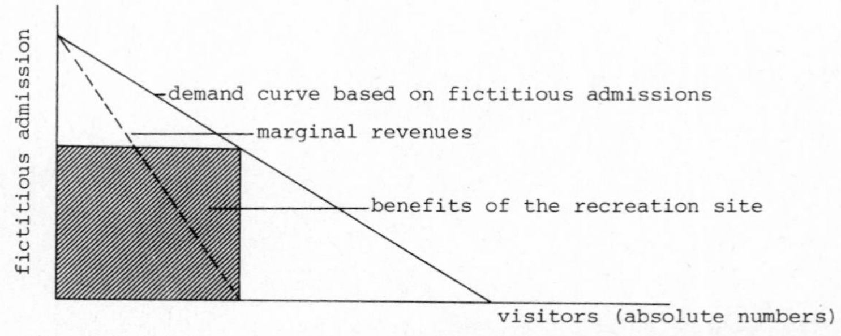

Figure 4.14. Demand curve for a recreation site based on fictitious admissions (Clawson).

Unlike the authors discussed above, Bouma starts from a number of recreation sites located at various distances from a residential centre. According to Bouma, the choice of a site depends on the nature of that site, the density of visitors and the distance from the residential centre. From research the connection can be obtained between, on the one hand, costs of travel and distance and, on the other, distance and density. From this the connection between costs of travel and density for each of the sites can be derived. On the assumption that the utility of a site is determined exclusively by the density of visitors, a recreationist will select that site of which the marginal utility equals the marginal costs of travel. The value of a certain recreation site is now equated to the additional costs entailed by distance that would have to be incurred if the site in question were to disappear, in order to provide the recreationists in question with the same level of utility as before.

The advantage of Bouma's method is that it is based on the opportunity cost principle, as a result of which the drawbacks of an approach via consumer's surplus is avoided (Clawson's method is not entirely free from these drawbacks either). However, the method is in fact out of place in a list of valuations of unimpaired functions. For Bouma starts from the (imaginary) situation that the function disappears, and therefore switches to determination of costs of compensation. Apart from its merits, the method has been mentioned here because it shows how the valuation of losses of function and the valuation of an unimpaired function can supplement one another.

In our investigation we shall not proceed for the time being to estimate the benefits of the restoration of function (by elimination) by means of the valuation of unimpaired functions. The main reasons for this are that the available methods are most laborious, have to be performed for each separate area and can be applied only for a few specific functions (mainly recreation). However, perhaps in due course grateful use can be made of the results of other investigations such as that by the Institute for Environmental Problems of the Free University, Amsterdam (F. Bouma) and that of the Institute for Land and Water Management Research, Wageningen (L. J. Locht).

As a second possible method of approximating the preferences for environmental functions in terms of money in addition to costs of compensation and financial damage, questioning has already been mentioned. The objections to this are self-evident.

Firstly, the information on the significance of environmental functions is deficient in many cases. This applies to the functions that serve as means of production. Individuals have inadequate insight into the importance of the environmental functions to the various production processes. It also applies to the functions that directly or indirectly determine health. Adverse effects on health often do not manifest themselves until years later, sometimes not until later generations (for example, damage to genes by radioactive radiation). Sometimes only a few experts are aware of the adverse effects. Sometimes adverse effects are suspected but cannot be demonstrated (such as deep-well discharges of chemical waste, aircraft contrails in the stratosphere). In the past, in a number of cases nobody was aware of certain adverse effects and it was not until later that these became evident (for instance, mercury poisoning by eating fish, accumulation of chlorinated hydrocarbons by way of the food chain). It is therefore not improbable that effects are also occurring today, the harm caused by which will not become evident till later. The lack of information is probably the greatest with the natural environment function. The relations within ecosystems are extremely complex. The consequences of the disturbances of ecosystems are difficult to gauge. Ecologists suspect that these consequences will be much greater than we realize so far.[27]

In all cases in which individuals have no awareness of the importance of an environmental function, the questioning method is pointless[28].* Only when loss of function is suffered directly by individuals is there no objection from the informative point of view to this method. This is the case, for instance, with noise, nuisance and stench.

A second obvious objection is the non-binding nature of the answers. There is a considerable difference between saying that one has money to spare for something and actually paying for it. This strong argument against the method of questioning needs no further explanation.

A third objection is that the respondents may feel that individuals may not be asked to make a contribution for the environment because in their opinion this is a task for the government or because the polluter should pay. The cry that people are 'entitled' to a clean environment is often heard. This opinion may influence the answers.

Finally, there is also the free rider problem.[29] Persons questioned may state low amounts on the assumption that others will 'bid' sufficiently high to restore the environmental function.

In the literature, few proposals for or examples of quantification in terms of money of preferences for environmental functions by questioning are to be found. Below, the method used in the

*J.B. Opschoor demonstrates with the aid of indifference curves that asking an uninformed consumer about his wishes means that one will get a non-optimal answer – from the consumer's point of view too.

investigation into the location of the third London airport and the method that has been suggested for environmental investigation of the Rhine Delta will be successively discussed.

In the report of the Commission on the Third London Airport – called the Roskill Report after the name of the chairman – the methods used by various research groups for estimating in terms of money the noise nuisance accompanying the four alternative locations of the third airport are discussed.[30] The method of estimating a fall in the value of houses by means of discussions with estate agents (realtors) need not be further considered here. After all, this amounts to estimating financial damage. In addition it has been attempted by questioning occupants to express in terms of money the disutility of moving to another part of the country and the disutility of the noise nuisance.

With regard to the disutility of moving house, the various research groups tried with the aid of three kinds of questioning techniques to find out what amount would be just sufficient to induce those questioned to move voluntarily to a comparable dwelling elsewhere. The percentages of the respondents who said that no amount, however great, would compensate them for having to move were 43, 38 or 8, depending on the method used. These results confirm my opinion that the objections stated above to questioning are real ones. In particular the non-binding nature of the answer if those questioned do not actually have to pay and the opinion that individuals ought not to have to pay are, I believe, the cause of the great differences in the results and also of the high percentages of respondents who state that no sum of money whatsoever could compensate them.

As regards the disutility of noise nuisance, persons in a quiet environment were asked what reduction in the price they would wish to have if they were to move to a house in an environment with noise nuisance, three different degrees of the latter being described. This question is an indirect attempt to estimate appreciation of peace and quiet in monetary terms. Depending on the level of noise, 40 to 60% of those questioned were not prepared to fill in an amount.[31] This result too makes it probable, to my way of thinking, that the objections to the questioning method listed above weigh heavily, in particular the non-binding nature and the opinion that individuals need not pay. A further disadvantage of this question is that the respondents have not themselves experienced the noise nuisance.

The Roskill Report states that it did not move on to the question of what amount one would be prepared to pay to stop construction of the airport. The authors of the report mention as the reason for this that the situation covered by the question rarely occurs in reality. According to the report, the amounts listed relate to the compensating consumer's surplus.[32]*

In my opinion, the latter remark is not correct. The amounts that the respondents are prepared to spend on keeping noise nuisance away are a direct expression of their preference for peace and quiet. The advantage of this form of questioning over the question what amount one would have to receive to put up with noise nuisance (see above) is the income restruction (since an unchanged real income is assumed).[32]* In principle this prevents the results from containing some consumer's surplus for the environmental good peace and quiet.

The comment that the situation rarely occurs in reality is of course correct. E. J. Mishan argues that this is precisely one of the big drawbacks of the whole structure of the Roskill Report. There is in fact no question of a real cost–benefit analysis of the construction or not of a third airport. All that happens is that alternative locations are considered; as far as the report is concerned, it is an established fact that a third airport is coming.[33]** Elsewhere Mishan states that there is no economic criterion for answering the question who has to compensate whom upon the occurrence of external effects. After all, this is a matter of distribution, on which economics cannot make any normative pronouncements. However, a sense of justice suggests that the originator must compensate the victim.[34] It is above all for this reason that the question as to how much one is willing to pay to avoid noise nuisance has great drawbacks.

In the Integrated Environmental Health Investigation of the Rhine Delta Authority a number of questions have also been included to obtain an impression of the willingness to make sacrifices. The present author has been involved in the compilation of a method for expressing the willingness to make sacrifices in terms of money. Initially, it was proposed that the wants for environmental functions be quantified by establishing their relation to produced goods, of which the price is known. When the want for the environmental function X proves to be greater than that for the market good A and less than that for the market good B, one would know that the subjects are prepared to spend a sum of money on function X lying between the price of A and that of B. This

*The variant of the consumer's surplus that Hicks calls the compensating variation relates to the maximum amount that the subjects are prepared to pay outside the market price to obtain a service. This variant contrasts with the equivalent variation, which represents the minimum amount that the subjects wish to receive outside the market price to relinquish a good.

**D. W. Pearce also points out that the Roskill Report merely contains a cost comparison between the four alternative locations. It implicitly assumes that the benefits are higher than the location with the lowest costs. The difficulties of measuring these benefits are clearly immense.

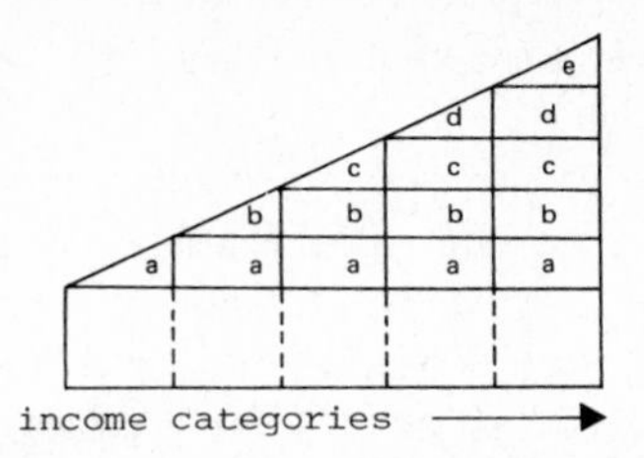

Figure 4.15. Diagram of expenditure on environmental goods above the lowest income category according to the coin game (Rhine Delta survey).

approach was not literally applied because an income restriction was absent here. Instead, a coin game has been chosen. Those questioned (divided into five income categories) get 40 coins, representing an expected 4% increase in income in the coming year. The coins may be spent on a number of goods, among which, in addition to several market goods, a few unpriced goods are included, such as clean water, clean air, absence of noise nuisance and safety of young people.* As a check on the reliability of the answers, the income elasticities calculated by means of the results can be compared with the income elasticities of the same goods calculated from budget surveys.

Since in this way only an impression can be obtained of what an individual is prepared to spend on environmental goods out of an – annual – increase in income, the following artifice will be applied. The sample is divided into five income categories. It is now assumed that the amount that indicates the difference between the lowest and the next highest class is spent in the same way as the 40 coins representing the 4% extra income of the lowest category. This assumption is likewise introduced into the difference between the lowest category but one and the following category, and so on. In other words, the pattern of expenditure of the 4% extra income is 'extrapolated' per category to the amount indicating the difference between two income categories. In this way, one can approximate the amount that the subjects wish to spend of that part of their income that is higher than that of the lowest category on the environmental goods mentioned in the survey. By way of explanation the above is reproduced in Figure 4.15. The amounts *a* are calculated from the percentage of the coins that the lowest income category wishes to spend on a given environmental function. The amounts *b* are

*These goods are not further specified; thus clean water is not related to a given – low – level of concentration of pollutants nor to a certain function of the water. Consequently, the Rhine Delta survey can furnish no more than a rough order of magnitude of the intensity of the preferences for environmental functions.

calculated from the percentage that the lowest income category but one wishes to spend, and so on.

The method used here has the following advantages. The persons questioned themselves suffer the disadvantages of the losses of function. No consumer's surplus is measured. The coin game incorporates an income restriction. A relation is established with market goods, of which the price is known. The drawbacks of insufficient information, of not really having to pay, the feeling that the polluter or the government ought to pay and the free rider problem still apply here too in full, however. Moreover, this method cannot be used to find out how much of the amount equal to the lowest income one is prepared to spend on environmental goods; an assumption will have to be made for that. For these reasons, and having regard in part to the limited manpower, our investigation will not proceed for the time being to establish preferences by the questioning method. However, in due course it may be possible to make use of investigations such as that of the Rhine Delta.

The Rhine Delta survey has already been held but not yet worked out, so that nothing can be said as yet about the results.

It emerges from the above that the possibilities of quantifying preferences for environmental functions in money are only slight. They can only very partially be derived by means of estimates of the costs of compensatory measures and of financial damage. Amplification of this by derivation from behaviour and by questioning is possible only to a limited extent, while questioning in particular encounters practically insurmountable objections. This means that in most cases the x of the curve $(c + d + x)$ is unknown and the shadow price of the environmental functions remains indeterminate. The only possibility then left is that the government estimates the value of the environmental functions. The next two sections are concerned with this.

4.6. The Shadow Price as the Great Unknown

It has been explained in Section 4.4 that the shadow price of environmental functions could be determined in principle from market data if all preferences for the functions were to be expressed in terms of compensatory measures and financial damage. But this is by no means the case. Consequently, as already remarked in Section 4.5, the level of the shadow price is partially dependent on the X amounts that the subjects would spend of their own volition on an environmental function if there were a market for that function. These amounts naturally vary with the degree of availability of the function, and therefore form a curve. The first derivative of this curve – the x curve – must be superimposed on the $(c + d)$ curve. In the previous section it was investigated to what extent the X amounts can be derived from behaviour and questioning. The possibilities proved limited.

It is therefore unavoidable that the government partly or even wholly estimates the X amounts – and thus the x curve – in many cases. In so doing the government can base itself on (verbal) descriptions of the importance of environmental functions and of the consequences of losses of function. For from these descriptions an impression may be obtained of the utility of the functions for individuals and of the disadvantage that loss of function entails. In addition, the government can allow itself to be guided by the information of the elimination cost curve. This method can best be defined as a *cost–effectiveness analysis*. The costs of the measures that may have to be taken can after all be weighed in the way described above against the effect to be achieved with them.

In Appendix I a description of this kind is given for the environmental components water and air.* This survey has been compiled from a literature survey, information from various research institutes and the personal observations of the staff of the Department for Environmental Statistics.

Filling in preferences on the strength of verbal information on the consequences of environmental deterioration can be defended on the following grounds.

Firstly, many environmental functions may be interpreted as collective goods; it is true of all functions that the way in which they are used, must be established by the community (see Section 4.2). In the case of other collective goods too the price is fixed on the strength of verbal descriptions. An instance is safety (expenditure on defence, police and dykes).

Secondly, it should be borne in mind that in a market economy as we know it most environmental functions remain outside the price mechanism. As a result, the functions are not priced and the goods and services produced are. E. J. Mishan describes how much trouble it would take, if peace and quiet were a market good and a journey by air an unpriced good, to demonstrate that the utility of such a flight in terms of money is worth the sacrifice of peace and quiet.[35] This consideration suggests that the government be recommended, when weighing the importance of produced goods and unpriced but scarce environmental

*As mentioned above, losses of function as a result of spatial competition are not considered here.

functions, either explicitly to estimate the shadow prices of the functions or, in the weighing, to replace the prices of the produced goods by the costs of their production. After all, both categories of goods may be regarded as each other's opportunity cost; they are always 'at the expense of each other'. However, the market price of a produced good expresses the urgency of the wants only in respect of other market goods, but *not* in respect of environmental functions, since the latter fall outside the market process. Consequently, when on the one hand the production costs of the produced goods and the costs of elimination (as 'production costs' of the environmental functions) are compared with one another and on the other hand the utility of the two categories of goods is directly weighed the one against the other, a more accurate comparison takes place than when a priced market good is weighed against an unpriced environmental function. In the latter case, one will be insufficiently aware of the fact that the price of the market does not give the slightest information on the ranking of the wants with regard to market goods *and* environmental functions; the priced market good will consciously or unconsciously acquire too great a weight.

Figure 4.10 presented in Section 4.4 assumes the shape of Figure 4.16 after allowance has been made for the amounts that individuals would

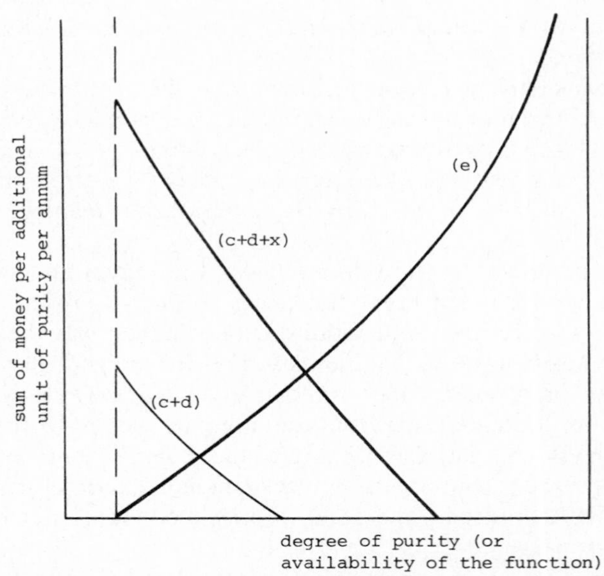

Figure 4.16. Shadow price of environmental functions taking into account all wants of individuals.

spend of their own volition on an environmental function if there were a market for that function.

As already mentioned, individuals have an insufficient knowledge of the importance (the objective value in use) of a number of environmental functions. It has therefore been stated in Section 4.5 that the government, in its valuation of the environmental functions, must not only estimate the amounts that individuals would spend of their own volition but must also allow its own preferences to count. In other words, in a number of cases there is reason to regard the environmental functions as *merit goods*.

Merit goods are goods the use of which the government wishes to encourage for certain reasons.[36] The following reasons are stated in the literature for this encouragement:[37]

(1) Individuals have insufficient knowledge of the merits of a good (lack of information).
(2) The goods have a considerable positive external effect that benefits the community (externality).
(3) Cultural heritage must be preserved (conservation).
(4) Allowance must be made for future wants.

Likewise the government can restrain the consumption of certain goods on account of inadequate knowledge of the harmful effect on the consumer or on account of the negative external effects on the community. Such goods are called *demerit goods*.

On the strength of the above criteria, there is every reason to regard most functions of the environment as merit goods.

Firstly, individuals have a great lack of information on the importance of a number of functions. As already mentioned in Section 4.5, this applies to functions serving as means of production, functions that directly or indirectly determine health and, above all, the function natural environment.[38]

Secondly, a number of functions have a high degree of externality. This applies in particular to the functions that are essential to health and to the function natural environment. The favourable side-effect of health for the community hardly needs further explanation. As for the positive external effects of the function natural environment, one must envisage factors such as the supply of gene material for the creation and improvement of field crops and livestock, the supply of medicines (vaccines, antitoxins), provision of the possibility of ecological study (which is required for insight into the interaction of, for instance, the human organism and nature) and above all the maintenance of biological equilibrium.[39] It is also true to say, notably with regard to the component water, that the degree of disturbance of the natural environment as regards qualitative competition determines the degree of availability of all other functions. For the reduced availability of water as a result of qualitative competition is in all cases caused by a disturbance of the existing biological and chemical composition of the water through human activities.

Thirdly, the function natural environment in particular may be regarded as one of the most important heritages of mankind. The conservation argument, which is often mentioned in connection with art subsidies, certainly also applies to the environment. The conservation of animal and plant species and of landscapes is too important to be left to private organizations like the World Wildlife Fund. Moreover, the objective of these organizations – the conservation of nature – is a static one. It amounts to the fact that all kinds of activities must be *omitted*. The whole production structure, on the other hand, is directed towards *doing*. The most vigorous impulse towards this is the remuneration system: the size of a person's income depends on his contribution to production. This leads to a pronounced dynamic development from wants to production and from production to new wants. In this dynamism static objectives such as the conservation of nature inevitably have to take a back seat.

This argument applies *a fortiori* when the future is at stake. As emphasized several times above, the uncontrolled growth of production and population makes inroads into vital environmental functions and thus leads to reduction of the possibilities of satisfying future wants.

R. A. Musgrave points out that in the case of merit goods and demerit goods there is a deliberate departure from individuals' preferences.[40,41] This is different from what happens in general with collective goods, for in supplying these the government tries in principle to approximate the preferences of the public as closely as possible.[41] According to Musgrave, in addition to the reasons usually stated in the literature,* there are two further reasons that justify deliberate departure from the preferences. The first is that an elected elite, on the basis of a better education or greater innate wisdom, may impose its preferences within certain limits on the public. The second is that it emerges from social behaviour itself that the community wishes to intervene to a considerable extent in the individual preferences of the consumers. Thus large sums of money are spent on individual amenities, such as low-rent housing and milk for babies.

*See p. 139.

Regarding the environmental functions as a merit good means that the government ought not only to estimate the X amounts (which individuals would spend of their own volition) but also the Y amounts by means of which it expresses its own preferences for certain vital environmental functions. These amounts naturally vary with the degree of availability of the function, and its first derivative – the y curve – can therefore be superimposed on the $(c + d + x)$ curve. This has been done in Figure 4.17.

The conclusion of this and the two previous sections must be that the level of the shadow price of environmental functions is largely indeterminate because insufficient information is available on the preferences for environmental functions. In the following section it will be explained that in practice the environmental functions are nevertheless valued, namely by the government. It remains an open question whether the government assigns the right value to the functions: the point of intersection of the e curve and the $(c + d + x + y)$ curve. Does it value them too highly? Or does valuation by the government lag behind the public's wants (x is estimated too low; a cultural lag occurs) and the government is remiss in its duty to coming generations (y is put too low)? A reasoned answer to this question cannot be given. It remains a matter of subjective appraisal. Such

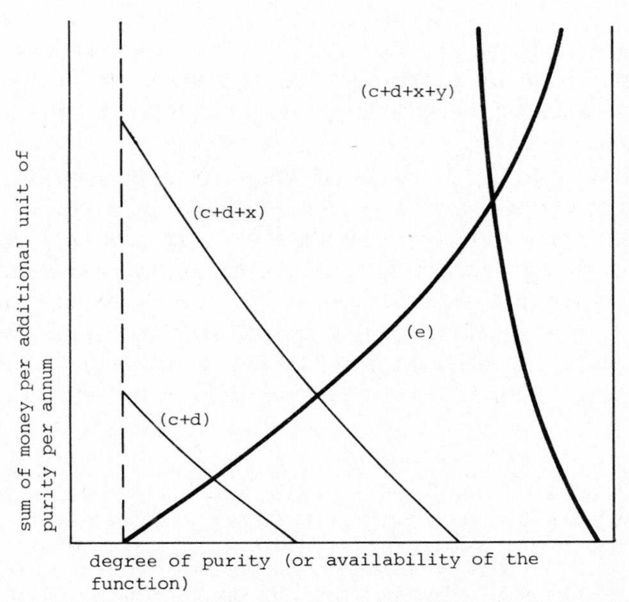

Figure 4.17. Shadow price of vital environmental functions regarded as merit goods.

situations, which in essence are not new, are usually solved in practice by setting objective standards that are derived from the natural sciences or from medical science. Such standards have already been in use for a considerable time in for instance the field of hygiene (toilets, drains, mains water). The next section will examine whether and to what extent this procedure can also be applied to the environment.

4.7. Effectuation of the Valuation of Environmental Functions by the Government; Standards

The extent to which the competing environmental functions are available at a given moment for the activities that can utilize them is, of course, determined by social forces. It follows from the above that wide availability of an environmental function is synonymous with a high valuation of that function, and vice versa. Investigation of the operation of the social forces leading ultimately to the valuation of the environmental functions is beyond the scope of this study. It can only be established here that when all is said and done it is the governments who, by the way in which they use their powers, have a decisive influence on the effectuation of the valuation of environmental functions.* The government decisions that effectuate the valuation amount to laying down rules for man's activities relating to production and consumption. The rules may consist of the prescription of provisions of all kinds (treatment of waste water, after-burners), of regulation of the use of substances by means of charges or prohibitions, of physical planning measures, etc.[42]

It is clear that, as a result of the spreading new scarcity, the government is acquiring a strongly growing influence on price determination and allocation of both the environmental functions and the goods produced. For by its decisions the government *simultaneously* values the environmental functions and the activities using these functions. It follows from this that the influence of individuals via the market mechanism is decreasing.** This may be explained as follows.

In qualitative competition the function water as a dumping ground for

*In principle it is also possible that others take a decision. An example is the mutual agreement of detergent manufacturers to produce only biodegradable detergents. Such agreements are relatively rare and moreover are more or less enforced by the government.

**Of course what is meant is that with regard to the valuation of environmental functions no spontaneous effect of the price mechanism is possible. Needless to say, the price mechanism can be brought to bear (in addition to physical regulations). But this can be done only via the budget mechanism.

waste, or air as a medium into which to release waste matter, is in competition with all other functions. We shall call the function dumping ground for waste (or medium into which to release waste matter) *A* and the other functions *B* to *Z*. Owing to the fact that the functions are competing with one another, assigning a high(er) value to functions *B* to *Z* at the same time means giving a low(er) value to function *A*, and vice versa. A high valuation for functions *B* to *Z* can be effectuated only by prescribing rules for the activities that utilize function *A*. The consequence of this is that more of functions *B* to *Z* and less of function *A* becomes available. The high rating of *B* to *Z* naturally has the consequence that the activities utilizing these functions become 'cheap' and thus expand, whereas the activities using function *A* become 'expensive' and thus contract. 'Expensive' and 'cheap' may mean the *de facto* payment of a high or a low (money) price, but often also the possibility of making worse or better use of a function. After all, for some functions, such as air for physiological functioning and natural environment, no price determination in the usual sense is possible (cf. Section 4.2).

When the government does not prescribe any rules for the activities making use of function *A*, a high value is automatically effectuated for function *A* and a low value for the other functions. The activities that utilize function *A* can continue to expand; use of the other functions becomes increasingly difficult. This development is unavoidable, since the activities that use function *A* can disturb the other functions, while the converse is not possible: breathing and making drinking water do not disturb the function dumping ground for waste.

Both non-intervention and intervention by the government are regarded as unpleasant and thus give rise to tension. The deeper cause of this is that competition between the functions in a country like the Netherlands is becoming increasingly fierce, which suggests that we are closely approaching the limits of the possible uses of the environment.

In essence, as regards the valuation aspect, the situation in physical and quantitiative competition does not differ from that in qualitative competition. Here too the influence of individuals on allocation via the price mechanism will decrease according as scarcity in the environment increases. Thus – to take a striking example – the allocation of land to motorways has far-reaching consequences. Activities like cycling, walking or playing are hampered, whereas motoring is facilitated. If the government restricts the space for motorways, the opposite is the case. Of course, this also has a far-reaching effect on the composition of the package of produced goods and services. It is therefore a precarious matter to speak of free consumer's choice within the framework of environmental problems. Choice by the consumer is preceded by a number of government decisions that largely influence that choice.

It follows from the above that the government cannot escape from implicit valuation of the environmental functions. Our investigation has shown that in so doing the government will be able to obtain little information on the preferences of the public. In general it will, however, be able to base its decisions on the information of the elimination cost curve and on verbal descriptions of the utility of environmental functions and the consequences of loss of function; the information will usually become available in the form of a cost–effectiveness analysis (see Section 4.6).

An obvious question is whether the government, in effectuating valuation of the environmental functions, must utilize objective standards derived from the natural sciences or from medical science. Standards are also used in other fields such as public health and social housing. Standardization has the disadvantage of invoking among the public the tendency to 'fill up' the standards set to the limit. The advantage of setting standards is that the discussion becomes factual and that sanctions can be attached. In fact, sanctions are a decisive argument for using standards: behaviour with regard to the environment can hardly be left to the social control that members of the public exercise with respect to one another.

In deriving environmental standards from the natural sciences particularly great difficulties are experienced. For the natural sciences will be able to indicate standards only for a number of specific functions, such as drinking water or water for swimming. However, science is not able to indicate what measures have to be taken to prevent a collapse of the environment and where exactly the thresholds lie that may not be crossed. This applies above all to the stability and the carrying capacity of the biosphere.

Recent publications, such as the M.I.T. report *Man's Impact on the Global Environment*, the *Blueprint for Survival* and the models of Forrester and Meadows, have strengthened the insight that the problem of environmental deterioration almost certainly cannot be solved merely by making provisions with regard to production processes and products. Estimating the costs of these measures and charging the amounts found to the polluting activity will probably not provide a sufficient brake on the undesired development. For this does not in itself solve the problem of the exhaustion of raw materials and sources of energy and the polluting effect of the consumption of energy. In addition, the increasing claim to space in itself involves an infringement of the natural environment. Consequently, direct intervention to reduce highly polluting, energy-consuming or space-swallowing activities will probably be necessary. There are as yet, however, no scientific criteria for calculating the level of activities to be aimed at.

Standards can, however, be set in a number of cases from the natural sciences with regard to the direct possible uses of an environmental component. Thus it is possible, for instance, to indicate what quantity of toxic substances may be contained in drinking water or at what concentration of sulphur dioxide or hydrogen fluoride harm to field crops begins to occur. However, these standards for the extent to which the burden of an environmental component by human activities is permissible, always relate to only one form of use of an environmental component determined by time and place. In other words, such a standard does not tell us anything about the effect of a certain burden if it occurs on more than a local scale or in the long term. Nor do these standards say anything about the effect that such a burden could have on other functions than the one for which it has been established. This applies *a fortiori* when functions are not only determined by chemical and/or physical properties of an environmental component but are also dependent on the functioning of the systems of interactions between the living organisms and the physico-chemical environmental factors within a given area, the ecosystems. The above-mentioned standards therefore tell us nothing about the influence that a burden on the environment that satisfies these standards will ultimately have on the stability of the biosphere or the separate ecosystems.

With regard to the influence that human activities could have on the ecosystems, E. P. Odum[43] describes the direction in which a solution for standard-setting can be sought. The point of departure is that ecosystems undergo a development from simple, rather unstructured systems with a small number of species and a large production in respect of the biomass present to complex, richly structured, mature systems with a great diversity of species and a limited production in respect of the biomass present. The young, rather unstructured systems are unstable. The mature, richly structured systems possess a great internal stability. As a result of human activities there is to an increasing extent a converse development going on from mature and stable to younger and less stable stages.

The mature systems are of great importance through their great stability and their stabilizing effect in respect of the surrounding systems; when systems are disturbed in the vicinity, recovery can be stimulated from here. In principle mature, stable systems can be used for all functions. Impairment means that fewer possible uses remain. According as the impairment continues, recovery becomes increasingly difficult and takes longer, and an ever-decreasing number of possible uses remain.

In order to keep the environment sufficiently stable, Odum believes that compartmentalization is required. He makes the following distinctions:

(1) protective environment, consisting of mature, undisturbed, stable ecosystems exerting a stabilizing effect;
(2) compromise environment, consisting of fairly highly developed systems that can be used for may purposes and in many ways;
(3) productive systems, consisting of young productive systems for agriculture and forestry;
(4) urban–industrial environment, consisting of non-vital systems.

For these compartments a balanced spatial distribution will have to be sought. On one hand, there is a rather unproductive but highly stable environment with many potential uses; on the other, there is a productive but highly unstable environment with few potential and actual possible uses. However the distribution may be, more of the one always means less of the other. How far we can continue burdening the environment by human activities is determined by the answer to the question of how far we can go on the downward path to an environment built up of an ever-increasing number of unstable and an ever-decreasing number of stabilizing elements. As long as this is not known, it is not possible to fix the limit of the level of human activities.

The argument outlined above amounts to the fact that only 'provisional' standards can be derived from the natural sciences for a number of specific functions. For the most vital function – that of the natural environment, on the quality of which the other functions basically depend – no standard can be given. It proves from the literature that ecology can indicate standards only for the conservation of separate nature areas; with regard to a standard for survival, ecology can merely warn that continuing to burden the environment may lead to an ecological crisis in which man's continued existence is at stake;[44] however, ecological literature does not state at what level of burden such a crisis will occur.[45]

In sum, the government cannot derive from the natural sciences any exact standards indicating how much we can burden the environment. However, the natural sciences do give clear indications that continuing along the path we are now following will lead to irreparable impairment of the function natural environment and thus of most of the other functions, without which human life is impossible. In my opinion, it must be concluded from this that a rule of conduct for survival in any case amounts to halting and diverting the growth of production and population. This is in accord with the recommendation of Boulding, Forrester and Meadows, discussed in Chapter 3. The natural sciences cannot indicate the exact level of activities at which we must aim. But they do contain a number of recommendations that could serve as starting points for establishing a level of activities at which the chance of disasters is minimized. These amount to the fact that, through the use of recirculation processes, human activities become part of the biological cycle. In this process, the level of activities is conditional on the degree of stability of this cycle not being decreased. In practice this will amount to recycling raw materials, switching to non-polluting, renewable sources of energy and to using land in such a way that sufficient room is left for the functioning of natural ecosystems.

4.8. References

[1]P. Hennipman. Nut, nuttigheid en objectieve gebruikswaarde. *De Economist*, 1943, pp. 433–438. Hennipman states that utility is also occasionally taken to mean the suitability of a concrete quantity of a good for meeting certain requirements, whereas usefulness relates to the property of a good as a kind to be desired.

[2]Cf. P.E. Rijtema. *Een Berekeningsmethode voor de Benadering van de Landbouwschade ten Gevolge van Grondwateronttrekking*. Nota 587 van het Instituut voor Cultuurtechniek en Waterhuishouding. Wageningen, 1971.

[3]Cf., among others, W. Drees Jr. and F.Th. Gubbi. *Overheidsuitgaven in Theorie en Praktijk*. Groningen, 1968, pp. 15–21, pp. 277–285; C. Goedhart. Waar de prijstheorie verstek laat gaan. *Orbis Economicus* 14, No. 1; P.A. Samuelson. A pure theory of public expenditure. In: *Public Finance*. Edited by R.W. Houghton. Harmondsworth, 1970; R.A. Musgrave. Provision for social goods. In: *Public Economics*. London, 1972, pp. 124–144; and C.M. Allan. *The Theory of Taxation*. Harmondsworth, 1971, p. 14 et seq.

[4]T. Scitovsky. Two concepts of external economics. *Journal of Political Economy* 62, 1954, p. 143 et seq.

[5]A. Marshall. *Principles of Economics*. Eighth Edition. London, 1969, p. 221 et seq. (First Edition, 1890).

[6]A.C. Pigou. *The Economics of Welfare*. New York, 1962, pp. 131–135, pp. 183–196 (First Edition, 1920).

[7]This effect is discussed at length in the well-known work by J.S. Duesenberry. *Income, Saving and the Theory of Consumer Behaviour*. Cambridge (Mass.), 1949.

[8]A.C. Pigou. Loc. cit., pp. 134–135.

[9]A.C. Pigou. Loc. cit., pp. 192 and 134.

[10]As introductions to the extensive literature that has been published in the last few decades in particular, mention may be made of: E.J. Mishan. The postwar literature on externalities: an interpretative essay. *Journal of Economic Literature* IX, 1971, No. 1; B. Goudzwaard. *Ongeprijsde Schaarste*. The Hague, 1970; and P. Hennipman. De externe effecten in de hedendaagse welvaartstheorie. *Economisch-Statistische Berichten*, 20 March 1968.

[11]P. Hennipman. See ref. 10. p. 250.

[12]Some points from the reasoning which follows have already been mentioned in: R.G. Ridker. *Economic Costs of Air Pollution. Studies in Measurement*. New York, 1967; cf. in particular Figure 1 on p. 5, showing the relation between costs of elimination and

costs of damage. This relation may also be found in: A.V. Kneese and B.T. Bower. *Managing Water Quality: Economics, Technology, Institutions*. Baltimore (Md.), 1968, Figure 14, p. 99. In the field of health care an elimination cost curve is used by: L. Merewitz and S. Soslick. *The Budget's New Clothes*. Chicago (Ill.), 1971, pp. 167–168. The latter authors take their figure from: R.N. Grosse. Problems of resource allocation in health. In: *Public Expenditure and Policy Analysis*. Edited by R.H. Haveman and J. Margolis. Chicago (Ill.), 1970, p.534.

[13]Cf. D.W. Pearce. *Cost—Benefit Analysis*. London, 1971, p. 52 et seq.

[14]E.J. Mishan. *Cost–Benefit Analysis*. London, 1971, p. 79 et seq.

[15]Cf. H.M.A. Jansen and J.B. Opschoor. *De Invloed van Geluidshinder op de Prijzen van Woningen – Verslag van een Enquête onder Makelaars in en rond de Haarlemmermeer*. Instituut voor Milieuvraagstukken van de Vrije Universiteit. Werknota No. 15. Amsterdam, 1972.

[16]A study in depth of this subject has been made by: F. Bouma. *Evaluatie van Natuurfuncties*. Verkenningen van het Instituut voor Milieuvraagstukken van de Vrije Universiteit. Series A, No. 3. Amsterdam, 1972.

[17]National Park Service (U.S.A.). *A Method of Evaluating Recreation Benefits and Costs of Water Control Projects*. August 1956.

[18]R.P. Marks and S. Myers. Outdoor recreation. In: *Measuring Benefits of Government Investments*. Edited by Dorfman. Washington (D.C.), 1965.

[19]See T.L. Burton and M.N. Fulcher. Measurement of recreation benefits – a survey. *Journal of Economic Studies* 3, 1968, No. 2.

[20]A.H. Trice and S.E. Wood. Measurement of recreation benefits. *Land Economics* XXXIV, 1958, No. 3.

[21]Cf. also T.L. Burton and M.N. Fulcher together with F. Bouma. Loc. cit.

[22]The figure, with a slight alteration, has been taken from: F. Bouma. Loc. cit.

[23]M. Clawson. *Method of Measuring the Demand for and Value of Outdoor Recreation*. Reprint No. 10. Resources for the Future, Washington (D.C.), 1959; cf. also M. Clawson and J.L. Knetsch. *Economics of Outdoor Recreation*. Baltimore (Md.), 1971, p. 77 et seq.

[24]J.L. Knetsch. Outdoor recreation demands and benefits. *Land Economics* XXXIX, 1963, No. 4.

[25]J.B. Stevens. Recreation benefits from water pollution control. *Water Resources Research* 2, 1966.

[26]F. Bouma. Loc. cit.

[27]Cf. also J. Lanjouw. Waar gaan we heen? In: *Het Verstoorde Evenwicht*. Utrecht, 1970, p. 281.

[28]See J.B. Opschoor. Opinie-enquêtering en informatie. *Economisch-Statistische Berichten*, 19 May 1971, p. 474 et seq.

[29]Cf., among others, J.M. Buchanan. *The Demand and Supply of Public Goods*. Chicago (Ill.), 1969, p. 89 et seq.

[30]Commission on the Third London Airport. *Report*. Chairman, The Hon. Mr. Justice Roskill. London, 1971, p. 268 et seq.

[31]Cf. also S. Plowden. *The Costs of Noise*. London, 1970, Figure 1, p. 6.

[32]Cf. J.R. Hicks. The four consumer's surpluses. *Review of Economic Studies* XI, 1943, pp. 31–41.

[33]See E.J. Mishan. What is wrong with Roskill? *Journal of Transport Economics and Policy* 4, 1970, No. 1, pp. 221–234; D.W. Pearce. *Cost–Benefit Analysis*. London, 1971, p. 68 et seq.

[34]E.J. Mishan. The postwar literature on externalities: an interpretative essay. *Journal of Economic Literature* IX, 1971, pp. 1–28, especially pp. 18–23.

[35]E.J. Mishan. What is wrong with Roskill? *Journal of Transport Economics and Policy* 4, 1970, No. 1, p. 230 et seq.

[36]See, among others, S.A. Marglin. *Public Investment Criteria*. London, 1969, p. 21.

[37]See, among others, C.M. Allan. *The Theory of Taxation*. Harmondsworth, 1971, p. 16 et

seq.; and J. Pen. Bijlage 3 van *Verslag van Werkzaamheden en Bevindingen over het Jaar 1964 van de Raad voor de Kunst*, p. 44.

[38]Cf., among others, K. Bakker. Het verstoorde evenwicht. In: *Mens contra Milieu*. Baarn, 1970, p. 85 et seq.

[39]Cf. R. Hueting. Moet de natuur worden gekwantificeerd? *Economisch-Statistische Berichten*, 21 January 1970, p. 80 et seq.

[40]R.A. Musgrave. Provision for social goods. In: *Public Economics*. London, 1972, p. 143 et seq.

[41]R.A. Musgrave. *The Theory of Public Finance: A Study in Public Economy*. New York, 1959, p. 13 et seq.

[42]See, for a survey of possible regulations: J. Pen. Zeven methoden van antivervuilingsbeleid: een poging tot systematiek. *Economisch Kwartaaloverzicht van de Amsterdam—Rotterdam Bank N.V.*, March 1971, p. 5 et seq.

[43]E.P. Odum. The Strategy of Ecosystem Development. *Science* 164, 1969, pp. 262–270; E.P. Odum. *Fundamentals of Ecology*. Third Edition. Philadelphia (Penn.), 1971, pp. 251–275.

[44]E.P. Odum. *Fundamentals of Ecology*. Third Edition. Philadelphia (Penn.), 1971, pp. 36 and 432; H.T. Odum. *Environment, Power and Society*. New York, 1971, pp. 7–9; R.H. Whittaker. *Communities and Ecosystems*. London, 1970, pp. 149–151.

[45]The author makes this pronouncement on the authority of the ecologists D.J. Kuenen and L. Vlijm.

Chapter 5

NATIONAL INCOME, ECONOMIC GROWTH AND LOSSES OF FUNCTION

5.1. The Relation between Growth and National Income; Definition of concepts

Starting from the subject matter of economics, economic growth should be defined as an increase in the satisfaction of wants insofar as this depends on the utilization of scarce means (welfare) or, which amounts to the same thing, as a reduction of the scarcity of economic goods. This also includes an improvement of allocation.

Since satisfaction of wants is not directly observable 'from outside' and thus is not in itself a cardinal measurable quantity, it has become customary to take a look at the changes in the quantities of economic goods becoming available. Both in part of economic literature and in the practice of statistical measurement this has been confined to looking at the production of goods and services (national income).

There are a number of objections from the point of view of welfare theory and statistics to the use of the changes in the amount of goods and services produced as an indication of the trend of welfare in the national economy. These objections will be discussed in Section 5.2. First, it should be asked whether in statistical measurement it is in fact permissible to link the satisfaction of wants to the means of satisfying wants – even in the wider meaning than exclusively production that is advocated here. The following objections may be made to this link:

(1) The wants can grow along with the increase in the means becoming available (or adjust to the decrease in the quantity of goods).
(2) The relative preferences may change.
(3) A reduction in the quantity of available economic goods may be caused by external factors, i.e. not brought about by individuals.

The first objection is of a psychological nature. Factors such as how we experience things and the possibility of getting accustomed to them lie outside the field of welfare theory. Nevertheless, in view of the undeniable importance of these factors I should like to say the following about them. It is in fact a question here of making the most obvious assumption with regard to a problem on which, theoretically speaking, no certainty can be obtained. Tinbergen gives the following advice for the solution of such dilemmas: 'The first methodological problem regarding which I should like to propose a choice is that, out of all possible theories for explaining economic phenomena and processes, we choose the simplest, as long as observation does not demonstrate to us that this is at variance with the facts'.[1] Now, economic theory proceeds implicitly from consistency between wants and actions. Further, I consider it permissible to assume that the endeavour to obtain more economic goods is a predominant tendency in the present-day culture of most countries. On the strength of these two assumptions, which are simpler than their converse, the change in the result of the obvious effort to obtain more goods may in my opinion be interpreted in principle as an indication of the level of satisfaction of wants reached (but see the remarks in Section 5.2). With regard to wants, the simplest assumption is that they develop less than proportionately to the increase in the quantity of economic goods becoming available. From the assumption that the wants increase proportionately or even more than proportionately, the conclusion follows that the effort to obtain more goods has no effect or even a negative effect on welfare. This is a less obvious point of departure. Of course, the above considerations do lead to relativization of the numerical values of statistical measurement.

The second objection (change in the relative preferences) is closely related to the problem of the composite index of prices discussed in Section 5.2. The assumption posited above about the parallelism between the quantity of goods and welfare is in my opinion the simplest one not only when it is a matter of changes in quantity in a package of goods of unchanged composition, but also in the case of a package that changes as a result of altered preferences.* For in the case of increasing productivity we can choose between more of the same goods, more newly introduced goods or a combination of the two possibilities. With the present-day measurement of the package of goods and services produced (national income) the term 'more' covers not only an increase in the existing quantity but also an improvement in quality and an expansion of the range of products. We may assume that with a price mechanism operating reasonably well the choice between exclusively more of the same or new products as well is made broadly in accordance with the wants of the subjects. The question whether in the latter case one can speak of 'new wants' cannot be answered. Have people always wanted to fly, or did this

*For changes solely as a result of change in relative prices see the problem of the composite index of prices dealt with in Section 5.2.

want only arise with the invention of the aeroplane? The fact that a number of people over the centuries endeavoured to build an aeroplane suggests that the former is the case. However, the decisive point is in the existence of a possibility of choice with regard to composition of the package of goods. The conclusion is practically the same as with regard to the price index problem: if in the new situation the factors of production are also capable of supplying a package of goods that satisfies wants in accordance with the former pattern, an increase in the volume of production may be considered indicative of an increase in welfare (*mutatis mutandis* the same conclusion applies to a reduction in the volume of production).

When making comparisons of welfare in time by means of the changes in the available quantity of economic goods it does in any case seem necessary to take the latter aspect into account. A natural disaster can destroy goods, and the threat of war* can reduce safety. The production to which this gives rise may not be regarded as an indication of increased welfare in comparisons in time. For this production serves only to restore the level of satisfaction of wants that had already been reached at the moment before occurrence of the external factor. It is therefore a good idea when making comparisons of welfare in time to correct for abrupt increases in expenditure on repair work as a result of disasters, etc.**

As far as I am aware, up to the thirties, with a few curious exceptions, the concept 'social product' was discussed only in the theoretical sense.[3] In the depression years there was a growing desire to obtain a statistical insight into the circular flow of the national economy. The thinking about the interrelation of macro-economic quantities initiated by J. M. Keynes additionally stimulated the wish to be able better to control the whole of economic events with the aid of econometric models. Time series are essential for this. At J. Tinbergen's request J. B. D. Derksen made the first calculations of national income in the Netherlands, published in the Central Bureau of Statistics' monograph *Enkele berekeningen over het nationale inkomen van Nederland* in the series *Speciale Onderzoekingen van De Nederlandse Conjunctuur*, in October 1939. In the war years the system for setting up national accounts was further considered and elaborated, especially in Britain and the Netherlands. J. B. D. Derksen

*A difficulty with the example of the threat of war is the uncertainty whether the factor is in fact external. In the course of history there have been countries that increased expenditure on armaments to expand their territory or sphere of influence. In that case one can hardly speak of an 'external factor'. Further, there are minorities that find that safety does not increase but decreases as a result of arming.

**This consideration also applies to international comparisons of welfare. Differences in natural conditions (e.g. climate) may lead to differences in production effort required to obtain the same level of satisfaction of wants.[2]

worked on this at the Netherlands Central Bureau of Statistics, and J. R. N. Stone did the same in Britain. In 1945 it proved that both countries had followed practically the same system. In 1947, under the auspices of the United Nations, the study *Measurement of National Income and the Construction of Social Accounts* was published, of which the appendix 'Definition and Measurement of the National Income and Related Totals' by J. R. N. Stone occupies the greater part.

Immediately after the war the Netherlands Central Bureau of Statistics made a start with replacing the initially approximate estimates by a structure of such detail and accuracy that the Central Planning Office and the policy-makers could utilize it as a springboard for their work. Among other things, use was made of input–output tables. The year 1953 saw the publication of the United Nations: *A System of National Accounts and Supporting Tables*, in which for the first time standard definitions, standard accounts and standard classifications are recommended for use by the member countries. This report is largely based on the report *A Standardized System of National Accounts* from 1952, by the National Accounts Research Unit of the O.E.E.C., under the direction of J. R. N. Stone. The continuing consultation at international level led to a further expansion and renewal of the system of National Accounts. The new conventions based on this are to be found in *A System of National Accounts*, published by the United Nations in 1968.

In considering the concept of social product, a distinction may be made between three phases. In the first phase, the social product is a mental construction in economic literature. In the second phase, various authors proceed to define the content of the concept. In the third phase, the statistical measurement of national income (as the social product had come to be called) is achieved.

The importance of the statistical work outlined above both to economic policy and to economic theory is evident. In my opinion too little emphasis falls on the fact that organizing the calculation of national income and, above all, the system of National Accounts does in fact itself entail quite some formulation of economic theory. Of particular importance to this study are the critical comments (discussed below) that have accompanied the genesis of the measurement of national income. These objections were partly of a theoretical and partly of a practical statistical nature. The discussions on the conception of national income in what was called above the second phase probably delayed the actual statistical measurement.[4]

As the reader will be aware, national income is now calculated by first measuring per class of industry the market value of the goods and services produced in one year. Next, the value of the raw materials and auxiliary materials consumed, the services rendered by third parties and the depreciation of the capital goods used in the production process are established. The difference gives the net value added at market prices of firms. For government services, the net value added is identified with the wages and social charges paid by the government. The sum of the net values added of firms and the government is equal to the domestic product at net market prices. When we add the balance of the primary incomes received from and paid to other countries, we get national income at net market prices.*

In brief, in national income the production of goods and services by business enterprises and the government is measured. An increase in national income therefore amounts to a growth in production. In economic literature, economic policy, journalism or daily usage the increase in deflated national income (often corrected for population growth, as a result of which the increase in production per head is obtained) is generally referred to as economic growth, and often as growth of welfare.[5]

In my opinion there are two reasons for the interpretation of the increase in national income as economic growth. In the first place, the rise in production has largely eliminated the poverty in which large sections of the population lived for centuries. To put it another way, the growth of production has done away with a great deal of scarcity. To that extent, growth of production is in fact indicative of growth of welfare. This has been discussed in Sections 2.1 and 2.2. In the second place, in the identification of growth of production with growth of welfare there is an echo of the definition of the subject matter of economics disputed in Section 1.2; the view that increasing the production of goods and services is the aim of economic action has long been abandoned by economic theory, but is still persistent in daily life (and among a few writers on economics).

The objections to identifying economic growth with an increase in national income will be discussed in the following two sections. Before doing so, a few very brief comments on the connection between the concepts economic growth, welfare, well-being, progress and happiness will be in order. For understandable reasons, these concepts occur so frequently in discussions on environmental deterioration that it seems sensible to consider them. In doing so, the first two concepts will be separated from those that follow. Then a simple definition of the concept of economic growth will be introduced which fits in as closely as possible

*At the same time consumption + capital investment + increase in stocks + exports − imports is determined, which also yields the national product. This second method and that of the value added are combined in input–output tables.

with the practice of statistical measurement but does not conflict with the 'modern' definition of the subject matter of economics.

Welfare has already been defined above as the degree of satisfaction of wants insofar as this depends on the use of scarce resources; economic growth as an increase in the satisfaction of wants. Now it seems to me that, insofar as people believe that their happiness depends on greater welfare, economic growth (defined as an increase in the satisfaction of wants) furthers human happiness. To what extent that is true is difficult to judge. In my opinion the same applies to the concept progress. Is progress the ever-increasing satisfaction of existing wants and the satisfaction of more and more new wants? The answer to that question may depend on our judgment of human objectives (the wants). As emphasized in Section 1.2, it is not for economists to make this judgment. It seems that an increase in the ability to satisfy wants is often all too easily equated with progress. Progress seems to me to be a quantity as yet indeterminate, an extremely subjective concept, historically, culturally and individually constrained. I should like to define well-being, regarded as a non-economic concept, as those aspects of human happiness that are not dependent on the use of scarce resources.[6]

We can now arrive at the following summary.[7] Economic growth in the sense of growth of welfare does not lend itself to direct statistical measurement. Nevertheless, in order to obtain *an indication* for welfare, it seems permissible to measure the volume of the economic goods becoming available. To be exact, the result of such measurement should not be interpreted as the trend of welfare but as the extent to which society has succeeded in increasing the availability of economic goods that are desired. This leads to the following definition of economic growth: *economic growth occurs only if and insofar as society succeeds in increasing the availability of economic goods (in the broad sense) desired by individuals.* This definition obviates the specific 'welfare criticism' (such as influencing individual welfare by income inequality) to be discussed below. With due observance of the restrictions and relativities discussed in this chapter the change in the quantity of scarce goods may be regarded as *one* of the indicators of the trend of welfare in time. This indicator will become relatively more important according as other conditions determining welfare are better satisfied. As long as the scarcity relates mainly to the goods and services produced by business and the government, the increase in national income can function as a reasonable indicator of economic growth (in the sense of increase in the quantity of goods). This has perhaps broadly been true in the past. But now that the impression is gaining ground that to an increasing extent important scarce goods remain outside the measurement of national income (notably the environmental functions), it will have to be considered to what extent correction of national income is possible and/or to what extent a presentation of the figures of the National Accounts can be given which excludes as far as possible the interpretation of the increase in national income as economic growth by the users of these statistics.

5.2. Old Objections to National Income as an Indicator of Growth

The theoretical and statistical shortcomings of the present calculation of national income are discussed below point by point. Most of them already played a part in the discussions among statisticians and between theoreticians and statisticians in the period that preceded the actual annual measurement of national income. Starting from the concepts defined above, the criticism may be subdivided into two categories:

- specific welfare criticism;
- the criticism relating to incomplete and incorrect registration of the volume of available economic goods (in the broad sense); in this category, the more technical statistical problem of the composite index of prices has also been placed.

The circumstance that the figures of national income cannot give a complete picture of the trend of welfare in the national economy is inherent in the approach chosen, in which after all it is not the satisfaction of wants itself that is measured but the means of satisfaction. J. Tinbergen commented as follows on this: 'We were very well aware that national income would not form a complete indicator of welfare. But, given a reasonable distribution of income and perfect competition it no longer matters what is produced, only how much of it is produced. Consequently, I attached great value to the compilation of a series of figures on the total production of goods and services. In the thirties, external effects, like environmental deterioration, did not yet play an important role'.[8] One could set the specific welfare criticism aside as improper criticism. But against this is the practical consideration that, as stated above, the increase in national income is often described as growth in welfare.

Specific welfare criticism consists of the following points:

(1) In national income the total value of the goods is found by multiplying the quantity of each of the goods by their respective prices and adding together the amounts found. Through this procedure the consumer's surplus which, as is known, relates to the difference between

the total utility of a good and the product of price (as the criterion of marginal utility) and quantity, is not expressed in the height of national income. Thus a doctor who saves a patient's life with the aid of a medicine creates a value which, whatever one may think about its exact size, is certainly higher than the values added that are recorded in national income (i.e. the doctor's fee and the incomes earned in the production of the medicine). The intra-marginal utility of goods which is ignored in national income will approach an infinite value. After all, the intra-marginal utility includes the utility of the first unit of food, drink, clothing, accommodation and medical care.[9]

(2) In national income the value added by production has been calculated at market prices. That is another reason why the results may not be interpreted as an indicator of welfare. The method of calculation – considered in the light of welfare theory – means that the (marginal) utility of goods of different subjects is added. Strictly speaking this is already impermissible with equal income distribution because it is impossible to compare utilities between individuals: some people attach greater value to goods than others. With inequality of incomes the addition procedure is not allowed *a fortiori* on account of the diminishing marginal utility of money as income grows.[10] Therefore, the welfare of society could increase through greater equality of income while national income remains the same. Income distribution is still recognized as an important factor in welfare. J. Wemelsfelder writes with reference to the study *Does Economic Growth Improve The Human Lot?* by R. A. Easterlin: 'When one considers both the number of people who feel happy and the number who do not, an obvious connection with the growth of welfare* cannot be discovered.** . . . On the other hand, connections between income and a sense of happiness do come to the fore when for each of the countries separately we correlate the happiness perceived with the income differences in those countries. This could point to the fact that it is not the absolute height of our income that is important, but the income in relation to that of others'.[11] The impossibility of comparing utilities between individuals further implies that, if one subject regresses and the rest of the group progresses, no pronouncement can be made on the final result.

(3) The law of diminishing marginal utility applies strictly speaking only to individuals. Nevertheless, a tendency towards decreasing marginal utility of produced goods is noticeable for the whole national economy. When everyone gets more of the same package of goods, that is very easy

*By growth of welfare is meant the increase of national income.

**The real national incomes of a number of countries and the average rating of the personal happiness of the inhabitants of those countries are being compared here.

to see. But, in my opinion, a tendency towards diminishing marginal utility of produced goods is also likely in the case of expansion of the package of goods. Thus Galbraith points out that some goods are acquired more readily than others and that the utility of goods for which a demand has to be created by extensive advertising campaigns is only slight.[12] Against this it could be argued that wants could increase in proportion to means. However, recent research by B.M.S. van Praag and A. Kapteyn indicates that this is not so. These investigators correlated the height of income with the subjective appreciation of it. Appreciation of income proves initially to rise strongly with income, but at a higher income level the marginal guilder leads to only slight additional satisfaction. The study also reveals that in the Netherlands 'a wage increase of *f* 100 net of which one has high expectations proves afterwards to be valued only as a net wage increase of *f* 35'. (This phenomenon is called the 'preference drift': the median income, stated as necessary for feeling that one has climbed halfway up the welfare ladder, changes with income; the individual welfare function thus shifts along with income.[13]) W. Siddré remarks that the time factor is in the process of forming a limit to possibilities of consumption for certain groups of people in some highly industrialized countries.[14] The resultant increasing consumption of several goods at the same time (such as 'Music to Read by') indicates that consumer goods are being less intensively used. This argument too suggests that the marginal utility of goods falls as national income rises. As a result, the increase in welfare is less than the growth of national income indicates.

(4) The degree of satisfaction derived from the working conditions in which production takes place is not expressed in the level of national income. When heavy and dull work is taken over by machines, welfare increases to a greater extent than national income shows. When, on the other hand, workers are prepared to accept a lower wage in return for a method of production that restores the bond between work and finished product and makes a greater call on the worker's skill, thus increasing job satisfaction, national income falls whereas welfare increases (scarce resources have deliberately been used to increase the satisfaction of wants). The increase in welfare that comes from the voluntary inclusion of women in production processes is not registered in national income.* Of course, the opposite may also occur: a wife stays at home, the income falls, but the satisfaction increases.

(5) The reduction of welfare as a result of involuntary unemployment is certainly much greater than the decrease in national product suggests.

*Cf. also point 2 on pp. 160–161.

The fact that not all economic goods are measured in national income and – proceeding from the criterion of scarcity – certain goods are not properly registered has also long been recognized by theoreticians and statisticians who have concerned themselves with the concept of national income. In my opinion this criticism must be taken more seriously than what has been stated above because, starting from the statistical approach chosen (measurement of the means for satisfying wants), it is directed towards the implementation thereof.

The criticism of national income as an indicator of economic growth (in the sense of increase in the means of satisfying wants) comprises the following points:

(1) For a changing package of goods, the numerical value of the growth of production cannot be established. This is a purely technical problem of statistics and not an objection from the viewpoint of economic theory to the use of national income as a growth indicator. It concerns the well-known problem of the composite index of prices. Real national income is obtained by expressing the income in current prices in an acceptable manner in constant prices, for instance by deflating the production per component by a price index computed for this purpose. The price index must be determined in theory by means of a constant package of goods. However, the package actually produced is constantly changing. Kuznets,[15] Hicks,[16] and Pigou[17] are among those who point out that, as a result, the calculated value of the price index varies, depending on the solution chosen for this problem. Over a short period the changes in the package of goods are relatively small; the problem therefore weighs less heavily over a short than over a long term.

Although the numerical value of the growth of production cannot be determined, it can often be established with great probability whether or not a real growth of production has occurred. Thus Pigou points out that, in a situation of growth resulting from an increase in productivity, the factors of production are in general capable in the year of comparison of producing a package of goods containing as much of each of the goods from the base year plus more of an arbitrary good (or goods). In that case, the factors of production are able to produce both more of the package in accordance with the pattern of the base year and more of the package in accordance with the package of the year of comparison. One can then speak of a real growth in national income, although this growth cannot be indicated by an exact percentage.[18] This comment by Pigou is doubtless valid with respect to the degree of growth of production that occurred in the industrialized countries in the postwar period.

(2) Not all production takes place in business enterprises or in

government agencies. A well-known example is the work of the housewife. We are concerned here not only with the level of national income but also with the changes in it. The present desire on the part of women to play a part in the social production process results in an unknown overestimation of the growth of production, as the housewife's work is taken over by paid domestic help and by crêches. In addition, the increased sales of labour-saving devices (such as dish-washers), greater frequency of eating out, etc. will lead to an over-rating of growth.* The often-cited marriage of the master of the house to his housekeeper operates in the opposite direction.

(3) Goods and services produced form only one category of economic goods. A well-known example of a scarce good not registered in national income is leisure time. This has greatly increased in recent decades. Leisure time and production can be swapped for one another. By not recording the increase in leisure time we underestimate economic growth (in the sense of increase of the availability of economic goods).

(4) In the calculation of national income in accordance with the present conventions, a number of activities are designated as final consumption which have a cost character and therefore ought to be booked as intermediate deliveries. S. Kuznets, who deserves mention as one of the great theoreticians of the conception of national income, emphasizes this.[19] Kuznets divides these activities into three categories.

(a) The first category is invoked by the fact that in industrial countries the dominant modes of production impose an urban pattern of living, which brings in its wake numerous services whose major purpose is to offset the disadvantages. Kuznets gives as examples the expenditure necessary for bridging the greater distance between home and work, and the money spent on compensation for the inconveniences entailed by living in dense agglomerations.

(b) The second category distinguished by Kuznets relates to expenditure that is inherent in participation in the technically and monetarily complex civilization of industrial countries. Payments to banks, employment agencies, unions, brokerage houses, etc., including such matters as education are not, according to Kuznets, payments for final consumer goods. They are activities necessary to eliminate the frictions of a complicated production system and not net contributions to ultimate consumption.

(c) As the third category the major part of governmental activity is

*Quite apart from this is the fact that working outside the home can contribute to the satisfaction of women's wants. This facet comes under point 4 on p. 159.

mentioned. The legislative, judicial, administrative, police and military functions of the state, according to Kuznets, are designed in order to create the conditions under which the economy can function. These services do not provide goods to ultimate consumers. It is wrong to count the whole of governmental activity as a net contribution to national income.

(5) Though in the calculation of national income allowance is made for the net addition to or withdrawal from the stock of capital goods, this is not the case with the exhaustion of natural resources. This point can be subdivided into three categories:

(a) exhaustion of replaceable and irreplaceable raw materials (timber, metals, phosphates);
(b) exhaustion of sources of energy (coal, oil, fissionable material for nuclear energy);
(c) loss of free consumer goods supplied by nature.

Attention had already been drawn to these shortcomings too in the discussions that preceded the actual measurement of national income. Thus the statistician W. I. King distinguishes between 'private wealth' (goods and services available to individuals and private firms), 'public wealth' (goods and services which the authorities have the right to dispose of) and 'social wealth'.[20] Under 'social wealth' come not only private and governmental goods but also the free goods of nature and the knowledge accumulated. In his considerations, King concludes that for practical reasons measurement of national income must be limited to estimating the value in terms of money of goods produced, as a result of which the free goods of nature unfortunately are left out of consideration. King warns against identifying increase in income with increase in wealth, because the people in the cities of industrialized societies must pay for a number of consumer goods given by nature that formerly could be freely enjoyed (like game, fruit, wood as a fuel for cooking, flowers, bird song and beautiful scenery),* whereas the building blocks supplied by nature for production, namely sources of energy (formed in millions of years of geological activity) and raw materials for primary and secondary production (phosphates, metals, timber) are being eaten into.

In later years proposals have repeatedly been made for taking this depletion of the stocks of energy sources and raw materials into account in the calculation of national income by means of depreciation. Thus S. Fabricant advocates that the above depletion be regarded as a cost factor. He opposes the U.S. Department of Commerce, which prefers to dispense with this correction. Fabricant argues that current (unrecorded)

*Cf. the critical comment on p. 165.

discoveries do not offset current depletion, if there is any truth in the widely held opinion that our mineral and other natural resources are shrinking. He considers it necessary to take that shrinkage into account in the estimate of national income. Both the depletion of farmland and that of mines and forests must enter into consideration. But depletion charges are of greater importance with regard to mines and forests than to farmland, on account of the relative stability of the latter type of depletion in comparison with that of mines and forests.[21]

Fabricant's co-discusser E. F. Denison does not share his views and believes that the production of raw materials is properly included in national income as a net factor income share, part of the economic rent accruing to the factor land.[22] The argument was settled in Denison's favour. In the publication *National Income*, 1954 edition, an extensive appendix on the conception of national income was included. This contains the following: 'Depletion is added to profits since it is not regarded as an element of capital consumption in the national income and product accounts; and capital gains and losses are eliminated from profits as not measuring incomes arising in current production'.[23]

5.3. *Economic Growth and Losses of Function*

In the period 1967–70 the present author published a number of articles criticizing the failure to take environmental deterioration (viewed as losses of function) into account in national income, or at least to do so correctly.[24] The reasoning of these articles is briefly as follows.

The changes in the figures of national income form an incomplete criterion for the trend of welfare. However, a theoretically exact yardstick cannot be given because – as already explained in Section 5.2 – the satisfaction of wants is a personal factor. It is therefore permissible, within certain restrictions, to derive the trend of the satisfaction of wants from the measurement of the means of satisfying those wants.

As regards the specific welfare aspects of the economic goods that are now measured in national income, the shortcomings of this procedure are not of such a nature that the great emphasis in economic policy on increasing national income steers society in an undesirable direction. Thus the problem of income distribution does not seriously interfere with the increase in national income, as long as certain groups do not become worse off in income in the absolute sense; in practice growth, at least viewed nationally, proves to go together with a more uniform income distribution.* The presumable decrease in the marginal utility of goods

*Cf. p. 18.

may make the numerical value of growth relative, but it does not summon up any doubt about the direction that growth is taking. The same applies to not measuring the consumer's surplus. A more or less conscious weighing of working conditions and production occurs; employment forms a separate point in economic policy.

Having regard to the deliberate neglect of the above aspects of welfare in statistical measurement, it is necessary to define economic growth as the extent to which the availability of economic goods is increased. Nor does the failure for practical reasons to take some economic goods into account in the calculation of national income give any reason for great concern about the direction that society is taking through the pronounced stress on increasing national income in economic policy. Thus the voluntary incorporation of married women in the market process leads to overestimation of growth, but this does not form a serious danger diverting economic events in an undesired direction. Leisure time and production are deliberately weighed against one another; one is sufficiently aware that potential growth of production is being sacrificed for more leisure time. The problem of the composite index of prices does make the numerical value of the growth percentages relative, but it does not cast serious doubt on the direction of that growth.

Expenditure on defence, police, etc., according to the articles summarized here, takes place with the consent of the majority of the population. The electorates are apparently of the opinion that this increases their security, and they are prepared to utilize scarce resources for this.* The expenditure relates to fundamental unpleasant properties of man and is among the regrettable necessities, like locks on doors and auditors. This expenditure too is deliberately weighed, and its size is known with exactitude. Of course, there is cause for investigation when there are well-founded suspicions that the changing structure of society leads to progressively increasing expenditure on police and the like.

All these shortcomings of the measurement of national income, according to the articles, call for strong relativization of the results and form reasons for the further development of statistical work, but they do not seem to be urgent problems. What is urgent is the problem of environmental deterioration. The losses of function form a considerable and rapidly increasing aspect of new scarcity that is not allowed for in the figures of national income. On the contrary, when measures of elimination and compensation are taken by private persons or the government, the costs contribute to the increase in national income. By

*I shall say nothing here about the thorny question of the minority who feel that defence expenditure leads to greater insecurity.

the identification of these results with the concept economic growth and the strong emphasis on growth in economic policy the danger is thus created of growth rates that, like a whirling compass, indicate that the national economy is proceeding along the desired course, whereas in reality society is drifting off in a different, undesired direction. It is therefore urgently necessary to calculate the size of environmental deterioration as far as possible in terms of money and to compare the results of these calculations with the figures of national income. It is definitely *not* the intention to replace the present figures by others, but merely to introduce alongside the current calculation an alternative one, in which the costs of measures of elimination and compensation are interpreted as intermediate deliveries. If this proves possible, insight into growth, interpreted as increase of the availability of economic goods, can at least be somewhat improved.

The criticism reproduced above – and also this study, which has taken the reasoning of the articles as its point of departure – ties in with the criticism by Kuznets and King discussed in the preceding section.* There is something of an overlap.

Our investigation describes the environment as functions and tries to assess the losses of function occurring through the competition between functions as a result of human activities. In this way no account is taken of the expenditure referred to by Kuznets that is inherent in a complex society, expenditure on police and similar functions of the State, and the depletion of raw materials and sources of energy.**

The examples that King gives of losses of consumer goods supplied by nature may be interpreted as losses of function.*** But they relate to only a few of the losses of potential use of the environment described – and then only partially – in this study. This is quite understandable, because in King's day there was hardly any question of an extensive environmental deterioration such as we have today. It must, however, be pointed out that hunting, picking fruit in the forest and felling timber call for human effort, so that game, fruit and timber were not free goods even in the days of the American frontierman mentioned by King, despite the fact that they did not go vìa the market.

The disadvantages attributed by Kuznets to the urban pattern of life, such as the greater distance between home and work,**** may be

*I should like to point out here that in the articles cited above the work of Kuznets and King is not mentioned, because in those days I was not yet familiar with it; my work then related to quite different matters from those dealt with here.

**See points 4b, 4c and 5a,b, respectively, on pp. 161–162.

***Point 5c on p. 162.

****See point 4a on p. 161.

interpreted as losses of function as a result of spatial competition, and the expenditure on this as the costs of compensatory measures. The same may be remarked with regard to Kuznets as was said about King. For understandable reasons Kuznets mentions only a few of the losses of function as a result of environmental deterioration; of the measures against this, only compensation is mentioned and not elimination. However, the reasoning followed in this chapter is already present in principle in Kuznets as also in King.

This reasoning – which will already have become clear from the above – is as follows. Production reduces the scarcity of economic goods, but at the same time creates a new scarcity of environmental functions; the same happens in the consumption of the goods and services produced. Since the increase in national income is generally interpreted as economic growth, the losses of function should be subtracted from national income. To know the amount that has to be deducted, they have to be valued. We found in Chapter 4 that the valuation of environmental functions is only very partially possible. A correction of national income for environmental deterioration is therefore also, unfortunately, only very partially possible. As a result national income loses much of its importance as an indicator of the trend of the means for the satisfaction of wants available to the public. We know that there is a rapidly increasing scarcity of environmental functions, some of which are of vital importance to man, but we can only partially quantify the preferences for these. In order at least to acquire some insight into the direction in which human activities are steering society from the point of view of scarcity, in addition to the existing national income an alternative figure should be presented, in the calculation of which the measures of compensation and elimination are not entered as a final product but as an intermediate delivery. For these measures do not yield a net increase of final goods. For this reason reference was always made in Chapter 4 to *costs* of compensation and elimination.

To make matters clear it may be repeated that the views presented here are in the context of a comparison of welfare in time, for which the trend of the quantity of scarce goods becoming available is considered as one of the possible indicators. It goes without saying that expenditure on measures of compensation and elimination in accordance with individual preferences contributes to welfare, and that this expenditure, given the parallelism between economic goods and welfare assumed in Section 5.1, represents an increase in welfare, counting from the moment at which the availability of environmental functions has already lessened. This view has been defended in Chapter 1, where the limited (productivistic) interpretation of the subject matter of economics has been challenged.

But in Chapter 4 the environment was defined as a collection of economic goods, the environmental functions, and losses of function were regarded as a new form of scarcity. In respect of the situation before the occurrence of the loss of function there is consequently no question of an increase in the quantity of final goods available to the public. In the event of complete restoration of function – which is seldom attained – the quantity of goods has remained the same in respect of the original state of affairs. The difficulties with regard to comparisons in time would not occur if it were possible to discount the losses of function themselves, at the moment they occur, as a negative item in the composition of national income. But this encounters two objections.

In the first place our environment, defined as a collection of possible uses, is not a flow quantity, like income. Within the present conventions of National Accounts it is only possible to apply depreciation to the (capital) goods made by man himself.*

More fundamental than this technical problem – after all, the conventions of the National Accounts can be changed – is the problem of valuation. We saw in Chapter 4 that, outside the actual expenditure on substitution or restoration of impaired functions (the costs of compensation and elimination), the urgency of the needs for the functions can hardly be established, if at all. Owing to the fact that in most cases the shadow price of the functions remains unknown, the inclusion of losses of function as a negative item in national income does not become possible until the expenditure on substitution or restoration of the function is made. At that moment, the occurrence of competition between functions (coming up against the limit of our finite environment) has consequences for the flow quantity income, which is a criterion of the volume of goods and services produced and outside which the environmental functions fall. That moment usually – not always – comes after the occurrence of the loss of function.

When the moment of taking measures coincides with the occurrence of

*Cf. point 5 on pp. 161–162. The term 'eating into capital' has been deliberately avoided in the discussion of losses of function and national income. In the occurrence of losses of function alternative costs almost always occur. Non-irreversible losses of function as a result of pollution (i.e., the use of the waste tip function) can be restored by the utilization of resources (elimination costs, see Chapter 4). In physical and quantitative competition of functions re-allocation is likewise almost always possible. Less use of the limited quantity of ground water for industry means more possibility of using it for households, agriculture, etc. (and vice versa). More urban space for cycling, children's play etc. means less space for the private car (and vice versa). Classifying the losses of function indicates where and how the limit of the possible uses of the environment – and thus of economic growth – is reached, but is not an inventory of losses of capital. An important exception to the above remarks is irreplaceable loss of the natural environment function. The latter can best be defined as destruction of capital.

loss of function, the problem of comparison in time does not occur. This case is elaborated below. Perhaps this at the same time makes it clear that the expenditure on measures for compensation and elimination of losses of function is called forth solely because it is no longer possible (fully) to meet the demand for the use of the environmental functions (as already explained in Chapter 4). As a result this expenditure is of an intermediate nature; it represents costs of substitution or restoration of the function and in a comparison in time does not represent an increase in final goods.

Suppose that the paper production of a country grows in 5 years by 10 units a year from 50 to 100 units a year. In this period 1 million people make use of the recreational water function. It is known that when the amount of waste water that accompanies the production of 100 units of paper is discharged, the limit of the self-purifying capacity of the water has been reached. It is now possible to decide first to build a treatment plant instead of stepping production up further. The construction of this plant – for instance in the sixth year – obviously does not increase the quantity of final goods available: paper production stays at the same level (100 units) and the recreational water function remains available to just as many swimmers (1 million). The problem of comparison in time does not occur: the expenditure on the plant is made at the moment when the loss of function would occur.

It is also possible to step up the production in the sixth year to 110. In that case the recreational water function is lost for 1 million swimmers. National income increases by the added value of the production of 10 units of paper. For reasons stated above, discounting the loss of function is not possible. In the following years swimming pools or a treatment plant are built. In the view defended here the expenditure on this is of an intermediate nature, since the need for the recreational water function has been demonstrated for the sum of the building costs of the swimming pools or the treatment plant. The basis for this is the assumption that after the fifth year the need for swimming remains about the same (cf. Section 5.1).

Briefly summarized, the reasoning defended here simply amounts to this: for the sake of other environmental functions desired by the public remaining available, when the waste tip function is used more factors of production must be utilized to obtain the same quantity of final goods.

In practice it will barely be possible to interrelate the time at which loss of function occurs and the resultant expenditure on compensation and elimination measures. This naturally introduces an inaccuracy into the alternative national income proposed here. This will be the less according as a longer period is considered. However, it is mainly the intention to illustrate the consequences of our economic activities for the environmental functions as far as possible by comparing the results of the two methods of calculation.*

To make it clear how the present (international) conventions of National Accounts are applied with respect to the functions of the environment, these functions can best be subdivided into consumer goods and means of production. Environmental functions that may be interpreted as consumer goods are, for instance, water used for recreation, air as a factor for human life (physiological functioning, sensory perception) and also water, air and soil as dumping grounds for waste (e.g. the emission of noxious substances by powerboats and cars). Environmental functions that may be regarded as means of production are for instance water used in agriculture, boiler feedwater, water as raw material for drinking water, farmland and water, air and soil as a dumping ground for waste (emission of harmful substances in production processes).

Reduction of the availability of functions that can be interpreted as consumer goods may be the result of activities by both consumers and producers (e.g. emissions by cars or factories). According to the conventions now in force, measures of compensation and elimination taken by the government and by private persons are regarded as final products. Examples of compensatory measures: the building of a swimming pool as a result of water pollution (government), fitting double glazing to reduce noise nuisance, extra travelling time between home and work and home and recreation, medical and material consequences of road accidents (private persons). Examples of eliminatory measures: waste water treatment plants (government), after-burners on car exhausts (private persons). On the other hand, the compensatory and eliminatory measures taken by industry are not regarded as final products. Examples: the construction of high stacks, the building of anti-noise walls on airfields (compensation), all self-undertaken treating measures (elimination). The loss in itself of consumptive possibilities of using the environment is left out of consideration. This loss of consumptive environmental functions therefore has consequences for national income only when some form or other of action to restore those functions is undertaken.

Loss of environmental functions serving as means of production may also be caused by the activities of both consumers and producers. In accordance with the present conventions measures of compensation and elimination by the government are regarded as final products. Examples are desalination canals for the Westland market gardening district (compensation) and water treatment plants (elimination). Compensatory

*See pp. 180–182.

and eliminatory measures by industry, on the other hand, are entered as intermediate deliveries. Examples are extra treatment measures on behalf of the drinking water supply (compensation)* and the switch to non-polluting processes (elimination). Loss of productive possibilities of using the environment for which no measures of compensation or elimination have yet been taken will sooner or later inhibit the increase in national income – insofar as the measures are not taken by the government. The loss of these environmental functions leads to higher production costs and, as a result, automatically diminishes the growth of national income, now or in the future. Examples are attack of ship's paint resulting in corrosion, extra measures necessary for the preparation of drinking water, corrosion of metals of factory plants by air pollution and reduction in the quality of agricultural water. The environmental functions that play the part of means of production may therefore be equated, as regards the growth aspect, with the other natural resources: the stock of sources of energy and raw materials. There too depletion leads to an automatic increase in the costs of production as a result of their greater scarcity. The costs of obtaining them increase. As a result, so does the price of the finished product. After deflation with the increased price index, the (volume of) national income has fallen.**

Finally, mention must be made of the complete omission of certain activities in view of the consideration that the limit of the capacity of the environment to absorb these has been reached. Stopping the building of roads through nature areas, the establishing of industry in regions that are already severely polluted, and restricting the use of private cars, etc., will lead, after a period of adjustment, to a different composition of national income (perhaps to more leisure time, too). In the reasoning followed here these are measures of environmental protection which are automatically reflected in the correct manner in national income in accordance with the present conventions as well. This may be supported by the following examples.

The public is beginning to understand that there just is not enough urban space for private cars *and* public transport *and* cycling *and* walking *and* safe play streets for children. The latter functions are valued more highly than the first one and are made available again by the authorities: public transport, cyclists, pedestrians and children regain the space they

*In National Accounts government enterprises do not come under the government sector but under that of business.

**In discussions the author is often asked: 'But surely the value added increases?' So it does. But against the increased value added there is a decreased or at least not proportionately increased final product. Hence the deflation with the price index. National income is an index of volume.The same applies to compensatory and eliminatory measures.

once had, the room for private cars is considerably reduced. As a result, the level of activities falls (less car-mileage, which requires more production than public transport and the bicycle) and with it national income.* This is quite logical, too. The limit of growth (as increase of the availability of scarce goods) has been reached. The result is that national income – as an indicator of the trend of the means of satisfying wants – can increase no further.

There is insufficient room between towns A and B to allow of leaving the existing rural area, with its natural riches and its peace and quiet, intact and of building a motorway. The recreational and natural function of the land is valued more highly than the communicational one. Consequently, the road is not built. The level of activities does not increase any further, nor does national income. And rightly so: the limit of growth (as increase of the availability of economic goods) has been reached here as well.

To elucidate the above it will now be illustrated by means of imaginary input–output tables how, in accordance with the present conventions of National Accounts, the costs of compensatory and eliminatory measures as a result of losses of function are entered in those accounts. The examples show that (as already explained) the way in which the entry is made depends on who bears the expenditure required for compensation or elimination of environmental functions lost wholly or partially. If the costs are to be borne by a firm, then from the point of view of the scarcity criterion double counting does not occur, but if private persons or the

*We assume that production for export necessary for the purchase of foreign cars and crude oil drops in proportion to the reduced number of car-miles. We also consider this case in isolation. We set it aside from the possibility that may exist of utilizing released factors of production elsewhere. This concerns the point not discussed here of the effect of environmental protection on employment. It is, incidentally, highly probable that environmentally acceptable production and consumption will increase employment. Installations for the purification of industrial and domestic waste water, the introduction of integrated control methods in agriculture to reduce the use of pesticides, flue gas desulphurization, dust catchers, responsible tipping and composting of waste, and the prevention of noise nuisance require the utilization of labour. The abolition of single-trip packaging, beakers, plates and cutlery and of vacuum-packed individual slices of ham, cheese and other products; the switch to durable goods that are geared to repair; the introduction of small-scale, biological farming, marketing its products in the vicinity of the farm; and the change to rail transport on balance create many more jobs than they destroy. As is known, the optimum allocation of the factors of production is reached when their marginal yields are equal to their respective prices. This condition is satisfied if the marginal substitution ratio of the factors of production is equal to their price ratio. Or, to put it another way, if the amounts of factors of production employed are inversely proportional to their prices. As the environmental functions become scarcer, then in a certain state of technology these functions will have to be sacrificed to a relatively smaller extent and relatively more labour will have to be put to work. To obtain the same package of goods and services, more workers will be needed. It is precisely in this way that a choice in favour of more environment and less production in general has to be made.

Table 5.1

	Intermediate deliveries			Final deliveries		Total production
	A	B	C	Household consumption	Government consumption	
Activity A	15	10	5			30
Activity B				100		100
Activity C[a]					20	20
Value added	15	90	15			
Total	30	100	20			150

[a]Government.

authorities pay double counting does occur and thus overestimation of growth too. A self-contained economy, full employment and the absence of frictions are assumed.[25]

Case I

Activity B produces with 100 men 100 units of $1 on behalf of households. Activity A produces 30 units; of these, the firms concerned with this activity deliver 15 to each other, 10 are supplied to B, and 5 to C. Activity C (the government) produces 20; this production is intended exclusively for what is considered to be the necessary partial elimination of losses of function caused by activity B as a result of the discharging of harmful substances. Activity C is entered in the National Accounts as final delivery. The national product equals $15 + 90 + 15 = 120$ (measured according to the values added), or $100 + 20 = 120$ (measured according to the final deliveries). See Table 5.1.

Case II

A law is adopted which lays down that the authorities should henceforth charge their services to those causing the losses of function. This can be done in the form of compulsory purchase by B. From the moment that the government charges B for his services, these are entered in the National Accounts, according to the current convention, as intermediate deliveries.* On the present assumptions the product of B

*The situation is different as regards levies, since there are after all taxes. The treatment plants built with the proceeds of levies are entered in the National Accounts (wrongly, according to the reasoning followed here) as final consumption by the government.

Table 5.2

	Intermediate deliveries			Final deliveries		Total production
	A	B	C	Household consumption	Government consumption	
Activity A	15	10	5			30
Activity B				120		120
Activity C[a]		20				20
Value added	15	90	15			
Total	30	120	20			170

[a]Government.

will undergo a price increase of 20%. The model will then look like Table 5.2. The inflated national income amounts to 120; after correction for price increases $Y = 100$. This result can be obtained direct by using a model in units of volume instead of current prices (Table 5.3). From this $Y = 100$ follows directly. For the sake of simplicity volumes will be used below.

The above models have in fact started from a price elasticity of the demand for the product of B equal to zero. This is an extreme supposition. At any other price elasticity of the demand (leaving aside positive elasticities), contraction of firm B will occur. To show this the model must be extended by firm X. We shall assume that X also pollutes to some extent, so that C has to deliver to X. After B and X have been charged with the costs of the restoration of function (eliminatory and/or compensatory measures), the picture might, for instance, be as shown in Table 5.4.

Table 5.3

	Intermediate deliveries			Final deliveries		Total production
	A	B	C	Household consumption	Government consumption	
Activity A	15	10	5			30
Activity B				100		100
Activity C[a]		20				20
Value added	15	70	15			
Total	30	100	20			150

[a]Government.

Table 5.4[a]

	Intermediate deliveries				Final deliveries		Total production
	A	B	C	X	Household consumption	Government consumption	
Activity A	15	9	5	1			30
Activity B					90		90
Activity C[b]		18		2			20
Activity X					10		10
Value added	15	63	15	7			
Total	30	90	20	10			150

[a] $Y = 100$.
[b] Government.

A comparison of case I with case II shows that, without any change having occurred in the result of production, a drop in national income occurs solely as a result of a change in the legal framework. For the sake of a better insight into what is going on in the community, it is advisable to arrive at a calculation of national income in accordance with case II. This national income can lead a life of its own alongside the one now current. The difference that then appears may be an aid in decisions regarding changes of the legal framework in the direction of further restriction of discharges by B. Only the latter naturally contributes to the change in allocation in favour of the environmental functions B to Z.* (For this the factors of production could be used that are now being utilized by X.)

5.4. *A Critical Examination of the Objections to Correction of National Income for Costs of Compensation and Elimination*

The discussions from the thirties and forties summarized in Section 5.2 on the measurement of national income have been revived in recent years with reference to environmental deterioration. In the discussions as to whether or not the decline of the environment should be taken into account in the figures of national income, the following arguments play a part:

(1) The principal objection to taking environmental deterioration into account in national income that comes to the fore in the discussions is, in

*Cf. p. 143.

my opinion, the problem of valuation. Thus the compilers of the E.C.E. report *The Treatment of Environmental Problems in the National Accounts and Balances*[26] rightly argue that the cost of prevention (corresponding to the costs of elimination used here) cannot serve as a possible deduction because these costs are not a criterion of the harm experienced by the public.* Sometimes considerable harm can be prevented at low cost, whereas in other cases a slight reduction in the harm involves high costs.

This brings us to the heart of the problem: the shadow price of the environmental functions is unknown because the public's wants of the functions can be quantified only very partially (see Chapter 4). However, this need not prevent us from taking into account that part of the wants which *can* be expressed in terms of money. This is, in any case, the private expenditure on measures of compensation and elimination, for this is irrefutable proof of the need for the functions. In addition, official expenditure on these measures can be taken into account. It is true that, as stated in Chapter 4, it cannot be established whether measures have been taken by the government in conformity with the public's preferences (has too much been done or – as ecological criticism suggests – much too little?), but such a procedure does fit in entirely with the conventions of National Accounts. The shadow price of other economic goods produced by the government is likewise unknown. Yet they are entered at cost in the National Accounts (for example, items such as dykes in the interest of security). In the case of business, similar costs are already being allowed for in the correct manner according to the reasoning followed above.

In my opinion the calculation of national income as practised at present conflicts with its own point of departure: recording the trend of the means of satisfying wants. To furnish at least some insight into the direction that society is taking from the point of view of scarcity, in addition to the existing national income at least a figure should be given in which the costs of measures of compensation and elimination have not been counted as a final product.

(2) Both the compilers of the above-mentioned E.C.E. report[27] and E.F. Denison[28] object that environmental effects are not linear. In the National Accounts ten eggs are always ten times as much as one egg, according to these authors. On the other hand a low CO content of the air is harmless, at a somewhat higher level it becomes a nuisance and above that level fatal; the first *x* dollars spent on pollution abatement may

*Harm in the sense of perception of the environmental deterioration by man; not to be confused with the much more limited concept of financial harm.

be of crucial importance, the second x dollars still important and the nth x dollars may have only a negligible effect on welfare.

In my opinion this argument is based on an incorrect comparison between produced goods and environmental functions; the fact is overlooked that in an economic respect environmental functions do not differ from produced goods. We are concerned here with the well-known problem of quality. Expenditure on an improved (or new) product is entered in the National Accounts as output equal to the quantity of already existing products that could be bought for the same expenditure. Ten eggs may always be ten times one egg in the National Accounts, but ten cars are by no means always ten times one car. Ten Deux Chevaux are in the National Accounts twice as much as BMW 3.0 S and half as much as a Rolls-Royce Silver Shadow, because a Rolls costs four times as much as a BMW and twenty times as much as a Deux Chevaux. And, in the same way, air with a carbon monoxide concentration x can cost twice as much as air with a CO concentration of $1\frac{1}{2}\,x$ and ten times as much as air with a concentration of $2\,x$: extra quality usually calls for progressively increasing costs. We saw in Chapter 4 that the elimination cost curve almost always has a progressively rising trend. Which part of these costs has to be taken into account in the calculation of national income depends on the urgency of the need for the function(s) being attacked by an agent (such as CO). The needs express themselves, in part, in the costs of measures of compensation and elimination. These amounts should therefore be taken into account.

The authors mentioned above apparently have in mind the assignment of a constant negative monetary value to a kilogram of CO introduced into the atmosphere. In that case, non-linearity does in fact present problems. However, in this study it is proposed that corrections be made for losses of function valued in terms of money; the problem of the non-linear effects disappears as a result.

(3) An objection frequently voiced to correcting national income is that it is difficult to determine how far this correction must go. This problem has three facets:

(a) It is possible that part of the expenditure on a given project compensating for environmental deterioration makes a real addition to the available means of satisfying wants.
(b) What amounts are spent on compensation or elimination of impaired environmental functions, or, in other words, how must environmental deterioration be demarcated?
(c) Which items, apart from those mentioned under b, must also be deducted?

Attention has been drawn to the facet of the problem of delimitation mentioned under (a) by J.B.D. Derksen,[29] among others. One of the examples that this author gives is the building of swimming pools to compensate for polluted sea water. The admission charges to these pools may mean that less use is made of them than was made of the free beach,* but alternatively, in such pools sports can be practised that are not possible in the open sea (swimming races, diving, water polo). According to Derksen it is not possible to draw a meaningful line between the compensatory and the other aspects of many measures of environmental conservation. Moreover, the calculations have to be repeated uniformly in successive years, because otherwise the final figures are not comparable. This leads to more arbitrary suppositions which again cast doubt on the comparability.

This argument certainly forms statistical difficulties in a number of cases. Kuznets, too, already pointed out that some items of expenditure have both a consumptive component and a cost component; for instance, it is difficult to make out which part of the high price of urban housing is the high cost of offsetting discomforts of living in a densely settled community, and how much represents greater facilities and comforts.[30] However, Kuznets adduces that with an estimate of the expenditure of a cost character, however broadly made, a considerably better approach to the real flow of final goods can be made because current measurement entails a huge duplication. He considers such a step of great importance both for comparisons between various countries and for comparisons within a country in the course of time. These arguments of Kuznets dating from the end of the forties, when there was not yet any question of a rapidly increasing environmental deterioration, now apply *a fortiori*: the figures of national income, which are generally interpreted as economic or welfare growth, are giving wrong signals. J. Tinbergen, too, prefers an approximate correction to the present situation, in which double counting clearly occurs.[31] Tinbergen writes that we must change our view that, for instance, medical aid to road accident victims and the production of anti-pollution installations form part of national income. Such additions to production have to be excluded from the calculations of national

*This point is connected with the allocation problem. In the exceptional case of everyone profiting equally from all functions (including the function of refuse dump, function A), this problem ceases to exist. In all other cases the limitation lies with the activity that pays. Derksen implicitly assumes that the former beach users pay. But when the users of oil (assuming that this is the only polluting agent) pay for the compensating swimming pool, the limitation lies in motoring and other oil-consuming activities. That a limit is imposed somewhere is precisely the consequence of the limit of potential use of the environment having been reached, or in other words, the limit of economic growth (in the sense of increase of the availability of economic goods).

income and be considered as necessary inputs to those components of national income which make for real happiness even if they are not measures of happiness.[32]

Whilst in the case of certain items of expenditure there is in fact some difficulty regarding the motives (partly for compensation or elimination of environmental deterioration, and partly not), with a large number of items this problem does not exist at all. The building of treatment plants for waste water serves only one purpose: the elimination of water pollution. The excavation of desalination canals serves only as a measure compensating for the salination of the Rhine. Playgrounds for city children endeavour only to compensate for the lost play facilities; according to the practitioners of social medicine this goal is barely attained.* When examined over a longer period of time, an increase in the expenditure on medical aid to road accident victims does not represent a net increase of the availability of economic goods.

The facet of the delimitation problem mentioned under (b) will also lead to agreements of a more or less arbitrary nature being arrived at. In my opinion this facet is more difficult and more fundamental than the one mentioned under (a). Environment and environmental deterioration and thus also measures of compensation and elimination are concepts difficult to define. A partial attempt at concrete demarcation has been undertaken in Appendix I of this study, where the losses of function as a result of qualitative and quantitative competition in water and qualitative competition in air are classified. At the same time, the possible measures of elimination and compensation are shown per loss of function. It is the intention, as this investigation proceeds, also to classify the losses of function in the soil and the losses of function resulting from spatial competition. If this proves successful, the whole will at the same time form a worked-out proposal for correction items for environmental deterioration. The present author is well aware that in this classification a number of arbitrary decisions have been taken. Thus, the room inside buildings has been left out of consideration (unless this is affected by outside agents). As a result, in Appendix I the consequences of, for instance, the use of asbestos and the presence of carbon monoxide have been classified outside buildings but not inside them. (It is known that the latter are much more serious as regards the immediate effect on health.) It is clear that the delimitation of the environment poses problems that can hardly, if at all, be solved on strictly logical grounds. However, in the author's opinion this need not prevent us from estimating the items on which there can be no doubt and arriving at (arbitrary) agreements about the others, all for the sake of the best possible information.

*Cf. p. 26.

The same procedure (corrections for items about which there is no doubt and conventional rules adopted for other items) may be applied for the facet mentioned under (c). This could for instance include the increase in expenditure as a result of industrial accidents, which have been left out of consideration in the classification in Appendix I. But must expenditure on keep-fit courses, home trainers and the medical aid after heart attacks be included, insofar as these are the result of the lack of exercise in our changed way of life? Perhaps there will be scope in our investigation in the future to work this facet out more closely.

(4) G. Jaszi is of the opinion that the fact that some forms of expenditure are made 'as a defence' against environmental deterioration is no reason for not regarding them as income. H. M. Peskin approvingly quotes Jaszi, who remarks in this context that food expenditures defend against hunger, clothing and housing expenditures against cold and rain, medical expenditures against sickness and religious outlays against the fires of hell.[33,34] Jaszi's remarks are aimed at F. T. Juster, who argues that 'defensive outlays' against pollution may not be regarded as part of the net output of national income. A car with an emission filter does not run any better or more efficiently than one without a filter, it simply costs more to get the same combination of vehicle services plus the desired constant environmental benefits* that society already had. According to Juster, such expenditure adds nothing to the flow of economic or social benefits produced by the system.[35]

In my opinion the remarks of Peskin and Jaszi reflect a lack of insight into the points of departure for measuring national income. One of the intentions of measurement was to register the available means of satisfying wants as an indication of the welfare of society.** For a long time production formed the most important part of these means. But when production (and consumption), as a negative and unintentional by-product, destroys means of satisfying wants already in existence (the environmental functions), it is not logical to regard the expenditure incurred in compensating for and eliminating these as income. For this spending does not mean a greater availability of economic goods in respect of the initial situation. Unlike the expenditure on housing, which reduces the scarcity of shelter and comfort that existed in the initial situation and unlike religious expenditure, which reduces the initial scarcity of the proclamation of God's word. A procedure that accords the same treatment to costs of compensation and elimination conjured up by man-made environmental deterioration and spending on food comes into

*Juster presupposes official regulations for a constant quality of the air.
**Cf. p. 157.

conflict with the – meaningful – point of departure of the measurement of national income.

(5) E. F. Denison adduces that the various forms of pollution cannot all be covered by a single index. For instance, it is not possible to combine the pollution of the Potomac and that of Lake Erie in a water pollution index, says Denison.[36]

To me this is a remarkable argument. For years now we have been adding together in national income a visit to the opera, the collection of refuse, medical treatment for a heart attack and a holiday in Majorca. The common denominator here is the utilization of scarce means, measured in money. As explained above, the same procedure can be followed with respect to the environmental functions.

We have now considered the most frequent objections to the publication of an alternative figure for national income, in which costs of compensation and elimination are not entered as a final product. In the present author's opinion, most of these objections resolve themselves into insufficient reflection on the points of departure of the measurement of national income, an incorrect interpretation of what economics is really all about, and failure to recognize the fact that the possible uses of the environment do not differ from goods and services produced as regards their scarcity. Further, the specific welfare aspects (what the goods mean to us) and the scarcity aspects (the degree of availability of the goods) are often confused, which does not make the discussions any the clearer.*

Most of the authors cited above stress that their objections to correction for environmental deterioration are quite unconnected with their concern about this problem. That is, of course, a good scientific starting point: concern may not influence statistical measurement. But this is by-passing the consequences of identifying the figures with the concept of economic growth. Economic growth – from the linguistic point of view too – can only mean that things are going well from an economic angle. In terms of the models of Forrester and Meadows, the identification of the increase in national income with economic growth gives a positive feedback to policy: continuing in the same direction, increasing production further. The ecological criticism discussed in this study arouses the well-founded suspicion that continuing growth of production will lead to catastrophes. A milestone on this downward path is the point at which an increase in production adds more scarcity than it alleviates. Comparison of a series of figures in which the costs caused by

*The author sees no point in going into this again after the above. The reader is invited to consult the literature cited.

environmental deterioration have been taken into account in the manner suggested here with the current series of national income figures may form one of the indicators of how far we have already travelled the dreaded road. The calculations proposed here form in the first place a particularly useful piece of information: they tell which part of our activities is directed only towards cancelling out the undesirable effects of our present consumption and production on the environment. In the second place, they can act as negative feedback in respect of the current behavioural pattern if it should prove that the compensatory part of our activities is on the increase. It is for this particular reason that D. L. Meadows too considers the calculations proposed here of great importance.[37]

If it should prove that an increasingly large part of our activities is confined to offsetting their effects, this may contribute towards a more critical view of the structure of our society. It could lead us to ask questions such as the following. Are monocultures really so remunerative? Must we keep on spraying insects to death? Must cities be as big as they are? Is the time we save by car and plane worth the trouble? And, perhaps, in conclusion: couldn't we try it another way? Above all, pricking the bubble of an aspect of 'economic growth' may also lead to protection of the environment because reduced production may become more acceptable to the public.

International statistical conventions do not allow of rapid change. But there are signs that the presentation of national income suggested here – side by side with the existing one – will one day become a fact.

In 1971, protection of the environment was accepted as the sixth objective of economic policy in the Netherlands.[38] This represents a recognition of the important economic facet that the environment forms for man, as well as a disconnection of the persistent identification of economics with production. A logical consequence of this step is to have the economic consequences of environmental management reflected in the macro-economic figures of national income.

A big step in the right direction is the recommendation by the Conference of European Statisticians to develop within the system of National Accounts a classification of intermediate consumption, primary inputs and gross fixed capital formation of industries by purpose, which would provide for the separation of outlays on the protection of environment from other outlays, and also to arrive at a further development of the classification of expenditure of government and private non-profit services by purpose with a view to separating outlays on the protection of environment.[39]

Finally, it is not without importance that leading authors like S.

Kuznets,* J. Tinbergen,** D.L. Meadows*** and P.A. Samuelson[40] have stated that they are in favour of an alternative national income in order to benefit from better information about macro-economic events.

5.5. References

[1]J. Tinbergen. Meetbaarheid van een rechtvaardige verdeling. *De Economist* 121, 1973, No. 2, p. 111.

[2]Cf. S. Kuznets. National income and industrial structure. In: *The Econometric Society Meeting, September 6–18, 1947, Washington, D.C., Proceedings of the International Statistical Conferences*. Volume V. Calcutta, undated, p. 205; and C.A. Oomens. *A Note on the International Comparison of National Income Figures*. Unpublished paper for the International Association for Research in Income and Wealth, 1965.

[3]In 1679, Sir William Petty estimated England's national income. In 1688, Gregory King did the same thing. Both calculations come to about £40 million. Gregory King's calculation is to be found in Natural and Political Observations and Conclusions upon the State and Condition of England, a manuscript which is unique in other respects as well, and is included in the booklet *Two Tracts*. Baltimore, 1936. At the beginning of the nineteenth century, estimates of national income were made by the Prussian L. Krug (*Betrachtungen über den National-Reichtum des Preussischen Staats und über den Wohlstand seiner Bewohner*. Berlin, 1805) and the Dutchman R. Metelerkamp (*De Toestand van Nederland, in Vergelijking Gebracht met die van Enige Andere Landen van Europa*. Rotterdam, 1804).

[4]J.B.D. Derksen. Personal information.

[5]Cf. F. de Roos and D.B.J. Schouten. *Groeitheorie*. Haarlem, 1960, p. 14; W.W. Rostow. *The Stages of Economic Growth, A Non-communist Manifesto*. London, 1960, p. 102; *Achtste Nota Inzake de Industrialisatie van Nederland*. The Hague, 1963, p. 89; *Nota Inzake Groei en Structuur van Onze Economie*. The Hague, 1966, p. 7; L.J. Zimmerman, *Arme en Rijke Landen*. The Hague, 1968, p. 21; A. Mey et al. *Encyclopedie van de Bedrijfseconomie*. In: *Algemene Economie*. Volume I. Bussum, 1969, p. 86; *Rijksbegroting voor het Dienstjaar 1971*. Chapter XIII. Economische zaken. Memorie van toelichting, p. 1; J. Wemelsfelder. Economie en menselijk geluk. *Economisch-Statistische Berichten*, 2 May 1973, p. 379.

[6]Cf. A. Heertje. Welvaart en welzijn, een schijntegenstelling. *Intermediair*, 15 January 1971.

[7]The thoughts mentioned hereafter were published by the author in a number of articles during the years 1967–70. These articles have been collected in the booklet *Wat is de natuur ons waard?* Baarn, 1970.

[8]J. Tinbergen. Personal information.

[9]Cf. J. Pen's reaction in the *Haagse Post* of 8 March, 1972, to an idea proposed by the Dutch progressive political parties to work with Gross National Utility and no longer with Gross National Product.

[10]Cf. F. Hartog. *Toegepaste Welvaartseconomie*. Leiden, 1973, p. 9.

[11]R.A. Easterlin. *Does Economic Growth Improve The Human Lot?* Mim. paper. University of Pennsylvania. Review of this paper by: J. Wemelsfelder. Economie en menselijk geluk. *Economisch-Statistische Berichten*, 2 May 1973, p. 379.

[12]J.K. Galbraith. *The Affluent Society*. London, 1958.

[13]B.M.S. van Praag and A. Kapteyn. Wat is ons inkomen ons waard? *Economisch-Statistische Berichten*, 25 April and 2 May 1973.

*See pp. 161, 177.
**See pp. 177–178.
***See p. 181.

[14]W. Siddré. De toenemende schaarste aan tijd. *Economisch-Statistische Berichten*, 25 August 1971, pp. 747–748.
[15]S. Kuznets. On the valuation of social income. *Economica*, February/May, 1948.
[16]J.R. Hicks. On the valuation of social income. *Economica*, August, 1948.
[17]A.C. Pigou. *Income*. London, 1949, p. 11.
[18]A.C. Pigou. Loc. cit.
[19]Cf. S. Kuznets. National income and industrial structure. In: *The Econometric Society Meeting, September 6–18, 1947, Washington, D.C., Proceedings of the International Statistical Conferences*, Volume V. Calcutta, undated, p. 205; and S. Kuznets. On the valuation of social income. *Economica*, February/May, 1948.
[20]W.I. King. *The Wealth and Income of the People of the United States*. New York/London, 1919, pp. 5–49.
[21]S. Fabricant. In: *Studies in Income and Wealth. Volume 10. Conference on Research in Income and Wealth*. New York, 1947, p. 50.
[22]E.F. Denison. Loc. cit., p. 77.
[23]The conceptual framework of national income statistics. In: *National Income*. 1954 Edition. U.S. Department of Commerce, Washington, 1954, p. 92.
[24]The articles have been collected in the booklet *Wat is de natuur ons waard?* Baarn, 1970.
[25]Cf. R. Hueting. Ruimtelijke ordening en het allocatievraagstuk. *Economisch-Statistische Berichten*, 21 May 1969.
[26]Statistical Commission and Economic Commission for Europe. Conference of European Statisticians. *The Treatment of Environmental Problems in the National Accounts and Balances*. CES/AC.40/4, 14 February 1973, pp. 6–7.
[27]Op. cit., p. 7.
[28]E.F. Denison, Welfare measurement and the GNP. U.S. Department of Commerce, Office of Business Economics. *Survey of Current Business* 51, 1971, No. 1, p. 15.
[29]J.B.D. Derksen. Zijn correcties van het begrip nationaal inkomen mogelijk en gewenst? *Economisch-Statistische Berichten*, 31 January 1973, pp. 97–100.
[30]S. Kuznets. National income and industrial structure. In: *The Econometric Society Meeting, September 6–18, 1947, Washington, D.C., Proceedings of the International Statistical Conferences*, Volume V. Calcutta, undated, pp. 218/219.
[31]J. Tinbergen. Personal information.
[32]J. Tinbergen. *Does the GNP of a Country Indicate its Happiness?* Written for a Japanese journal in 1970.
[33]H.M. Peskin. *National Accounting and the Environment*. Norwegian Central Bureau of Statistics. Oslo, 1972, p. 12.
[34]G. Jaszi. *Comments on F. Thomas Juster, 'A Framework for the Measurement of Economic and Social Performance'*. Unpublished paper prepared for National Bureau of Economic Research Conference on the Measurement of Economic and Social Performance. Princeton (N.J.), 4–6 November 1971, p. 11. Later Published in: M. Moss. *The Measurement of Economic and Social Performance*. New York, 1973.
[35]F.T. Juster. *A Framework for the Measurement of Economic and Social Performance*. Princeton (N.J.), 1971, pp. 50–51.
[36]E.F. Denison. Loc. cit., p. 15.
[37]D.L. Meadows. Personal information.
[38]*Rijksbegroting voor het Dienstjaar 1972*. Chapter XIII. Economische zaken. Memorie van toelichting, p. 4.
[39]Statistical Commission and Economic Commission for Europe. Conference of European Statisticians. *Report of the Meeting held in Geneva, 19–23 March 1973*, CES/AC. 40/5, p. 13.
[40]P.A. Samuelson. *Economics*. Ninth Edition. New York, 1973, pp. 195–198. This author mentions with approval a study by: W. Nordhaus and J. Tobin. Is growth obsolete? In: *Economic Growth. Fiftieth Anniversary Colloquium V*. New York, 1972. Samuelson rather suggests that in this study corrections were made not only for factors such as leisure time but also for environmental deterioration. However, Nordhaus and Tobin state that they were not able to correct for encroachment upon the environment (p. 49). They

correct merely for the inconveniences of the city. These are estimated by means of the wage differentials between town and country. The assumption is made that everyone is free to choose where he lives (p. 50). In my opinion this assumption is not tenable. In the first place people are tied to their work. In the second place there is not enough room in the countryside to house all the town-dwellers (certainly in a country like the Netherlands). A calculation of this kind is not in the slightest way a criterion of the degree of environmental deterioration nor of the costs of compensation and elimination.

Further

C.B.S. Enkele berekeningen over het nationale inkomen van Nederland. In: *Speciale Onderzoekingen van de Nederlandse Conjunctuur*. The Hague, 1939.

United Nations. *Measurement of National Income and the Construction of Social Accounts*. New York, 1947.

C.B.S. *Het Nationale Inkomen van Nederland 1921–1939*. Utrecht, 1948.

United Nations. *A System of National Accounts and Supporting Tables*. New York, 1953.

O.E.E.C. *A Standardised System of National Accounts*. Paris, 1952.

C.B.S. *Statistische en Econometrische Onderzoekingen 2e/3e kwartaal 1958*.

United Nations. *A System of National Accounts*. New York, 1968.

Chapter 6

SUMMARY OF CONCLUSIONS

For many (and in fact for the author too) this study will not have yielded the result expected of it. True, a theoretical connection has been established between environment and economics. However, the quantitative elaboration of this proves only partly possible. Though in most cases it will be possible to calculate costs of elimination, the preferences can be expressed only very partially, through compensatory costs and financial damage. The crucial question 'What is nature worth to us?' cannot be answered by means of the instruments available to us. But in my opinion the study has shown that at the same time another question remains unanswered, namely 'What is the worth to us of goods that are produced and consumed at the expense of the environment?'. For when the value of the environment cannot be determined in the conflict between production and environment, the market price of produced goods may no longer be accepted as an indicator of the economic value of these goods. It is therefore advisable, when weighing produced goods and environmental functions against one another, deliberately to forget the (market) prices of the produced goods, and further to rely on the one hand on a verbal description of the utility of both categories of goods, and on the other on the utilization of scarce resources (measured in terms of money) required to obtain or maintain both categories of goods.

With regard to this reliance the study already gives some information. The functions of water and air have been described; the losses of function as a result of qualitative and quantitative competition in water and of qualitative competition in air have been classified. It has been indicated what measures of compensation and financial damage result from the loss of an environmental function and by what measures of elimination this loss can be made good. At the same time, the costs of elimination have been calculated for a number of agents. For one agent, salination, the costs of measures of compensation and the financial damage could also be estimated. It was therefore possible to perform a complete cost–benefit analysis for salination and to indicate the optimum point of treatment with the aid of market data. Unfortunately, this situation is an exception.

An important aspect of the problem posed is the question whether, when the environmental deterioration is taken into account, economic growth still occurs. In this study this question has been divided into two: 'Is the availability of means of satisfying wants still increasing' and 'Is the satisfaction of wants still increasing?'

As regards the first question the following conclusions may be drawn from the study. The shadow prices of environmental functions cannot usually be tracked down because the wants for these functions are only very partially reflected on the market. We must assume that the shadow prices of vital environmental functions are very high, but we do not possess the instruments for measuring exactly how high. Corrections to national income (in order to arrive at a series of figures to place alongside the existing ones) are possible only for losses of function in which the want for the function may be derived from market data. These are the amounts spent by private persons on measures of compensation and elimination. In accordance with the conventions of National Accounts, the costs of compensation and elimination incurred by the government also qualify as correction items. Costs incurred by business have already been entered in the right way according to the scarcity criterion applied here. From the corrections advocated here, at least some insight can be gained into the direction in which society is heading as a result of environmental deterioration from the viewpoint of scarcity.

The first results of our study, presented in Appendix II, and based on estimates, are too incomplete to make it possible at this stage to arrive at a broad correction over a given period. For the performance of corrections from year to year a regular flow of data is required, which will largely have to be obtained from polls. These have not yet been held. In addition to a national income corrected for compensatory and elimination costs, there are of course many other data. In this study mention has already been made of emission and concentration data, the incidence of plant and animal species, the elimination cost curves (which indicate how much it costs to eliminate a certain agent, irrespective of the preferences), and financial damage. The investigation is also directed towards these. In addition, one could think of indicators like population density, fragmentation of space, etc.

On the strength of the considerations in Chapter 5, it must be concluded that the second question posed above ('Is the satisfaction of wants still increasing?') cannot be answered by means of statistical measurement.

In conclusion, the study has brought me to a number of personal insights of a far-reaching nature.

In my opinion human activities are leading to increasingly violent competition between the functions of the environment. In a country like the Netherlands, hardly any further increase in activities is possible without considerable impairment of environmental functions of which other activities are already making use (in other words, without leading to a considerable loss of function). If this is correct, it means that the limits of the qualitative, quantitative and spatial possibilities of using our environment have been reached or already exceeded. Since no economic activity is possible without making use of the environment, it follows from this that the limits to growth in the sense of increase of the availability of scarce goods are probably close at hand.

I consider the most serious conflict that is occurring as we reach the limits of possible use of the environment – the competition of functions – to be that between the present generation and those to come. All the information now available suggests that an unchanged continuation of growth of production and of population will almost certainly lead to ecological or climatic disasters or to a collapse of our civilization as a result of the exhaustion of energy and natural resources, shortage of food, pollution or lack of space. This amounts to the fact that our level of consumption is most probably at the expense of the consumption by, and indeed the very possibilities of life of, our children and grandchildren. Environmental deterioration is therefore above all a problem of future generations, for which this generation is responsible. Most members of the present generation either are not capable of giving expression to their concern for the future in their conduct because they cannot escape as individuals from the prevailing institutional framework, or are simply not interested in the future ('The future will just have to look after itself').

In this situation, which has no precedent in the history of mankind, the level of activities will, in my opinion, have to be limited to such an extent, on the strength of ethical considerations, that the future is given a fair chance. Mention is made in the last section of Chapter 4 of the type of measure that would restrict the activities to an acceptable level.

Little imagination is required to see that implementation of such measures will mean considerable interferences with daily life. They comprise much more than 'just' taking measures of elimination. In the short term, on a geographically limited scale and in a situation without growth, the elimination cost curve used in this study can still be interpreted as the costs of anti-pollution measures. At worldwide level and in the long term such a curve expresses above all a reduction in the level of activities. For almost every anti-pollution measure entails pollution in another form and requires space, raw materials and energy. Finally, almost every activity imposes a burden on the environment. Seen in a wider perspective, therefore, the elimination cost curve represents much more the effect of for instance changing from private cars to public transport or bicycles, or changing to a society as recommended in the *Blueprint for Survival*, than the costs of treatment plants.

The question who would have to intervene so drastically in everyday life remains unanswered. Should it be the government, whose composition and therefore powers of decision depend on the wishes of the citizens? Or a board of experts? The concept of merit good, which in fact forms the basis of the problem of intergenerational distribution, rests, according to Musgrave, on a belief in an elite and on a tendency in society to keep the freedom of choice offered by the market mechanism within certain limits. But if authors like Forrester, Meadows, Boulding, Odum and the compilers of the report *Man's Impact on the Global Environment* are right, such a rigorous restriction of the subjects' freedom of choice will have to be imposed that little will remain of the free market mechanism.

However, the following comments may be made on this prospect. Man's wants are to a considerable extent determined historically and culturally. They are also open to influence to a high degree. On the whole, the influence being exerted at present is in the direction of more production and less environment. However, recently there have been spontaneous campaigns among the population in the opposite direction. This suggests that a drastic change in the pattern of wants is quite feasible. If this view is correct, optimism with regard to human happiness is justified, even if the availability of means of satisfying wants decreases.

Furthermore, the basis rooted in our society of having the result of economic activity determined by the preferences of the subjects is defensible only as long as it concerns the production and consumption of goods and services with no far-reaching effect on either third persons or future generations. As long as there is no such effect, the argument that the consumer does not know what is good for him can be countered by the argument that free people must be able to make their own decisions or their own choices of their own free will, since this freedom forms an integral part of human existence. But in a situation in which the sum of the individual decisions threatens to result in an unlivable world for coming generations it is permissible, to my way of thinking, to correct the individual preferences. In such a case it can be adduced as an argument for limiting human freedom that many believe that man derives much of the meaning of his life from his relation with others, notably with his children and grandchildren. It is above all for this reason that setting standards for human activity in the given situation is permissible, even though it probably runs counter to what many people now want. The policy that must now be followed in the name of future generations makes an appeal to the public's 'better self'.

This study deals with a sombre subject, but its message is certainly not one of despondency. The hope for a livable environment for our children seems best served by optimism regarding human imagination and ingenuity, which are great, and pessimism regarding human institutions, which are slow to react.

Appendix I

THE SYSTEM OF TABLES DEVELOPED BY THE NETHERLANDS CENTRAL BUREAU OF STATISTICS*

AI.1. System of Tables for the Component Water

Of the three aspects of competition of functions stated in Section 4.1, the quantitative and qualitative aspects will be discussed here for the component water. Spatial competition will be dealt with at a later stage in the study. 'Water' here means both surface water and ground water. It has already been explained in Section 4.1 how quantitative competition (the amount of water) and qualitative competition (the quality of the water) of the functions of the component water are described in a system of tables. This system is to be found in this appendix, and will be further explained below.

In Table AI.1 all the separate functions of water are compared with one another. In the cells of the table loss of function is indicated by a plus sign and no loss of function by a minus sign. The names of the functions of the component water speak for themselves on the whole. Only three of them need a brief explanation. Water for agriculture includes fishing water. Water in the natural environment is not only a function whose availability is desired by man for its own sake but also – as regards the qualitative aspects – an indicator of the degree of availability of all other functions. For the reduced availability of water as a result of qualitative competition is always caused by a disturbance of the existing biological and chemical composition of the water by human activities. The function 'utilization of water for construction' relates to the fact that certain parts of structures depend on the quantity or the quality of the water. Thus a fall in the ground water level as a result of abstraction of ground water may cause wooden piles to rot and buildings to subside through shrinkage of the soil. Furthermore, sulphates in particular may attack the concrete foundations of quay walls and buildings.

*The CBS Department of Environmental Statistics.

Table AI.1

Competitive use of water, by function.

		2. Industrial water								
	Drinking water	Cooling water	Water for flushing and transport	Process water	Water for agriculture	Water for recreation	Water in the natural environment	Water for navigation	Water as an element in the social environment	Utilization of water for construction
	1	2.1	2.2	2.3	3	4	5	6	7	8
1. Drinking water	+	+	+	+	+	–	+	+	–	+
2. Industrial water										
2.1 Cooling water	+	+	+	+	+	–	+	–	–	+
2.2 Water for flushing and transport	+	+	+	+	+	–	+	–	–	+
2.3 Process water	+	+	+	+	+	–	+	–	–	+
3. Water for agriculture	+	+	+	+	+	–	+	+	–	–
4. Water for recreation	–	–	–	–	–	–	–	–	–	–
5. Water in the natural environment	+	+	+	+	+	–	–	–	–	–
6. Water for navigation	+	–	–	–	+	–	–	+	–	–
7. Water as an element in the social environment	–	–	–	–	–	–	–	–	–	–
8. Utilization of water for construction	+	+	+	+	–	–	–	–	–	+
9. Water as a dumping ground for waste	+	+	+	+	+	+	+	+	+	+

Table AI.2

Losses of function as a result of quantitative competition in water, by function.

		2. Industrial water								
	Drinking water	Cooling water	Water for flushing and transport	Process water	Water for agriculture	Water for recreation	Water in the natural environment	Water for navigation	Water as an element in the social environment	Utilization of water for construction
	1	2.1	2.2	2.3	3	4	5	6	7	8
1. Drinking water	1	2	3	4	5	—	6	7	—	8
2. Industrial water										
2.1 Cooling water		9	10	11	12	—	13	—	—	14
2.2 Water for flushing and transport			15	16	17	—	18	—	—	19
2.3 Process water				20	21	—	22	—	—	23
3. Water for agriculture					24	—	25	26	—	—
4. Water for recreation						—	—	—	—	—
5. Water in the natural environment							—	—	—	—
6. Water for navigation								27	—	—
7. Water as an element in the social environment									—	—
8. Utilization of water for construction										28

List AI.2.1

Description of the losses of function as a result of quantitative competition in water, by function (some examples).

Cell no. Table AI.2	Competitive functions	Description of losses of function	Financial damage (D) Compensatory measures (C)[a]
1	Drinking water – Drinking water	When so much drinking water is pumped out of the ground water that the maximum capacity is attained, other methods will have to be applied.	C: Build new installations; switch to surface water (extra treatment costs).
5	Drinking water – Water for agriculture	Abstraction of ground water lowers the ground water level.	D: Lower crop yield. C: Bring in water from elsewhere (ground or surface water).
6	Drinking water – Water in the natural environment	Owing to the abstraction of water, nature areas may acquire a lowered ground water level. This may lead to impoverishment of the natural environment.	C: Bring in water from elsewhere (ground or surface water).
8	Drinking water – Utilization of water for construction.	A fall in the ground water level may cause wooden piles to rot.	D: Reduction in value of buildings. C: Bring in water from elsewhere (surface water); repair buildings.
25	Water for agriculture – Water in the natural environment.	The use of water by the agricultural sector may lead to nature areas drying out or becoming too wet. Water management on behalf of nature areas may lead to a change in the water level of farmland.	D: Drop in crop yield; drop in value of farmland. C: Activities of adjustment; bring in water from elsewhere.
29	All functions	Because of bottlenecks a number of bodies have begun to concern themselves with problems of quantitative competition.	Buildings, salaries, etc.

[a]Since quantitative competition is not a matter of degree but is absolute in nature, no elimination measures are possible here. Once no further compensatory measures can be taken, the use of water on behalf of one or more functions will necessarily have to be restricted.

As stated already in Section 4.1, the losses of function as a result of quantitative competition are described in rows 1–8 of Table AI.1. These losses of function are elaborated in Table AI.2. The losses of function as a result of qualitative competition occur on row 9 of Table AI.1 and are elaborated in Tables AI.3 and AI.4.

Quantitative competition of functions is absolute. The quantity of the component is insufficient to provide for every use or intended use. The functions are therefore directly in competition with one another. Use on behalf of one function means withdrawal from another function and vice versa. As a result, if all the cells in Table AI.2 are completely filled in, each loss of function occurring will appear twice. For simplicity's sake a presentation has consequently been chosen showing half of the cells in which loss of function appears as a result of quantitative competition. The losses of function traced are numbered. These numbers refer to List AI.2.1.*

In this list the losses of function traced as a result of quantitative competition in the water are briefly described, together with a concise indication of the accompanying financial damage, compensatory measures that can be taken and the cost factors occurring. The losses of function naturally amount to shortages of water for various functions. The financial damage usually boils down to a lower crop yield and damage to buildings. Compensatory measures consist mainly of bringing in water from elsewhere. Elimination in the form of taking measures is, of course, not possible in quantitative competition: the quantity of an environmental component cannot be increased. All that can be done is to make the most efficient use possible of the quantity available and to weigh the different possible uses against one another. In quantitative competition even more than in qualitative competition – where standards are apparently elastic – the limits of the environment find expression.

In Table AI.3 – the first of two tables describing *qualitative competition* in water – the cells indicate which agents are discharged into the water by which originators. A plus sign in one of the cells means that the originator discharges that agent into the water; a minus sign means that the originator does not discharge the agent, or does so to only a negligible extent.

The agents are subdivided into biological, chemical and physical ones. As explained in Section 4.1, by 'an agent' is meant a constituent which

*In the translation the lists of the losses of function have been abridged to a few striking cases. The reader interested in the complete elaboration should contact the author c/o Central Bureau of Statistics, Prinses Beatrixlaan 428, Voorburg (ZH), The Netherlands.

Table AI.3

Qualitative competition in water, by agent and by originator.

Agent	Biological			Chemical											Physical			
	Pathogens	Animals	Plants	Biodegradable organic substances	Persistent organic substances	Other organic poisons	Oil	Oxygen-binding inorganic substances	Heavy metals	Other organic poisons	Salts	Sweetening	Change in pH value	Eutrophicating substances	Rise in temperature	Radioactivity	Current and Wash	Silt and coarse insolubles
Direct originators	101	102	103	201	202	203	204	205	206	207	208	209	210	211	301	302	303	304
1 *PRODUCTION*																		
1.1 *Auxiliary and general processes*																		
1.1.1 Land transport	−	−	−	−	+	+	+	+	+	+	+	−	+	+	−	−	−	+
1.1.2 Water transport	+	+	−	+	+	+	+	+	+	+	+	−	+	+	−	−	+	+
1.1.3 Heating and cooling	−	+	−	+	−	+	+	−	−	+	+	−	−	+	+	−	+	+
1.1.4 Generation of energy (not in 1.1.3)	−	+	−	+	−	+	+	−	−	+	−	−	−	+	+	+	+	+
1.1.5 Commerce	−	−	−	+	−	−	−	−	−	−	−	−	−	+	−	−	−	+
1.1.6 Packaging	−	−	−	+	−	−	−	−	+	−	−	−	−	+	−	−	−	+
1.1.7 Cleaning	+	+	−	+	+	+	+	−	−	+	−	−	+	+	−	−	−	+
1.1.8 Government services and other services	−	+	−	+	+	−	+	−	−	−	+	+	−	+	−	−	+	+
1.2 *Specific processes*																		
1.2.1 Agriculture and horticulture	+	+	+	+	+	+	−	+	+	+	+	−	+	+	−	−	+	+

1.2.2 Building trade																		
1.2.2.1 Structural engineering	–	–	+	+	–	–	+	+	–	+	+	–	–	–	–	–	+	+
1.2.2.2. Civil engineering	–	–	+	+	–	–	+	+	–	+	+	–	+	–	–	–	+	+
1.2.3 Industry and mining	+	–	–	+	+	+	+	+	+	+	+	–	+	+	–	+	–	+
1.2.4 Land improvement, earth-moving and open-cast mining	–	–	+	+	–	+	+	+	–	+	+	–	–	+	–	–	+	+
1.2.5 Catering trade	+	–	–	+	–	–	–	–	–	–	–	–	–	+	–	–	–	+
1.2.6 Fat-stock farms	+	–	–	+	+	–	–	–	+	+	–	–	+	+	–	–	–	+
2 *HOUSEHOLD CONSUMPTION*																		
2.1 Land transport	–	–	–	–	+	+	+	–	+	+	+	–	+	+	–	–	–	+
2.2 Water transport	+	–	+	+	–	+	+	–	+	+	+	–	+	+	–	–	+	+
2.3 Sewage	+	–	–	+	–	+	–	–	+	+	+	–	+	+	+	–	+	+
2.4 Time spent outside the home	+	+	–	+	–	–	–	–	–	–	–	–	–	+	–	–	–	+
3 *INTERCHANGE WITH SOIL*																		
3.1 From soil	+	–	–	+	+	+	+	+	+	+	+	–	+	+	–	–	–	+
3.2 To soil	+	–	–	+	+	+	–	–	+	+	+	+	–	+	–	–	–	+
4 *INTERCHANGE WITH AIR*																		
4.1 From air	–	–	–	+	+	+	–	+	+	+	–	–	+	+	–	+	–	+
4.2 To air	–	–	–	+	+	+	+	+	–	+	–	–	–	–	+	–	–	–
5 *FOREIGN COUNTRIES*																		
5.1 Imports of pollution	+	+	+	+	+	+	+	+	+	+	+	+	+	+	+	+	–	+
5.2 Exports of pollution	–	–	–	+	–	–	+	+	+	+	+	–	–	–	+	+	–	+

may cause loss of function by either its addition to or withdrawal from the environment by man. Through the agent a change in the environment often occurs, which in fact causes the loss of function. In the system of tables the agents and the changes are not distinguished from one another; the nomenclature has been based as far as possible on the agent.

The biological agents are in turn subdivided into pathogens, animals and plants. The animal and plant agents lead to environmental changes as a result of their planting, and catching or withdrawal. Thus release of the musk-rat in the Netherlands has resulted in an undesirable spread of this species which is not a native, the consequence being loss of function in the form of damage to dykes threatening whole systems of these defences. For the function 'natural environment', addition or withdrawal of plants and animals often means a loss of function in itself. Thus large-scale removal of sundew and mushrooms has led to local eradication of these species. In general the chemical agents speak for themselves. It may, however, be remarked that the classification has been made according to effect of the agent, so that a certain substance and the products of its decomposition may appear among different groups of agents. With regard to the physical agents, it may be commented that with respect to silt only its properties such as turbidity and light interception are considered.

The activities that cause the discharge of the agents into the water are subdivided into production processes, households, interchange with other environmental components and foreign countries. The production processes are subdivided in turn into auxiliary and general processes on the one hand and specific processes on the other. This has been done because activities like transport and packaging or agriculture, horticulture and specific industrial processes often have their own type of pollutants. The category 'foreign countries' covers imports and exports of agents. By 'export' is meant discharge of an agent in such a way that this no longer has any effect on the national economy. Export in this sense will in general occur for only part of the total quantity discharged. Thus, of the quantity of biodegradable organic matter discharged into the sea, only part will be decomposed far out from the coast; much of this matter moves with the coastal current along the coast as far as the Wadden Sea, causing oxygen deficiency as it goes. Only in cases such as the dumping of common salt in the sea can one speak of export of the whole quantity dumped.

When loss of function occurs through the effect of the agents on the functions of the water, this is indicated by a figure in the relevant cell of Table AI.4. The figure refers to List AI.4.1, where the losses of function traced in the water are listed and briefly described. In the elaboration, as complete a description as possible will of course be given. A concise

Table AI.4

Losses of function as a result of qualitative competition in water, by agent and by function.

Function		2. Industrial water								
	Drinking water	Cooling water	Water for flushing and transport	Process water	Water for agriculture	Water for recreation	Water in the natural environment	Water for navigation	Water as an element in the social environment	Utilization of water for construction
Agent	1	2.1	2.2	2.3	3	4	5	6	7	8
100 *BIOLOGICAL*										
101 Pathogens	1	—	2	3	4	5	—	—	—	—
102 Animals	—	—	—	—	6, 7, 8, 9	6	6, 10, 11 to 19	7	7	—
103 Plants	—	—	—	20	20	20	20 to 23	21	20, 21	—
200 *CHEMICAL*										
201 Biodegradable organic substances	24, 27	25	24	24	26	26, 27, 28	26, 29	—	27	—
202 Persistent organic substances	30, 31	30	30, 31	30, 31	30, 32 to 35	30, 32, 36	30, 32	37	30, 32	—
203 Other organic poisons	38, 39	38	38, 39	38, 39	38, 40, 41	38, 40, 42	38, 40	—	38, 40	—
204 Oil	43, 44	43	43, 44	43, 44	43, 45, 46	43, 47	43, 45, 48	47, 49	43, 47	47
205 Oxygen-binding inorganic substances	50, 51	50, 51	50, 51	50, 51	50, 51	50, 51	50, 51	—	50, 51	—
206 Heavy metals	52, 53	52	52, 53	52, 53	52, 54, 55, 56	52, 54, 57	52, 54	—	52, 54	—
207 Other inorganic poisons	58, 59	58	58, 59	58, 59	58, 60, 61	58, 60, 62	58, 60	—	58, 60	—
208 Salts	63	63	63	63	64	—	65	—	—	66
209 Sweetening	—	—	—	—	67	—	67	—	—	—
210 Change in pH value	68, 69	68, 69	68, 69	68, 69	68, 69	68,69	68, 69	—	68, 69	68, 69
211 Eutrophicating substances	70, 71	70, 71	70, 71	70, 71	70, 72 to 75	70, 72 to 76	70, 72 to 75	76	70, 72, 73	77
300 *PHYSICAL*										
301 Rise in temperature	78	78	78	78	78	78, 79	78, 80	—	78, 81	—
302 Radioactivity	82	—	82	82	82	82	82	—	82	—
303 Current and wash	83	83	83	83	83, 84	83, 84, 85	83, 84	86	83, 84	—
304 Silt and coarse insolubles	87, 88	87	87, 88	87, 88	87, 89	87, 89, 90	87, 89	87	87, 90	—
All agents	91	91	91	91	91	91	91	91	91	91

List AI.4.1

Description of losses of function as a result of qualitative competition in water, by agent and by function (some examples).

Cell no. Table AI.4	Agents	Functions in which the loss occurs	Description of losses of function	Financial damage (D)[a] Compensatory measures (C) Elimination measures (E)
	BIOLOGICAL			
1	Pathogens	Drinking water	The presence of pathogens in water makes it less suitable as raw material for drinking water.	C: Extra treatment measures. E: Build treatment plants; chlorinate the effluent.
4		Water for agriculture	The presence of pathogens in surface water makes it unsuitable as drinking water for livestock and makes molluscs inedible.	D: Lower yield. C: Bring in water from elsewhere. E: Build treatment plants; chlorinate the effluent.
5		Water for recreation	By discharging treated or untreated water near a swimming place, the water becomes unfit to swim in.	D: Drop in value of recreation areas. C: Build new swimming pools elsewhere. E: Take treating measures.
8	Animals	Water for agriculture	Overfishing leads to a reduction in catches in later years.	D: Reduction of yield. C: Stock with fish.
10		Water in the natural environment	The escape of commercially bred musk-rats leads to a disturbance of the existing biological equilibrium.	E: Control.
16			The construction of dykes to islands and roads to isolated marshy areas makes it possible for foreign animals (rats, fieldmice) to enter. As a result, autochthonous animals (e.g. the Nordic vole) are threatened, since they can survive only in isolation.	E: Restore the isolation.

20	Plants	Process water Water for agriculture Water for recreation Water in the natural environment Water as an element in the social environment	Azolla and Elodea are imported exotic plants. They propagate quickly in already disturbed water and cover this completely, thus interfering with aeration. The result is a reduction in the water's self-purifying capacity.	E: Remove the plants.
	CHEMICAL			
24	Biodegradable organic substances	Drinking water Water for flushing and transport Process water	The discharge of biodegradable organic substances reduces the oxygen content of the water and often spoils the taste.	C: Extra treatment. E: Treat waste water; apply another manufacturing process; use other raw materials.
30	Persistent organic substances	All functions excl. water for navigation and utilization of water for construction	The occurence of persistent organic substances in water harms the natural purification process, thus making the water less suitable for all the functions stated.	C: Extra treatment. E: Remove persistent substances from waste water; make more careful or less use of pesticides.
31		Drinking water Water for flushing and transport Process water	Persistent organic substances in water impart a poor quality for the functions stated through their toxic effect and taste-spoiling effect.	See 30.
32		Water for agriculture Water for recreation Water in the natural environment Water as an element in the social environment	Discharge or flushing of persistent organic substances leads to a low level of water organisms and, in the event of large-scale discharges, to fatality. This phenomenon may be acute, but may also occur as a result of cumulation in food chains.	D: Lower yields; drop in value of recreation areas. C: Stock with fish; close off areas from contaminated water. E: See 30.
34		Water for agriculture	Discharge of persistent organic substances makes water unsuitable as drinking water for livestock.	D: Lower yield of milk. C: Bring in water from elsewhere. E: See 30.

List AI.4.1 *continued*

Cell no. Table AI.4	Agents	Functions in which the loss occurs	Description of losses of function	Financial damage (D)[a] Compensatory measures (C) Elimination measures (E)
38	Other organic poisons	All functions excl. water for navigation and utilization of water for construction	The discharge of poisons harms the natural purification process, thus making the water less suitable for all the functions stated.	C: Extra treatment. E: Remove poisons from waste water.
43	Oil		A thin coating of oil prevents oxygen from penetrating the water, thus lowering its quality.	C: Remove oil. E: Use oil more carefully.
44		Drinking water Water for flushing and transport Process water	Oil spoils the taste of water.	C: Filter oil or remove it in some other way. E: Use oil more carefully.
47		Water for recreation Water for navigation Water as an element in the social environment Utilization of water for construction	Oil pollutes shores, beaches, water, ships etc.	D: Reduction of the value of recreation areas. C: Cleaning of beaches, etc. E: Use oil more carefully.
48		Water in the natural environment	Oil pollution causes increased mortality of birds and other animals.	C: Therapy. E: Use oil more carefully.
50	Oxygen-binding inorganic substances	All functions excl. water for navigation and utilization of water for construction	Discharge of oxygen-binding inorganic substances leads to a lower oxygen content of the water, making it less suitable for all the functions stated.	C: See 24. E: See 24.
52	Heavy metals	All functions excl. water for navigation and utilization of water for construction	The occurrence of heavy metals in water harms the natural purification process, thus making the water less suitable for all the functions stated.	C: Extra treatment measures. E: Remove heavy metals from waste water; other manufacturing processes; use other raw materials; reduce or cease polluting activities; use pesticides more carefully.

54		Water for agriculture Water for recreation Water in the natural environment Water as an element in the social environment	Discharge of heavy metals leads to a low level of water organisms and, in the event of large-scale discharges, to fatality. This phenomenon may be acute, but may also occur as a result of cumulation in food chains.	D: Lower agricultural yield; drop in value of recreation areas and social environment. C: Close off areas from polluted water. E: See 52.
58	Other inorganic poisons	All functions excl. water for navigation and utilization of water for construction	The discharge of poisons disturbs the natural purification process, thus making the water less suitable for all the functions stated.	C: Extra treating measures.
64	Salts	Water for agriculture	Salination of the surface water makes this water less suitable for use in the agricultural sector because growth is stunted and lime scale forms in spraying (both in the pipes and on the plants).	D: Reduced yield. C: Combat salination by introducing fresh water; bring in water from elsewhere. E: Reduce discharge of salts by other manufacturing processes; other raw materials; store waste water; direct discharge into the sea of e.g. NaCl; reduce or cease the polluting activity; air-bubble screens in sluices; sill in waterways in open connection with the sea; close off gas sources.
66		Utilization of water for construction	As a result of a higher salt content of water, materials are damaged more quickly; of particular importance are sulphates in connection with damage to concrete.	D: Drop in value of buildings. C: Apply protective coatings; use special materials. E: Reduce discharge of salts by other manufacturing processes; other raw materials; store waste water; Direct discharge into the sea of e.g. NaCl; reduce or cease the polluting activity.

List AI.4.1 *continued*

Cell no. Table AI.4	Agents	Functions in which the loss occurs	Description of losses of function	Financial damage (D)[a] Compensatory measures (C) Elimination measures (E)
68	Change in pH value	All functions excl. water for navigation	The discharge of various substances leads to a change in the pH value of the water, making it less suitable for all the functions stated.	C: Extra treatment measures. E: Stop acids. Other manufacturing processes; other raw materials; reduce or cease the polluting activity.
69			Through the emission of SO_2 in the atmosphere, rain water acquires a lower pH. As a result, the surface water acidifies.	C: Extra treatment measures. E: Limit SO_2 emission.
70	Eutrophicating substances	All functions excl. water for navigation and utilization of water for construction	Eutrophication leads to very strong fluctuations in oxygen content. In addition the oxygen content decreases because as a result of duck-weed growing rapidly the surface of the water is covered, thus hampering aeration. This makes the water less suitable for all the functions stated.	D: Reduced yield; drop in value of recreation areas; etc. C: Extra treatment measures; dredge watercourses. E: Apply tertiary treatment; other manufacturing processes; other raw materials; reduce or cease the polluting activities.
72		Water for agriculture Water for recreation Water in the natural environment Water for navigation	As a result of eutrophication, strong plant growth occurs, through which the use of water for the functions stated is hampered.	D: See 70. C: Remove plants. E: See 70.

75		Water for agriculture Water for recreation Water in the natural environment	Eutrophication may lead to bloom of toxic blue algae, as a result of which the water becomes unsuitable, for instance, as drinking water for livestock.	D: Drop in value of recreation areas. C: Bring in water from elsewhere; build swimming pools elsewhere. E: See 70.
	PHYSICAL			
78	Rise in temperature	All functions excl. water for navigation and utilization of water for construction	At a higher temperature the oxygen content of the water falls, making the water less suitable for all the functions stated.	C: Aerate the water to be used. E: Use other cooling systems.
80		Water in the natural environment	Rise in temperature disturbs the ecosystem existing in the water.	E: Use other cooling systems.
82	Radioactivity	All functions excl. cooling water, water for navigation and utilization of water for construction	Radioactivity can make water unsuitable for the functions stated.	E: Reduce or stop radioactive discharge; apply other processes.
89	Silt and coarse insolubles	Water for agriculture Water for recreation Water in the natural environment	An increase in silt reduces photosynthesis. At the same time shellfish and other bottom animals are covered. The gills of fish may be damaged.	D: Drop in value of fishing water. E: Reduce discharge of dirt.
91	All disturbances	All functions	Since losses of function occur, many bodies have to concern themselves with these problems.	Salaries, buildings, monitoring networks, etc.

[a]As emphasized in the text, losses of function are only partly reflected in financial damage and compensatory measures, and in many cases elimination is impossible or only partly possible (see Sections 4.5 and 4.6). This applies in particular to the natural environment.

indication has also been given in the column 'financial damage, compensatory measures, elimination measures'.*

The losses of function as a result of qualitative competition in the water – which are arranged by agent – are very different in nature and cannot be easily summarized in a few sentences. The most important losses of function as a result of water pollution are the impairment of the natural environment, the endangering of the drinking water supply, the decline in possibilities of recreational use of water and impairment of the quality of water for agriculture. Viewed in the long term, the impairment of the natural environment is of decisive importance among these losses of function. As explained at the beginning of this section, this function determines the availability of all other functions. However, the natural sciences cannot give any standards for the exact limit of the carrying capacity of ecosystems. It can merely be established that the present pollution is initiating a development in which a transition is taking place from varied stable systems to unstable systems with only a limited range of species. This is contrary to natural development.

The financial damage as a result of water pollution amounts broadly to reduction of the yield particularly of farms and a drop in the value of among other things buildings, farmland and recreation areas. Compensatory measures consist in general of the treatment of water for use as, for example, drinking water, of the construction of alternative facilities (such as swimming pools) and of utilizing the water at less polluted places. Elimination measures amount to the installation of treatment equipment, switching to other raw materials and to other processes, or reducing or ceasing the activity causing the pollution.

Two or more agents can have a joint effect that is unequal to the sum of the parts. A number of these double effects are known in water pollution: in highly polluted water botulism (that can kill birds and cause disease in men) can occur when this water is strongly heated. Some poisons (for instance, Endosulfan) have a stronger effect in salt water than in fresh. There are probably very many of these multiple effects. As very few quantitative data yet exist on multiple effects, the tables 'Qualitative competition in water; synergisms caused by the effect of two or more agents' and 'Losses of function as a result of qualitative competition in water, by synergism and by function', and the corresponding list, cannot as yet be produced by statisticians.

*In the translation the lists of the losses of function have been abridged to a few striking cases. The reader interested in the complete elaboration should contact the author c/o Central Bureau of Statistics, Prinses Beatrixlaan 428, Voorburg (ZH), The Netherlands.

AI.2. System of Tables for the Component Air

As already stated in Section 4.1, each environmental component has three aspects: a quantitive, a spatial and a qualitative one. In the case of the component air the quantitative aspect plays no part; the spatial aspect (which plays only a subordinate role) will be dealt with at a later stage of our study. Consequently, the qualitative aspect (air pollution and noise nuisance) alone remains. It has already been briefly indicated in Section 4.1 how air pollution and noise nuisance are produced in a system of tables. This system of tables and lists is to be found and will be explained below.

As in the case of the component water, environmental deterioration in respect of the component air is described with the aid of its functions (possibilities of use possessing usefulness). As explained in Section 4.1, the functions relate only to the qualitative aspect (air pollution and noise nuisance). It has also already been explained there that, as a result, Table AI.5 for the component air is of a different form from Table AI.1 for the component water. The whole Table AI.5 for air corresponds to the bottom row of Table AI.1 for water; the other rows from the water table disappear in the case of air on account of the absence of the quantitative aspect.

A list follows of the various functions of the component air, with a short explanation of the content.

Table AI.5
Competitive use of air, by function.

To the benefit of the function	At the expense of the function												
	1 *Air as a factor in human life*	1.1 For physiological functioning	1.2 For sensory perception	1.2.1 Hearing	1.2.2 Smell	1.2.3 Sight	2 *Air as a factor in agriculture*	2.1 Animals	2.2 Plants	3 *Air as a factor in the natural environment*	4 *Air as a factor in technical processes*	5 *Air as a medium for radio waves*	6 *Air as a medium for storing matter*
7 *Air as a medium into which to release waste matter*		+		+	+	+		+	+	+	+	+	+

1. Air as a factor in human life

1.1. For physiological functioning

In this category comes respiration and the absorption of air by the skin and mucous membranes. It also covers the precipitation of particles on human beings and the absorption of sunlight (for the latter may be hampered by air pollution, with possible adverse effects on health). The absorption and emission of heat via the air also comes under this function. Air pollution can in some cases seriously impair the physiological functioning of man.

1.2. For sensory perception

1.2.1. Hearing

The function hearing is hindered above all by disturbing sources of sound. This may result in failure to receive useful information. Moreover, disturbing sound sources may have a negative psychical or psychosomatic effect.

1.2.2. Smell

The function smell relates to the negative psychical consequences of stench. Possible damage to the olfactory organ has been placed under physiological functioning.

1.2.3. Sight

Vision can also be disturbed by air pollution (solid and liquid particles or non-colourless gases like NO_2). Eye irritation comes under physiological functioning.

2. Air as a factor in agriculture

2.1. Animals

Air pollution can be especially harmful to grazing livestock, which, as they graze, may absorb precipitated pollution, thus ingesting considerably more pollution than they inhale directly.

2.2. Plants

A plant uses oxygen for combustion and carbon dioxide and sunlight for photosynthesis. The air absorbed contains pollutants, frequently resulting in serious damage to the plant, especially the leaves. In addition, air pollution can absorb light, thus slowing down photosynthesis.

3. Air as a factor in the natural environment

Since in the short term the importance of the natural environment, viewed regionally, is less than that of agriculture, this function has not been further subdivided. However, it must be borne in mind that, regarded worldwide, it is of vital importance in the long term to maintain a sufficiently large part of the natural environment.*

4. *Air as a factor in technical processes*

In various production processes air pollution may have a disturbing influence. This is immediately clear in the manufacture of photographic emulsions. Another instance: when chemical reactions take place in furnaces with air as base material and with the aid of catalysts, the latter may become inoperative through air pollution.

5. *Air as a medium for radio waves***

Under this function come radio reception, television reception, interception of radar beams etc.; in general, all information transmitted with an electromagnetic wave as carrier. Radio disturbance is described here by considering the disturbing wave as an agent.

6. *Air as a medium for storing matter*

Sulphur oxides, among other agents, cause metals to corrode more quickly than in an unpolluted atmosphere; other materials are attacked too. Moreover, among other effects of pollution, buildings become dirty and fabrics lose their strength more quickly. In effect, polluted air stores matter less well than non-polluted air.

7. *Air as a medium into which to release waste matter*

Functions 1–6 have been described by means of disturbances that occur in the use of air by human beings, by animals and plants in agriculture, by animals and plants in the natural environment and in technical processes. Function 7 is of an entirely different nature. This function describes the release of waste matter into air: the causing of air pollution and noise nuisance.*** The utilization of this function is therefore at the expense of the other functions, or (in other words) the confrontation of function 7 with the other functions causes losses of function. This confrontation has been demonstrated in Table A1.5; when loss of function takes place this is indicated in the cells of the table by a plus sign.

*Cf. pp. 144–147.

**The word medium is not meant to suggest that air is necessary for the propagation of radio waves.

***When air is absorbed on behalf of one of the functions 1–6, it often happens that this air, not containing pollutants, is emitted again. When this happens, the absoprtion of air is always considered in detachment from the emission of air; the emission of polluted air is classified under function 7.

Table AI.6

Qualitative competition in air, by agent and by originator.

Agents	BIOLOGICAL	CHEMICAL																			PHYSICAL				
Originators	Organisms or parts of them	Aliphatic hydrocarbons	Aromatic hydrocarbons	Aldehydes	SO_2, SO_3, H_2SO_4	H_2S	CO	NxOy	NH_3	CO_2, H_2O	Inorganic fluorine compounds	Inorganic chlorine compounds	Other inorganic acids	Pesticides	Lead and lead compounds	Other metals and their compounds	Asbestos	Other substances causing stench	Other substances causing loss of function	Other elements for photochemical reactions	Sound	Radio waves	Change in temperature	Solid and liquid particles	Radioactive radiation
1 *PRODUCTION*																									
1.1 *Auxiliary and general processes*																									
– Land transport	–	+	+	+	+	–	+	+	–	+	–	–	–	+	+	+	+	+	+	+	+	+	+	+	–
– Water transport	–	+	+	+	+	–	+	+	–	+	–	–	–	+	+	–	+	+	+	+	+	+	+	+	+
– Air transport	–	+	+	+	+	–	+	+	–	+	–	–	–	–	+	–	+	+	+	+	+	+	+	+	–
– Heating	–	+	+	+	+	–	+	+	–	+	–	–	–	–	–	+	–	+	+	+	+	–	+	+	–
– Generation of energy	–	+	+	+	+	–	+	+	–	+	–	–	–	–	–	+	–	+	+	+	+	+	+	+	+
– Processing of waste	–	+	+	+	+	+	+	+	+	+	–	+	+	+	+	+	+	+	+	+	+	–	+	+	+
– Transhipment of goods	–	+	+	+	–	–	–	–	–	–	–	–	–	+	+	+	+	+	+	+	+	–	–	+	+
1.2 *Specific processes*																									
– Agriculture and horticulture	+	–	–	–	–	+	+	–	+	+	–	–	–	+	–	–	+	+	?	?	+	–	–	+	–
– Mining	–	+	+	–	–	–	–	–	–	–	–	–	–	–	–	–	–	+	?	+	+	+	–	+	–
– Building trade	–	–	–	–	–	–	–	–	–	–	–	–	–	+	–	–	+	+	?	–	+	+	–	+	–
– Chemical industry																									
– Oil refineries and petrochemical industry	–	+	+	+	+	+	+	+	+	+	+	+	–	+	+	+	?	+	+	+	+	+	+	+	–
– Plastics and rayon industry	–	+	+	–	–	+	–	–	–	–	–	+	–	–	–	–	+	+	+	?	+	+	–	–	–
– Pigment industry	–	–	–	–	–	–	–	–	–	–	–	–	–	+	–	–	?	+	+	–	+	+	–	–	–
– Paint industry	–	+	+	–	–	–	–	–	–	–	–	–	–	–	+	+	–	–	–	+	+	+	–	+	–

– Manufacture of inorganic acids	−	−	−	−	+	+	−	+	+	+	+	+	+	−	−	−	?	−	+	−	+	+	−	+	−
– Manufacture of fertilizers	−	−	−	−	+	−	−	+	+	−	+	−	+	−	−	+	?	+	+	−	+	+	−	+	−
– Other chemical industry	?	+	+	+	+	+	+	+	+	+	+	+	+	+	+	+	+	+	+	+	+	+	+	+	+
– Metallurgical industry	−	−	−	−	+	+	+	+	+	+	+	+	+	−	+	+	?	+	+	−	+	+	+	+	−
– Manufacture of asbestos, cement, bricks, pottery and glass	−	−	−	−	−	−	−	+	−	+	+	+	+	−	−	+	+	−	+	−	+	+	+	+	−
– Rubber manufacture and processing	−	+	+	?	+	+	+	?	?	−	−	?	?	−	−	?	+	+	+	?	+	+	+	+	−
– Pulp and paper industry	−	+	+	−	+	+	−	−	−	−	−	+	−	−	−	−	−	+	−	−	+	+	+	+	−
– Food and feed industry	+	+	+	+	−	+	−	−	+	+	−	−	−	−	−	−	−	+	?	−	+	+	+	+	−
– Other specific processes	+	+	+	+	+	+	+	+	+	+	+	+	+	+	+	+	−	+	+	+	+	+	+	+	+
2 *HOUSEHOLD CONSUMPTION*																									
2.1 Transport	−	+	+	+	+	−	+	+	−	+	−	−	−	−	+	+	+	+	+	+	+	+	+	+	−
2.2 Heating	−	+	+	+	+	−	+	+	−	+	−	−	−	−	−	+	−	+	+	+	−	−	+	+	−
2.3 Cooking	−	+	+	−	−	−	−	+	−	+	−	−	−	−	−	−	+	+	+	?	+	−	+	+	−
2.4 Other activities of households	+	+	+	−	+	+	+	+	+	+	−	+	?	+	+	+	+	+	+	+	+	+	−	+	−
3 *INTERCHANGE WITH SOIL*																									
3.1 From soil	+	+	+	+	+	+	+	+	+	+	?	+	?	+	+	+	+	+	+	+	+	+	+	+	+
3.2 To soil	+	+	+	+	+	+	+	+	+	+	+	+	+	+	+	+	+	+	+	+	+	+	+	+	+
4 *INTERCHANGE WITH WATER*																									
4.1 From water	+	+	+	+	+	+	+	+	+	+	?	+	+	+	?	?	−	+	+	+	+	+	+	+	+
4.2 To water	+	+	+	+	+	+	+	+	+	+	+	+	+	+	+	+	+	+	+	+	+	+	+	+	+
5 *FOREIGN COUNTRIES*																									
5.1 Imports of pollution	+	+	+	+	+	+	+	+	+	+	+	+	+	+	+	+	+	+	+	+	+	+	+	+	+
5.2 Exports of pollution	+	+	+	+	+	+	+	+	+	+	+	+	+	+	+	+	+	+	+	+	+	+	+	+	+

Table AI.7

Losses of function as a result of qualitative competition in air, by agent and by function.

Agent / Function	1 Air as a factor in human life: 1.1 For physiological functioning	1.2 For sensory perception: 1.2.1 Hearing	1.2.2 Smell	1.2.3 Vision	2 Air as a factor in agriculture: 2.1 Animals	2.2 Plants	3 Air as a factor in the natural environment	4 Air as a factor in technical processes	5 Air as a medium for radio waves	6 Air as a medium for storing matter
BIOLOGICAL										
Organisms or parts of them	1	—	—	—	42	65	82	91	—	—
CHEMICAL										
Aliphatic hydrocarbons	—	—	25	—	31	51	82	91	—	—
Aromatic hydrocarbons	2	—	25	—	31, 42	—	82	91	—	—
Aldehydes	3	—	25	—	31, 42	61	73, 82	91	—	101
SO_2, SO_3, H_2SO_4	4	—	25	—	31, 32	52	71, 72	91	—	101 to 111
H_2S	20	—	25	—	31	61	73, 82	91	—	103, 112, 113
CO	5	—	—	—	42	—	82	91	—	—
N_xO_y	20	—	25	26	31, 33, 34	53, 61	74, 82	91	—	101, 104, 105, 111
NH_3	20	—	25	—	31, 42	61	73, 82	91	—	101
CO_2, H_2O	6, 7	—	—	—	34	—	—	—	—	101, 104
Inorganic fluorine compounds	20	—	—	—	35	54	75, 76	91	—	101, 114
Inorganic chlorine compounds	20	—	25	—	31, 36	55	73, 82	91	—	101, 103, 104, 105
Other inorganic acids	20	—	—	—	42	61	82	91	—	104, 105

Pesticides	8	—	—	—	37	56	77, 78	91	—	—
Lead and lead compounds	9	—	—	—	38	57	82	91	—	101
Other metals and their compounds	10	—	—	—	39	58	82	91	—	—
Asbestos	11	—	—	—	42	—	82	91	—	—
Other substances causing stench	—	—	25	—	31	—	73	—	—	—
Other substances causing loss of function	20	—	—	—	42	61	82	91	—	112, 115
Photochemical smog										
O_3	12	—	25	—	31, 34, 40	59	73, 74, 79, 80	91	—	101, 111, 116
Peroxyacyl nitrates	13	—	—	—	40	59	79, 80	91	—	101
Aldehydes	3	—	25	—	40	59	73, 79, 80	91	—	—
Other photochemical reaction products	13	—	25	—	40	59	73, 79, 80	91	—	—
PHYSICAL										
Sound	14	14	—	—	31	—	73	91	—	117
Radio waves	—	—	—	—	—	—	—	91	95	—
Change in temperature	7	—	—	—	—	—	—	91	—	—
Solid and liquid particles	4, 6, 7	—	—	26	31, 34	60	74, 81, 82	92, 93	—	101, 102, 104, 105, 107, 118, 119
Radioactive radiation	15	—	—	—	41	61	82	91	—	—
All agents	121	121	121	121	121	121	121	121	121	121

List AI.7.1

Description of losses of function as a result of qualitative competition in air, by agent and by function (some examples).

Cell no. Table AI.7	Agents	Functions in which the loss occurs	Description of losses of function	Financial damage (D)[a] Compensatory measures (C) Elimination measures (E)
4	SO_2, SO_3, H_2SO_4; possibly together with physical action of particles	Humans: Physiological functioning	High concentrations of sulphur oxides may increase mortality and prove troublesome to patients with respiratory diseases. Probably SO_2 and H_2SO_4 in particular have these effects.	D: Reduction of productivity; drop in value of buildings and of land. C: Therapy; move to less polluted area; treat air admitted to buildings. E: Install treatment equipment; switch to other raw materials; switch to other processes; reduce or cease the polluting activity.
6	CO_2, (H_2O), particles	Humans: Physiological functioning	The CO_2 concentration in the atmosphere increases through human agency; as a result the temperature rises. The effect of particles is less and presumably results in cooling (worldwide effects).	E: Reduce emissions.
12	O_3	Humans: Physiological functioning	At the highest concentrations of O_3 recorded in the Netherlands during photochemical smog the following effects are to be expected: irritation of nose and throat; decrease in visual acuity at low light intensities; difficulties with respiration for sensitive individuals (e.g. asthma and emphysema patients).	D: Reduction of productivity. C: Therapy. E: Restrict emission of elements for photochemical reactions.

14	Sound	Humans: Physiological functioning; hearing	Noise nuisance is regarded by the practitioners of social medicine as one of the most important forms of environmental pollution. At very high volumes loss of hearing occurs; at lower volumes psychical effects occur (from minor irritation to psychiatric syndromes). Places where high volumes occur are unsuitable for housing, work or recreation.	D: Reduction of productivity; drop in value of houses and the price of land. C: Therapy; sound insulation of building; move; go elsewhere for recreation. E: Insulate; move and/or remove sources of noise.
15	Radioactive radiation	Humans: Physiological functioning	Radioactive radiation is a health risk; through human agency (nuclear explosions and reactors) the radioactivity of the atmosphere has increased. Above all genetic risk.	D: Reduction of productivity. E: Limit emission of radioactive material, locally but also worldwide.
25	Aliphatic hydrocarbons Aromatic hydrocarbons Aldehydes SO_2, SO_3, H_2SO_4 H_2S N_xO_y NH_3 Inorganic chlorine compounds Other substances causing stench (incl. mercaptans, alkyl sulphides, amines, esters, CS_2) O_3 Other substances created in the photochemical smog process	Humans: Smell	Stench has mainly a psychical effect; it is unpleasant to unbearable to live, work or relax in areas where stench prevails. Among other things, the power of concentration declines. On a secondary basis this has financial consequences.	D: Reduction of productivity; drop in value of houses or the price of land. C: Not possible in general; sometimes move; go elsewhere for recreation; treat air admitted into buildings. E: Limit emissions.

List AI.7.1 *continued*

Cell no. Table AI.7	Agents	Functions in which the loss occurs	Description of losses of function	Financial damage (D)[a] Compensatory measures (C) Elimination measures (E)
35	Inorganic fluorine compounds	Agricultural sector (animals)	HF and fluorine compounds are necessary in small amounts but toxic to livestock in large amounts. In descending sensitivity: cattle, sheep, horses, pigs, poultry. The skeleton becomes weaker, the developing teeth are affected, food is ingested less well.	D: Drop in milk yield; damage to meat. C: Provision of cattle cake containing aluminium sulphate; periodically move stock to 'clean' pastures. E: Limit emissions.
38	Lead and lead compounds	Agricultural sector (animals)	Lead compounds that have settled on grass and hay cause among cattle loss of appetite, diseases of the intestinal tract, reduced defence mechanisms of the lungs, brain damage. Stunted growth and reduced milk yield result; the milk produced contains lead compounds: danger to human health. Also sensitive: sheep, goats, pigs and horses.	D: Drop in milk yield; damage to meat; drop in value of pastures beside motorways. C: Use feed not poisoned by lead; use other pastures than those beside busy motorways. E: Limit use of petrol; limit lead content of petrol.
54	Inorganic fluorine compounds	Agricultural sector (plants)	Plants are highly sensitive to fluorine compounds, notably fruit trees (peach and plum) and ornamental plants (gladioli, freesias and tulips). Results may be leaf damage and reduced yield.	D: Reduction of yield; drop in value of land. C: Do not grow in highly polluted areas; switch to less sensitive varieties; possibly also: human therapy. E: Limit emissions.
57	Lead and lead compounds	Agricultural sector (plants)	Lead compounds that have settled on crops may make them less suitable or unsuitable for consumption. This may occur with cereals, beets, cabbage varieties, lettuce and other vegetables.	D: Reduce yield. C: Do not grow the crops mentioned close to motorways. E: Limit emissions (among other measures taken, produce no-lead petrol).

72	SO_2, SO_3, H_2SO_4	Natural environment	Lower plants: mosses and lichens are highly sensitive to SO_2. Higher plants: those sensitive to SO_2 include poplar, beech, spruce, white clover, black nightshade.	E: Limit emissions.
76	Inorganic fluorine compounds	Natural environment	Fluorine compounds act as cumulative plant poisons. Various higher plants are highly sensitive, such as maple and fir species, Solomon's seal, knot-grass and St. John's wort. Of the lower plants, lichens are highly sensitive.	E: Limit emissions.
77	Pesticides	Natural environment	A number of animal species in the natural environment suffer from pesticides (especially predators). In part the pesticides are spread via the air (and absorbed directly or via the food chain).	E: Apply pesticides more carefully; use less persistent pesticides or no pesticides; switch to biological control methods; switch to a system of smaller monocultures.
93	Physical effect of particles	Technical processes	In many industrial premises strict requirements have to be made of air purity, especially freedom from dust (e.g. manufacturers of photographic material, laboratories). Often most of the pollution to be removed is of non-natural origin.	D: Reduction of productivity; loss of material. C: Treat air supplied. E: Limit emissions.
101	Aldehydes SO_2, SO_3, H_2SO_4 N_xO_y NH_3 CO_2, H_2O Inorganic fluorine compounds Inorganic chlorine compounds Lead and lead compounds	Materials	Aldehydes oxidize into organic acids; acid-forming oxides may form salts with NH_3. These substances, together with SO_2, SO_3 and H_2SO_4, and also oxidants from photochemical smog, may attack steel. The effect depends greatly on the humidity and is reinforced by solid and liquid particles. Soluble iron salts are formed; if paint is applied afterwards, blistering and rusting beneath the paint occur.	D: Drop in value of structures. C: Replace structures more quickly; make them stronger; protect them (or protect them better) by paint systems (with a good pretreatment); larger storage sheds to prevent rusting; use materials that corrode less quickly. E: Limit emissions.

List AI.7.1 *continued*

Cell no. Table AI.7	Agents	Functions in which the loss occurs	Description of losses of function	Financial damage (D)[a] Compensatory measures (C) Elimination measures (E)
	O_3 Peroxyacyl nitrates possibly together with physical action of particles			
105	SO_2, SO_3, H_2SO_4 N_xO_y Inorganic chlorine compounds Other inorganic acids possibly together with physical action of particles	Materials	Soluble calcium salts are formed in both mortar and sand-lime brick; these salts wash out.	D: Drop in value of buildings. C: Extra maintenance. E: Limit emissions.
107	SO_2, SO_3, H_2SO_4 possibly together with physical action of particles	Materials	Objects of art (paintings, books, etc.) are affected (deterioration of important historical works of art).	D: Drop in value. C: Restore; air filters in museums. E: Limit emissions.
116	O_3	Materials	Cracks may occur in natural rubber and various kinds of synthetic rubber.	D: Drop in value. C: Extra maintenance; switch to resistant materials. E: Limit emissions of elements for photochemical smog.
121	All agents	All functions	Since air pollution occurs, various bodies are obliged to concern themselves with these problems.	Setting up and operating institutes; monitoring networks; salaries.

[a]As emphasized in the text, losses of function are only partly reflected in financial damage and compensatory measures, and in many cases elimination is impossible or only partly possible (see Sections 4.5 and 4.6). This applies in particular to the natural environment.

As stated in Chapter 4, the functions do not act directly on one another but through an intermediate step, the agent. An agent has been defined as a constituent or amount of energy which may cause loss of function either by its addition to or by its withdrawal from the environment by man. This may, for example, be a chemical substance, an organism, heat or radioactivity. Human activities (the originators) introduce agents into the air (function 7), and these bring about the loss of function (functions 1–6) directly or indirectly. Introduction of the agents into the air is represented in Table AI.6. The left-hand column and the heading list the originators and the agents respectively. Next the occurrence of losses of function has been classified in Table AI.7; the left-hand column and the heading list the agents and the functions respectively; in the cells it is stated which losses of function occur. The losses of function thus traced are briefly described in List AI.7.1.

In Table AI.6, the cells show which agents are introduced into the air by which originators. A plus sign in one of the cells means that the originator introduces that agent into the air. A minus sign means that the originator does not introduce that agent into the air, or does so to only a negligible extent. If the information was insufficient, a question mark has been placed. The classification of the agents and that of the originators used in the table will be explained below.

The agents have been divided into three categories: chemical, physical and biological.

Chemical substances are the principal agents. They can enter the air through leakage or as the waste product of technical processes (from stacks, exhausts, etc.). Sometimes they are deliberately applied, as in the spraying of insecticides. They can also suddenly enter the air in large quantities as a result of accidents.

Some of the chemical agents are organic ('aliphatic hydrocarbons' to 'aldehydes') and some inorganic ('SO_2, SO_3, H_2SO_4' to 'other inorganic acids'). Finally, there is also a mixed group (pesticides' to 'other elements for photochemical reactions'). A number of agents of the last group call for a further description.

Under the heading 'pesticides' not only pesticides themselves (irrespective of their chemical composition) are included but also substances like polychlorinated biphenyls (PCBs); the latter have a comparable effect but are produced for other purposes. The metals have been divided into lead and lead compounds and other metals and their compounds. The latter group includes mercury and cadmium, metals which in the environment as a whole are at least as dangerous as lead. However, only in the case of lead does a considerable part of the total intake in the body come from the air, which is why only this metal has been listed separately. The category labelled 'other elements for photochemical reactions' includes hydrogen peroxide and organic peroxides; in general every substance which has not been singled out as an agent in itself but which can be an element for photochemical reactions.

The physical agents are much more heterogeneous than the chemical ones. The most important physical agent is sound (a state of vibration of the air). Dust, ash, soot, liquid droplets etc. are not distinguished separately, but summarized as 'solid and liquid particles'. These particles may cause losses of function through their physical properties (e.g. the ability to intercept sunlight, to absorb gases), but the chemical composition may also be the cause of the loss of function. In the latter case, the chemical substance of which the particle consists is stated as agent in Table AI.7, to be discussed below. In the former case, 'solid and liquid particles' are stated as agent; in list AI.7.1 (likewise to be discussed) this is indicated somewhat more specifically as the physical effect of particles.

The biological agents are organisms or parts of organisms such as pollen grains. The majority of these are introduced into the air by natural causes and therefore are not dealt with in this study. The change in the quantity or the composition of the biological material caused by human agency has, however, been included in the tables.

The originators of the above agents are to be found in the left-hand column of Table AI.6. The division into production processes, households, interchange with other environmental components and foreign countries is the same as for water, but the subdivision of these groups is somewhat different. For instance, industry has been split up. On the other hand, for example, the catering trade is no longer distinguished as a separate originator, but classified under other specific processes.

In a specific process (such as manufacture of pulp and paper) use is often made of an auxiliary process or a general process (such as heating). In such a case, the emissions which result from heating are stated only under the heading 'heating' and not under the heading 'manufacture of pulp and paper'. The same applies to transport, generation of energy etc., in brief, for every auxiliary process distinguished in Table AI.6.

The same table indicates which agents are introduced into the air by the various categories of originators. The basis taken for this is the state of the agents at the moment when they leave the stack, exhaust and so on.

Movement of the agents

In general, an agent introduced into the air moves and is simultaneously weakened. This applies to sound – except in special cases (such as reflections of sound) the volume decreases with increasing distance from the source – but also to changes in temperature (a packet of heated air is moved and mixed with cold air). For chemical substances spreading is more complicated; this is discussed below.

(a) *Spreading of gases*

Gases introduced into the air are carried by the wind and are at the same time diluted. The method of spreading depends on the wind velocity and direction and the variations in these, and on the vertical temperature gradient of the atmosphere. The concentration reached at a given place can be roughly calculated by means of emissions and meteorological data.

(b) *Inversion: photochemical reactions*

When the temperature of air increases with height, one speaks of an inversion. In an inversion the air barely moves in a vertical direction. It regularly happens that an inversion is operative at a height of 100 to 1000 m, whereas below that height the air is well mixed. This is an inversion ceiling. Most emissions occur at a height lower than this inversion ceiling. If such an inversion ceiling persists for a number of days in succession, the concentrations of the pollutants in the layer of air beneath that ceiling may greatly increase. And when in such circumstances ultraviolet radiation from sunlight breaks down nitrogen dioxide, aldehydes, etc., the reaction products can in turn initiate chemical reactions. In this way a number of new substances are created, the principal ones being ozone and peroxyacetyl nitrate (PAN). These substances can cause losses of function such as watering eyes, damage to plants, etc.

The phenomenon is known as photochemical smog. It was first observed in Los Angeles, where it has been studied closely. The phenomenon is not yet fully understood, but the most important reaction mechanisms are known with reasonable certainty. The smog in the Rotterdam area is not exactly the same as that in Los Angeles; among other things, the ozone concentrations in the Rotterdam area are lower. However, it is highly probable that the principal photochemical reactions occurring in Los Angeles also happen in the Rotterdam area, though not to the same extent.

On this assumption, the principal reactants and reaction products of photochemical smog are set against one another (in Figure AI.1). The reaction mechanisms have not been included in this diagram. Footnotes to Figure AI.1 show how the various substances have been classified as agents. The substances on the right are not found in Table AI.6 unless they are substances that have a direct harmful effect outside smog

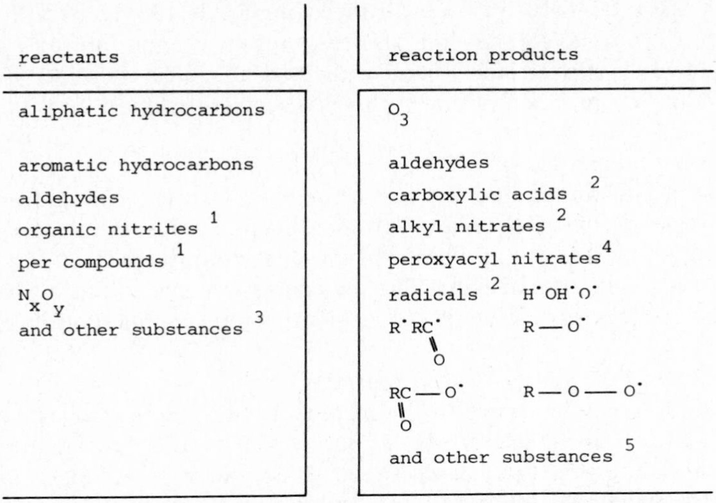

reactants	reaction products
aliphatic hydrocarbons	O_3
aromatic hydrocarbons	aldehydes
aldehydes	carboxylic acids [2]
organic nitrites [1]	alkyl nitrates [2]
per compounds [1]	peroxyacyl nitrates [4]
N_xO_y	radicals [2] $H^\cdot$ $OH^\cdot$ $O^\cdot$
and other substances [3]	$R^\cdot$ $RC^\cdot$(=O) $R-O^\cdot$
	$RC(=O)-O^\cdot$ $R-O-O^\cdot$
	and other substances [5]

Figure AI.1. Photochemical reactions. Reactants and reaction products classified by agents. [1]Included as: Other elements for photochemical reactions. [2]Included as: Other photochemical reaction products. [3]Various substances are suspected of participation in photochemical reactions, for instance CO and metal oxides; these have not been included in the diagram. [4]The most common is PAN. [5]Not all substances formed in the photochemical smog process are known.

formation; however, they cause losses of function and are therefore agents. These agents have been included in Table AI.7, to be discussed below, under the heading 'photochemical smog'.

(c) *Other chemical reactions in air*

Photochemical reactions are not the only ones in air. For instance, sulphur dioxide is oxidized to sulphur trioxide, which together with water yields sulphuric acid. In these reactions it is often impossible to investigate whether a substance as such has been introduced into or formed in the air. However, for a completely systematic classification this ought to be known. Consequently, a less rigid classification has been opted for; the other reactions have not been included in Figure AI.1, and in Table AI.7 the reaction products and the substances introduced directly into the air have been treated alike.

(d) *Spreading of particles*

For a survey of the movement of agents, the spreading of particles is also of importance. This closely resembles the spreading of gases, the main difference being that particles also sink down, at a velocity dependent on their size.

(e) *Disappearance of gases and particles from the atmosphere*

If the substances did not disappear from the atmosphere after a certain time, every form of air pollution would attain an unacceptably high concentration in the course of time. However, there are various mechanisms for disappearance. Particles do not only sink slowly down; they also fall along with rain. Gases may disappear from the atmosphere through chemical reactions. Besides the reactions already mentioned, the breakdown of organic molecules to water, carbon monoxide and carbon dioxide in the upper atmosphere plays an important part. In addition, gases may attach themselves to solid particles or dissolve in liquid droplets, and disperse along with these. They may then end up in the water or be absorbed in the soil (and are then further dealt with under those components), but may also end up on human beings, animals, plants and objects. In that case they continue to be dealt with under the component air; doubtful cases of plant damage will also be treated under the component air.

The net result of the processes stated under (a) to (e) determines the strength of the losses of function by chemical substances; for this see

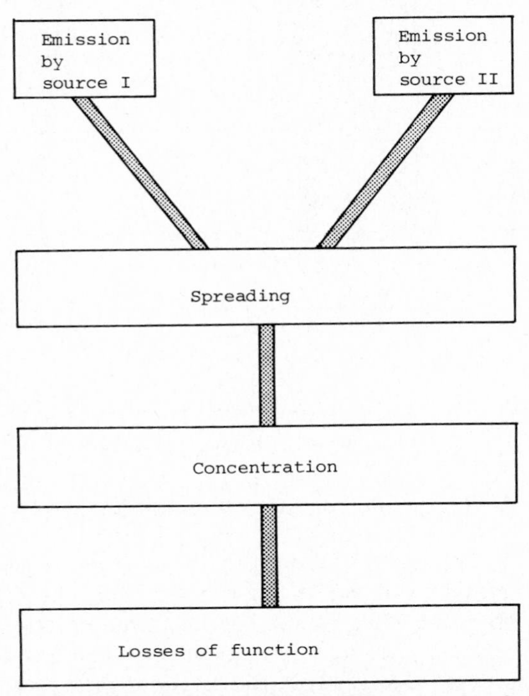

Figure AI.2. Air pollution by one chemical substance.

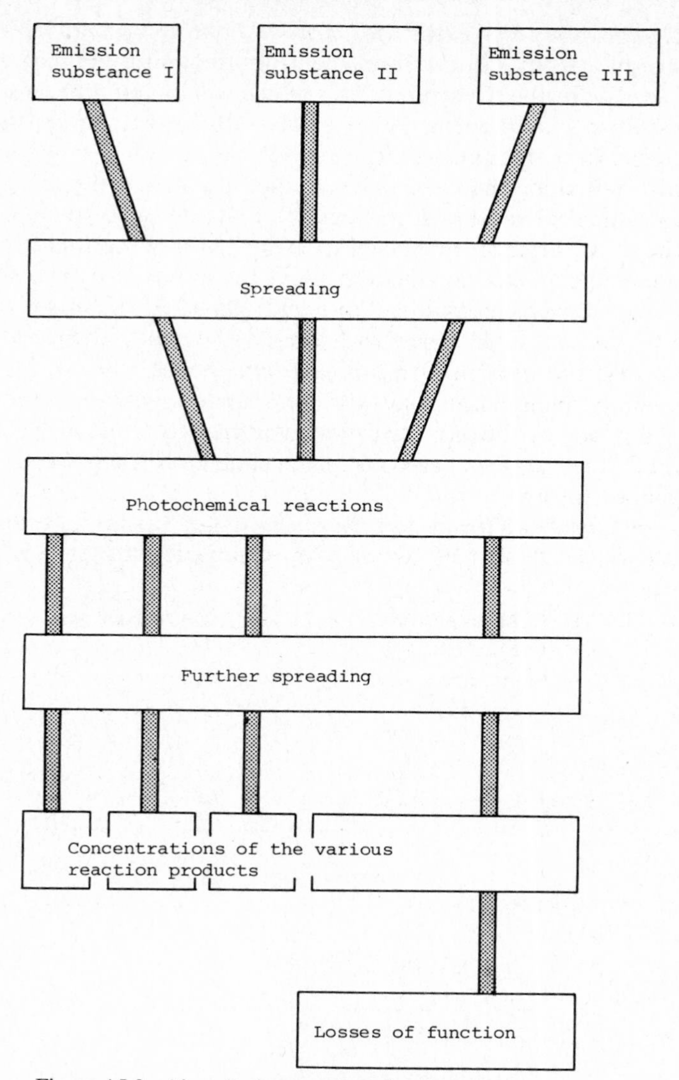

Figure AI.3. Air pollution by photochemical smog.

Table AI.7. For chemical substances the path from originator to loss of function is schematically shown in Figures AI.2 and AI.3.

Table AI.7 shows the effect of the agents on the functions. As chemical agents mention is made in the first place of substances which do not undergo any chemical change from the moment they enter the air to the moment that they cause loss of function. In the second place, under a separate heading, come the substances formed in air by photochemical smog, and in the third place substances formed by other chemical reactions in the air. No separate classification has been made for this third category; the substances have been classified together with those introduced directly into the air.

When a loss of function occurs, this is indicated by a figure in the relevant cell of Table AI.7; when no loss of function occurs, this is indicated in the cell by a minus sign. The figure refers to a brief description of the loss of function given in List AI.7.1. In three cases the same figure may appear in more than one cell. Firstly, different agents cause the same loss of function. Secondly, impairment of more than one function (by one or more agents) is interpreted as one case of loss of function. This happens, for instance, if the weather is influenced, in which case both the functions physiological functioning and vision may be impaired. Thirdly, two different agents can often have an effect that is unequal to the sum of the separate effects. A number of these synergistic effects are known in air pollution: the effect on certain plants of the simultaneous occurrence of air pollution with SO_2 and NO_2 is more harmful than the sum of the effects of each of those pollutants separately. The same applies to SO_2 and O_3. Probably many more synergistic effects exist. However, quantitative information on them is so scanty that separate mention of singular and synergistic effects was considered to be pointless. Consequently, no separate table has been included for the synergistic effects.

In List AI.7.1, the losses of function given in Table AI.7 are briefly described. Broadly speaking, the losses of function are classified as follows:

- humans
- animals (agricultural)
- plants (agricultural)
- animals and plants (natural environment)
- other losses of function.

The losses of function will be explained below in the above order.

Humans

A number of episodes of air pollution have had serious consequences for human beings and without any doubt have caused deaths (as, for example, in Donora, Pennsylvania, in 1948, and in London in 1952). A more recent report from Tokyo (May 1972) speaks *inter alia* of symptoms of paralysis among hundreds of schoolchildren.

Fortunately, air pollution of such a severity has not yet occurred in the

Netherlands. And yet there are probably consequences for public health. Data on this can be obtained in two ways.

In the first place animals and also humans may be exposed experimentally to a certain concentration of the polluting substance, and the consequences recorded. In such experiments no adverse effects are usually noted at the concentrations now occurring in the ambient atmosphere. However, from the results of experiments with higher concentrations one can gain an impression of the danger to health presented by the concentrations occurring in the ambient atmosphere.

Secondly, evidence can be gathered by epidemiological research; the correlation of health parameters (mortality, incidence of various diseases, sickness absenteeism) with measured concentrations of pollution in a given area. In the Netherlands, it cannot generally be deduced for certain from research in this field that a correlation does in fact exist between health and air pollution.[1] In view of the fact that only the concentrations of sulphur dioxide and soot are measured on a large scale, that the results to be expected are small ones and that other variables than air pollution have a more pronounced influence, this is not surprising.

Financial damage usually amounts to reduction of productivity, reduction of income, a fall in the value of buildings or of land. Compensatory measures consist in general of therapy, moving to a less polluted area, engaging in recreation in a less polluted area, or treating air admitted into buildings. Elimination measures amount to the installation of equipment for treatment, switching to other base materials or other processes, or reducing or ceasing the activity causing the pollution. These measures are briefly stated in List AI.7.1.*

Three additional remarks remain to be made about the description of financial damage, compensatory measures and elimination measures. Firstly, the description concentrates on financial consequences; this is the reason why deterioration of health itself, which is much more drastic for the person suffering from it than the resultant loss of productivity, is not mentioned here. In Chapter 4 the direct want for an unpolluted environment is explicitly stated.** Secondly, in the case of the elimination measures it has not been indicated by which of the originators these measures were taken. Thirdly, it has already been remarked that the data on impairment of health are very uncertain. This applies equally to the corresponding damage and measures. In the case of noise nuisance matters are much clearer. Psychical effects of this are demonstrable, and

*In the translation the lists of the losses of function have been abridged to a few striking cases. The reader interested in the complete elaboration should contact the author, c/o Central Bureau of Statistics, Prinses Beatrixlaan 428, Voorburg (ZH), The Netherlands.

**See, inter alia, p. 125.

someone exposed to excessive noise will be inclined to take concrete measures to improve his circumstances. Damage and measures are here of the same kind as listed above.

Animals (agricultural)

Grazing livestock are harmed more severely by air pollution than humans, because air pollution that settles on grass attains a much higher concentration there than in the air. A connection can therefore be established between air pollution and disease symptoms for livestock with much greater certainty than for human beings. Most of the damage is done by fluorides; a broad relation can be indicated between the concentration of fluorine in the grass and the extent to which, for instance, the health of cattle is affected. The financial damage consists in general of a drop in milk yield, damage to meat, damage to wool or a drop in value of the land. Compensatory measures here are therapy for animals, therapy for humans (in the event of meat or milk becoming unhealthy for humans), not using highly polluted areas for stockbreeding or the acquisition of new stock. Elimination measures amount here to the installation of treatment equipment, switching to other base materials or other processes or reducing or ceasing the activity causing the pollution. For the separate losses of function only a brief statement will be made on what damage is done and what measures can be taken against it.

Plants (agricultural)

Most consequences of air pollution for plants begin as damage to the leaves. Usually this amounts to plasmolysis of cells (in the case of dicotyledons: spongy or palissade parenchyma) and chlorosis (decrease in the quantity of chlorophyll in the leaf). In addition, abnormalities of growth occur in the plant. The various pollutants cause a more or less specific pattern of damage.

The sensitivity to each substance varies greatly per plant species. Even specimens of the same species display great differences from one another. Furthermore, the sensitivity depends on humidity, amount of sunlight and many other variables. Finally, other plant diseases, insects, etc. may cause comparable damage. For all these reasons it is often difficult to distinguish damage by air pollution from other causes.

In the Netherlands damage to plants is caused mainly by fluorides and by dust that has settled on the panes of glasshouses (the plant receives less light and thus grows more slowly). Financial damage consists mainly of a drop in the yield or the value of land. Compensatory measures here are switching to the cultivation of crops in areas that are not severely polluted (if necessary moving farms and market gardens), switching to less sensitive crops, therapy for humans (if substances toxic to man occur on or in plants). Here too elimination measures amount to the installation of equipment for treatment, changing to other base materials or other processes, or reducing or ceasing the activity causing the pollution.

Animals and plants in the natural environment

There are fewer data on attacks by pollutants on animals and plants in the natural environment than on attacks on livestock and crops. Although relatively few wild animals and plants are known for certain to be attacked by air pollution, it may be assumed on the strength of the data on livestock and crops that many wild animals and plants suffer from air pollution. The instances given in List AI.7.1 therefore need in no way be the most important losses of function.

It has already been stated that, from the worldwide viewpoint, it is vital that a sufficiently large part of the natural environment continues to exist. As explained in Section 4.7, there are still no closely defined ecological standards to which the level of human activities could be geared. In addition, only the government can give substance to the preferences of individuals to leave a livable world behind them. For these reasons, the danger entailed in attacks of the natural environment has not been included in the list. However, in many cases an estimate of the elimination costs is possible; the calculations will relate mainly to this.

Other losses of function

As regards air as a factor in technical processes, the following remarks may be made. A loss of function that is probably important here is disturbance of chemical production processes by air pollution. Further, engines and other moving mechanical parts may be damaged or, for instance, the manufacture of photographic material may be upset in air that is not dust-free. Financial damage and measures of compensation and elimination have been given for each loss of function separately in List AI.7.1; insofar as these amount to filtration of the air drawn in, it should be borne in mind that a certain degree of filtration would also have been necessary in the case of air not polluted by human activities; only part of the costs of filtration are a consequence of air pollution.

In the case of this last category of loss of function (e.g. corrosion of metals or damage to building materials) it is often possible to indicate which agents cause material damage and of which type this damage is, but not the extent to which this damage is attributable to air pollution (e.g. sulphur dioxide) and to natural influences (e.g. salt along the coast). However, a rough breakdown is possible. The concentration of the pollution and the time for which the material is exposed to the pollution are by no means the only variables determining attack. Thus humidity plays a dominant role. Financial damage, measures and costs are in all cases separately stated for these losses of function.

AI.3. Reference

[1]See, among others, K. Biersteker. *Verontreinigde Lucht.* Assen, 1966.

Appendix II

SOME QUANTITATIVE RESULTS

A brief summary is given below of the first results of the work in the Department of Environmental Statistics of the Central Bureau of Statistics.*

*AII.1. Biodegradable Organic Matter in Water***

The quality of surface water is largely determined by the quantity of oxygen dissolved in it. For good management of surface water it is therefore important to have an insight into the burden imposed on the water by substances directly or indirectly influencing the oxygen balance. The most important substances are biodegradable organic materials. In addition to the natural supply, the following sources, whose volume is determined wholly or partially by man, are important in this respect:

(a) untreated domestic sewage;
(b) untreated industrial discharges;
(c) discharges by bio-industry;
(d) discharge of the effluent of treatment plants;
(e) international rivers (import);

*Rates of exchange of currencies were as follows during the period covered by this study:

	£1 = Dfl.	US $1 = Dfl.
1969	8.66	3.62
1970	8.66	3.62
1971	8.53	3.49
1972	8.03	3.21
1973	6.82	2.79
1974	6.28	2.69
1975	5.60	2.53
1976	4.77	2.64
1977	4.28	2.45
1978	4.15	2.16

**In this section a short summary is given of pp. 1–85 of the C.B.S. publication *Waterverontreiniging met afbreekbaar organisch en eutrofiërend materiaal* (Water pollution with biodegradable organic and eutrophicating material), The Hague, 1972.

(f) discharge into the sea (export);
(g) precipitation of matter from the atmosphere;
(h) supply of material from the surface of the soil or from below the surface;
(i) oil dumping by shipping;
(j) waste disposal in the water by recreationists;
(k) stirring-up of silt from the bottom;
(l) bloom and death of algae and water plants;
(m) discharge of toxins;
(n) run-off of rainwater and entry into operation of storm water overflows;
(o) discharge of ground water deficient in oxygen;
(p) discharge of cooling water;
(q) fertilization by farms with natural manure.

For sources (a) to (e) an estimate has been made of the size of the emissions; for sources (a) to (d) the sums of money required for eliminating the emissions have also been estimated. For some of the other sources an estimate has been made of the order of magnitude of the emission, while for the remaining ones a qualitative description had to suffice.

The polluting capacity of biodegradable organic substances in waste water can be expressed in population equivalents. By a population equivalent we mean the quantity of biodegradable organic matter which, as regards its oxidizing capacity, corresponds to that of the sewage of one member of the population. The oxidizing capacity can be determined chemically (chemical oxygen demand, COD) or by measuring the quantity of oxygen required for biological breakdown (biochemical oxygen demand, BOD).* The emission of domestic sewage follows directly from the size of the population, while the emission of industrial waste water has been calculated by means of waste water coefficients. These give per unit of product, per unit of raw material or per other unit the number of population equivalents discharged in the production process.

The waste water coefficients are based on measurements of the chemical oxygen demand of the effluent from the various production processes. The burden on the surface water in which the degradation takes place through biological processes is best approximated by determining the biochemical oxygen demand. The difficulty that now occurs is that the number of population equivalents (PEs) of industrial

*The time required for complete biological breakdown may be very long, depending on the substance. Consequently, in practice one confines oneself to measuring the oxygen consumption for 5 days at a temperature of 20°C (BOD_5^{20}).

waste water determined in accordance with the COD is not the same as the number measured in accordance with the BOD. The sewage of one member of the population per day has a polluting capacity expressed in COD of 135 grams and in BOD_5^{20} of 54 grams. Domestic sewage therefore has a fixed COD–BOD ratio of 2.5 : 1. As a result of the differences in rate of degradation, this ratio varies for different types of industrial waste water, both between these types and in respect of domestic sewage. In general industrial waste water is more easily biodegradable, with the result that degradation proceeds more quickly, and the BOD per unit of time is higher.* As a result of this, the COD–BOD ratio is lower than 2.5 : 1. For industrial waste water the average ratio is 1.6 : 1, for potato flour production 1.5 : 1 and for strawboard manufacture 1.8 : 1. The population equivalents calculated by means of waste water coefficients have therefore been corrected by 2.5/1.6, 2.5/1.5 and 2.5/1.8 respectively. In the estimates, use has been made of the waste water coefficients stated in the Implementing Order of the Surface Waters Pollution Act.

Corrections have also been made for fluctuations in production during the year, for the waste water coefficient is based on a uniform discharge for 250 normal working days a year. In the case of discharge concentrated in a shorter period (season) the burden is therefore greater than emerges from the coefficient, whereas in more scattered discharge (continuous-process industries) the burden is lower. Finally, a correction has been made for the mobility of the population (commuting, holidays, etc.) and for the fact that the pollution of the branches of industry that have been put at 0.5 PE per employee has in theory already been included in the number of PEs calculated for the population.

The estimate has been made for 1969. In that year the size of the population was around 13,000,000 and the sewage of 4,260,000 inhabitants was being biologically or mechanically treated. The installed treating capacity for industrial waste water was around 3,000,000 PEs. On the basis of an average efficiency of 35% for the mechanical installations and of 90% for the biological ones, the effluent discharge of treatment plants was approximately 1,400,000 PEs. According to measurements by the Government Water Control Department the importation of biodegradable organic matter (including the natural burden) was 28–29 million PEs via the Rhine, 2–3 million PEs via the Maas and its tributaries and 2–3 million PEs via the other rivers. A summary of the estimate of the net emission of biodegradable organic

*This is mainly because industrial waste water contains less organic silt than domestic sewage. Sometimes industrial waste water contains no silt at all.

Table AII.1
Net emission of biodegradable organic matter, 1969.

		Population equivalents[a]
Population		8,740,000
Businesses		45,600,000 + U.Q.
of which:		
Fen-colony farms	15,100,000	
Stockbreeding farms[b]	2,500,000	
Other businesses	28,000,000 + U.Q.	
Effluent of treatment plants		1,400,000
International rivers		32 to 35,000,000
Export		U.Q.
Other sources		U.Q.
Total (approx.)		90,000,000 + U.Q.

[a]U.Q. = unknown quantity.

[b]Through the advent of the bio-industry, with little land, a local surplus of manure has come into being. This surplus enters the natural environment, either by over-fertilization, or by dumping, or by discharge into the water. It is estimated that 2,500,000 PEs are discharged direct into the water. It is assumed that, of this quantity, 400,000 PEs qualify for elimination via treatment plants. A publication on the overall problem of the bio-industry is in preparation.

matter is given in Table AII.1. The discharge of biodegradable organic matter may impair the quality of the water. Depending on the degree of severity, the result may be partial or complete loss of all functions of the water.

The cost calculations have been confined to the costs of elimination proceeding from the estimated emission. No estimates have been made of the costs of compensatory measures and of financial damage as a result of the loss of functions. The influence of the discharge of biodegradable organic matter on the compensatory measures calculated in Section AII.3 for the preparation of drinking water cannot be isolated from the influence of other agents.

The expenditure on elimination measures already taken may be subdivided into the following items:

- sewage system;
- the plant (i.e., the electro-mechanical and architectural part of the plant);
- the branch and main sewers of the plant;
- the land required for the plant;
- overheads (office building, technical staff, collection of treatment charges, etc.).

Table AII.2
Costs of elimination measures taken, 1969 (millions of guilders, 1970 prices).

	Capital investment[a]	Annual costs[a]
Population		
Sewage system	U.Q.	U.Q.
Treatment	650	100
Industry		
Sewage system	U.Q.	U.Q.
Rehabilitation	U.Q.	U.Q.
Treatment	500	75
Total (rounded off)	1200 + U.Q.	200 + U.Q.

[a]U.Q. = unknown quantity.

In many cases expenditure on sewage systems already in existence was incurred so long ago that it is hardly possible to fix the level of this expenditure. Such cases have therefore been left out of consideration.

If we call plants, branch and main sewers, land and overheads together treatment, the estimate of the costs of elimination measures already taken in 1969 can be summarized, as shown in Table AII.2. In estimating the costs of eliminating the emission estimated in the table, the point of departure has been the situation in 1969 – as for the emission itself – since this is the last year on which sufficiently reliable data were available.* All the sums of money mentioned are given in 1970 prices.

To eliminate the emission of biodegradable organic substances the following measures can be taken:

- installation and improvement of sewage systems, for both population and industry;
- internal rehabilitation measures by firms, consisting of recycling, recovery of raw materials, etc.;
- construction of treatment plants.

The total capital investment required for sewage systems has been estimated at Dfl. 2,000 to 2,900 million, with annual costs of Dfl. 200 to 290 million.

In the construction of the elimination cost curve (Figure AII.1) the costs of sewage systems have been left out of consideration, since no well-founded assumptions can be made about which part of the sewage

*However, in 1978 an enquiry has been made into the discharge of biodegradable organic matter which will yield more recent data with a greater degree of reliability than this estimate can supply.

systems must be installed in each of the phases of elimination to be discussed below. With regard to phasing of the other elimination measures, it has been assumed that a start will be made with rehabilitation (of which the costs per PE are by far the lowest), followed by the construction of large treatment plants in areas of concentration and, finally, the building of either small treatment plants or larger ones with longer branch and main sewers in areas with less concentrated discharges (the latter two cases have considerably higher costs per PE than large treatment plants in areas of concentration). An elimination cost curve constructed in this way assumes that the average cost curve for rehabilitation or treating per branch of industry (or even per firm) is linear. In principle this minimization problem can be solved if the cost structure per firm or branch of industry is known. In some cases use can be made, for instance, of mathematical programming models for calculating the minimum costs at each level of pollution; the points found in this way form the *E* curve. Moreover, from what has been said in Chapter 4 it follows that arranging measures in order of increasing costs ought possibly to proceed differently in practice from the curve constructed here. For the optimal approach in time will have to depend on the difference in benefits and costs (whereby the benefits have to be estimated by the authorities, in the absence of market data) in the sense that measures will have to be taken first at the place where the positive difference in costs and benefits is the greatest; this may of course differ from region to region.

The elimination cost curve is based exclusively on the annual costs. No assumption has been made about the period over which the treatment plants that may or will have to be built will extend; capital investments are therefore not considered in the curve. Thus, on the abscissa of the system of axes of the graph, only population equivalents appear; on the ordinate are the total annual costs.

Rehabilitation is possible only for firms. Possible rehabilitation measures are given below in the order of increasing annual costs per PE. The number of PEs to be eliminated by these rehabilitation measures could only be established on a COD basis. However, for the construction of the elimination cost curve the numbers of PEs per branch of industry on a BOD basis are necessary, since after all these show the actual burdening and thus also the unburdening of the water with biodegradable organic matter. As the COD–BOD ratio may differ per branch of industry from the average for the whole of industry,* the points calculated below for the elimination cost curve are theoretically not entirely correct. However, the differences will be small.

*See p. 233.

Successively, the annual costs and the numbers of PEs thus avoided by possible (whole or partial) rehabilitation in the strawboard industry, the dairy industry, potato-flour factories and the sugar industry have been calculated. This yields points 1 to 5 in Figure AII.1, where point 1 relates to elimination by the strawboard industry, point 2 to strawboard plus dairy industry, and so on. Point 6 has been obtained by adding the estimated costs of discharges by the bio-industry qualifying for treatment and point 7 by calculating the costs of the remaining numbers of PEs to be eliminated by normal treatment.

In the cost calculation it has been assumed that with the plants still to be built the average investments and annual costs per PE are equal to those of the plants built in 1968, 1969 and 1970. It is, however, probable that all kinds of changes will occur; what effect these will ultimately have is difficult to see. The following may be regarded as the most important influences:

- In a general approach to the pollution problem a tendency will develop to build larger plants. This leads to lower sums for investment and costs.

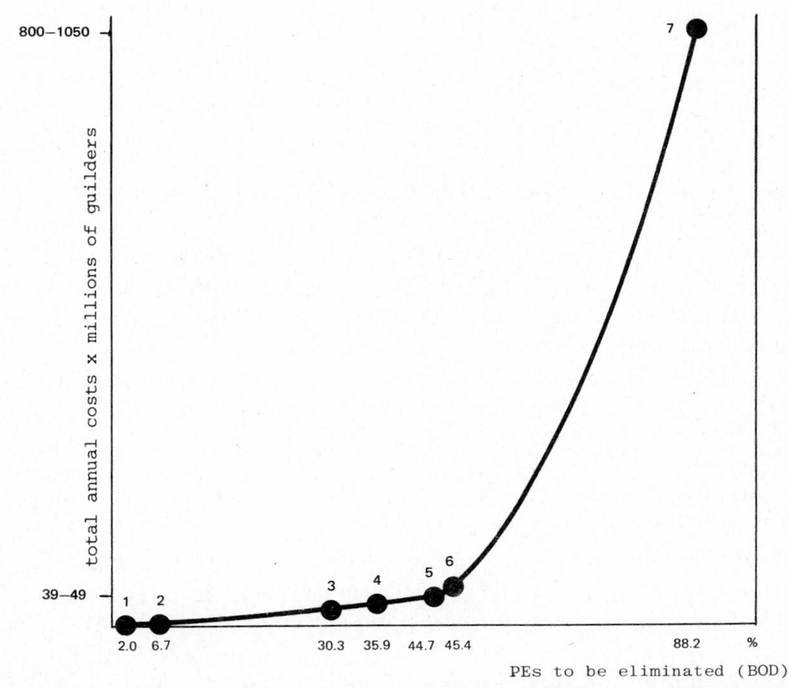

Figure AII.1. Elimination cost curve for biodegradable organic matter. Point 1 relates to elimination by the strawboard industry, point 2 to strawboard plus dairy industry, and so on (see text).

- The part played by oxidation ditches has been growing in recent years. They require less capital investment and have somewhat lower operating costs.
- The interest rate and energy prices have a considerable influence on the annual costs and thus also on the type of plant chosen.
- The problem of silt processing will probably increase as a result of increasing quantities of silt and manure surpluses. This will entail higher costs.
- The economic situation considerably influences the level of the price quoted.

Table AII.3
Costs of elimination measures still to be taken, 1969 (millions of guilders, 1970 prices).

	Capital investment[a]	Annual costs[a]
Population		
Sewage	1700–2500	170–250
Treatment		
Plants	850–1050	150–190
Branch and main sewers	425– 525	50– 65
Land	124– 130	12– 13
Overheads	65– 140	9– 19
Total (rounded off)	1500–1800	220–290
Total of population	3200–4300	390–540
Firms		
Sewage	300– 400	30– 40
Rehabilitation	125– 200	20– 30
Treatment		
Plants	2000–2400	360–440
Branch and main sewers	1000–1200	120–150
Land	290– 330	29– 33
Overheads	160– 330	22– 44
Total (rounded off)	3500–4300	530–670
Potato-flour and strawboard industry		
Rehabilitation	170	20
Treatment	250– 280	30– 35
Bio-industry		
Treatment	26	4
Other measures	U.Q.	U.Q.
Total of firms (rounded off)	4400–5400	630–800
Effluent of treatment plants	U.Q.	U.Q.
International rivers	U.Q.	U.Q.
Grand total	7600–9700 + U.Q.	1000–1350 + U.Q.

[a]U.Q. = unknown quantity.

Taking these uncertainties into account, a margin has been adhered to in the amounts for investment and annual costs per PE for biological treatment plants. The results are summarized in Table AII.3.

The annual costs involved in elimination of biodegradable organic matter correspond to approximately 1% of national income in 1970 (net, market prices). The investments required for elimination of the untreated discharged biodegradable organic matter amount to 7–10% of national income in 1970 (net, market prices).

After rehabilitation and treatment of part of the net emission stated in Table AII.1, a residual pollution still remains which consists of the following items. Firstly, there is the pollution by international rivers. This has been left out of consideration in the curve, since it could not be indicated which elimination measures have to be taken against this abroad. Secondly, 2.1 million PEs remain from the bio-industry that cannot be treated. Thirdly, the effluents remain of the existing biological treatment plants and of the plants still to be built. Finally, there are the 1.3 million PEs of households which can be connected to the sewage system only at extremely high cost.

The calculated data for the construction of the elimination cost curve (Figure AII.1) are summarized (excluding sewers) in Table AII.4.

*AII.2. Eutrophicating Substances in Water**

The influence exerted by the occurrence of eutrophy on the quality of surface water is partly the same as that of biodegradable organic matter. In the compilation of the C.B.S. publication, it has been assumed that in fresh surface water in the Netherlands phosphates are the limiting factor. As a result of the occurrence of eutrophy there is a pronounced increase in the biomass in the water, so that at night, when oxygen is not produced but is consumed for respiration, considerable oxygen deficiencies are possible. In addition, when organisms die off, a larger biomass leads to a greater burden on the surface water with biodegradable organic matter, and excessive algal bloom may lead to excretion of toxic substances. Depending on the severity of the above phenomena, the result may be partial or complete loss of all functions of the water.

The text of the C.B.S. report, in which an explanation is given of how a phosphorus balance sheet was drawn up, is rather technical and difficult

*In this section a short summary is given of pp. 86–108 of the C.B.S. publication *Waterverontreiniging met afbreekbaar organisch en eutrofiërend materiaal* (Water pollution with biodegradable organic and eutrophicating material), The Hague, 1972.

Table AII.4
Data for the elimination curve for biodegradable organic matter (millions of guilders, 1970 prices).

	Population equivalents[a]		Annual costs[b]
Rehabilitation			
Strawboard industry	1.1	2.0%	—
Dairy industry	2.6	4.7	3
Potato-flour industry	13.2	23.6	19
Sugar industry	3.1	5.6	10
Other firms	4.9	8.8	7–17
Subtotal	24.9	44.7	39–49
Treatment			
Bio-industry (part)	0.4	0.7	3
Firms (incl. residual pollution by the strawboard industry, the effluent of treatment of the bio-industry and the waste discharge pipe for East Groningen)	16.4	29.4	563–706
Population	7.5	13.4	220–290
Subtotal	24.3	43.5	786–999
Residual pollution			
Bio-industry (part)	2.1	3.8	U.Q.
Effluent of existing treatment plants	0.6	1.1	U.Q.
Effluent of treatment plants still to be built			
– Firms	1.8	3.2	U.Q.
– Population	0.8	1.4	U.Q.
Population not connected to sewage system	1.3	2.3	—
Subtotal	6.6	11.8	U.Q.
Grand total	55.8	100	800–1050 + U.Q.

[a]Left-hand column in millions of PEs, right-hand column in percent.
[b]U.Q. = unknown quantity.

to summarize. For clarity's sake it is given here in a somewhat simplified form (Table AII.5). The phosphate burden of the fresh surface water, expressed in kg of phosphorus, is about 15 million kg of phosphorus a year (the item *Accumulation in surface water and bottom silt*). According to the balance sheet, the gross supply is 66–89 million kg of phosphorus, and the net supply 63–88 million kg of phosphorus. Of the supply, the following items qualify for elimination of the phosphorus by treatment plants (tertiary treatment): domestic sewage (detergents, faeces

Table AII.5

Phosphorus balance sheet for fresh surface water, 1969/70 (millions of kg of P).

Supply			Withdrawal	
Detergents		8.5–9.1	Outflow to sea and dredging of rivers	39–63
Total discharge	9.2–9.8		Sluices discharging into the sea	5.5–7.5
Arrested by treatment	0.6–0.8		Direct discharge of domestic seqage into the sea	1.4–1.8
Human faeces and urine		5.7–6.1	Direct discharge of industrial waste water into the sea	0.1–0.3
Total discharge	6.1–6.7		Dredging and cleaning of watercourses	0.0
Arrested by treatment	0.4–.06		Withdrawal via biomass of animals	0.1
Industry		2.5–3.4	Treatment in drinking water processing	0.1
Potato-flour	0.6–1.4		Irrigation of horticultural land	0.3–0.7
Dairy	ca. 0.4			
Other foods	ca. 0.3		*Accumulation in surface water and bottom silt*	12–21
Engineering	0.1–0.4			
Other heavy and processing industry	ca. 1.0			
Arrested by treatment	0.0–0.2			
Solid and liquid manure		0.8–1.4		
Erosion of agricultural land		0.7–0.9		
Erosion of other land		0.2–0.4		
Imported via Rhine		40–60		
Imported via Maas		2.0–4.0		
Imported by other international rivers[a]		2.0–3.0		
Precipitation		0.5–1.5		
Total (net)[b]		63–88	Total (net)[b]	63–88

[a]Excl. Scheldt.

[b]The average of the total is determined by adding together the averages of the individual items. The inaccuracy in the total is then calculated by squaring the inaccuracies of the individual items, adding them together and then extracting the square root of the whole. As a result of this method the sum of the separate minima is not equal to the minimum of the total. The same applies to the maxima.

and urine), industrial waste water and some of the liquid manure (0.1 million kg of P).

For the Netherlands, the following two methods of phosphate disposal enter into consideration. The first method consists of dosing ferrous sulphate into the aeration circuit and the second of treating the effluent with ferric chloride. This requires a separate after-settling tank. One the assumption that half of the waste water will be treated by the first method and the other half by the second one, the following estimate may be made of the investment for and annual costs of elimination of the phosphorus emissions.

As the cost calculations are based on population equivalents, it has been estimated how many PEs are contained in the waste water that qualifies for phosphorus elimination. The estimate appears in Table AII.6.

On the assumptions mentioned above, the total investment for tertiary treatment of all the waste water amounts to approximately Dfl. 180 million, while the annual costs are approximately Dfl. 60 million (1970 prices).

With the aid of tertiary treatment of the waste water a considerable percentage of the phosphates can be arrested. Which exactly these phosphates will be cannot be stated with exactitude, since notably it is not yet known whether the polyphosphates from the detergents can likewise be arrested. On the assumption that these polyphosphates too are eliminated and that the efficiency of tertiary treatment is 80% on average, the gross emission of 66–89 million kg of P a year falls by 14–16 million kg of P a year. It is difficult to establish what effect this ultimately has on the quantity of phosphorus accumulated in the fresh surface water because it is not known whether and to what extent export is reduced as a result

Table AII.6
Waste water qualifying for P elimination (millions of BOD PEs).

	PE[a]
Domestic sewage	13.0
Industrial waste water	
Food and drink and tobacco industry	5.6
Chemical industry	0.7
Engineering industry	U.Q.
Potato-flour and strawboard industry	U.Q.
Total (rounded off)	21

[a]U.Q. = unknown quantity.

of reduced emission. It is estimated that the burden of 12–21 million kg of P a year will fall to 5–10 million kg of P a year. This therefore means that, taken over the Netherlands as a whole, the situation continues to deteriorate, though less quickly.

Of the burden approximated in the balance sheet as the balance, some 50% can therefore be eliminated by tertiary treatment. In theory, almost complete elimination can be achieved by eliminating the phosphate discharges that result from imports via the international rivers, by increasing the efficiency of tertiary treatment and by reducing the use of detergents and cleaners.

The latter can be attained by switching to detergents without phosphates (e.g. green soap and soda or detergents containing phosphate substitutes) or by using smaller quantities of detergents. In areas with soft water, the same washing result can be obtained with a reduction of 10% in respect of the quantity of detergents prescribed in 1970. The area within which this is possible can be extended by central water softening. The costs of water softening are compensated for by the advantages. A much greater reduction of detergent use can be obtained when less stringent requirements are made of the 'whiteness' of the wash. Depending on how dirty the wash is and the requirements made of 'whiteness', a reduction by 50–60% is possible.

As already stated, large quantities of phosphate can be absorbed on bottom silt. This phosphate can be released again for primary production. As a result, an elimination of phosphate discharges will not have an effect until a considerable time has elapsed, namely when the quantity of phosphate attached to the silt has reached a much lower level. For a quick solution on behalf of highly eutrophicated waters, the elimination of phosphate sources should therefore be accompanied by dredging of the water in question. Obviously, it is impossible to dredge all waters. Apart from the problem of dredging the whole of the IJsselmeer (the former Zuider Zee), for example, it is after all not possible to store so large a quantity of silt, except in the sea. Consequently, dredging can present only a local solution for very strongly eutrophicated waters.

It follows from the above that the solution to the eutrophy problem must in general be sought in elimination of the emissions. However, this solution will not yield results until the phosphate absorbed on the silt has been washed out to sea. This may take several decades.

No attention has been devoted above to the consequences of the export of phosphates out to sea. It is not yet sufficiently clear what factors can play a part in the eutrophication of sea water. If it should prove that phosphates are of importance in this, the balance sheet compiled above will have to be adapted accordingly.

AII.3. Salination of Water*

Salination means in all cases here the pollution of water by inorganic salts. In the Netherlands a certain degree of salination is of ancient occurrence as a result of salt water seepage. This has come about through the fall in level of the land which occurs in peat-digging and consolidation of the soil. The latter process is the result of artificial lowering of the ground water level, which is necessary to drain the soil sufficiently for agricultural purposes. To counter the drawback of salt-water seepage, fresh water has been introduced from the Rhine system.

The flushing function of the Rhine water has been seriously impaired. There are two causes: the first is salination of the Rhine as a result of all kinds of discharges into it, and the second is the further penetration inland of the salt wedge of the New Waterway, resulting from deepening the fairway for shipping and from constructing new harbours.

The occurrence of salt water seepage has been taken as given. After all, this seepage is largely inherent in the reclamation of agricultural land. With our present technical knowledge it is not possible to eliminate the seepage at an acceptable cost. The study therefore takes as its starting point the situation in which fresh water from the Rhine system is used to reduce the consequences of the salt burden of the seepage.

As stated, the salination of the Rhine system is caused by the salt wedge of the New Waterway and by discharges into the Rhine. These discharges originate largely from the potassium mines in the French Alsace and the mines and industry in the Ruhr District, further consisting of industrial and domestic sewage along the entire river basin. Moreover, of course, the Rhine carries its own salt of natural origin.

In addition to salt water seepage and the discharges from the Rhine system, the following sources of salination may be mentioned: water passed and leaked through sea locks and sluices, industrial waste water and domestic sewage discharged into waters outside the Rhine system, gas wells, driven wells, precipitation, artificial fertilizers, and salt scattered on icy roads.

The size of the salt burden could be derived largely from existing literature. The quantities by weight relate in all cases to the weight of chloride (Cl^-) ions, since these are used in general as indicators of the total salt burden.

The chloride burden through salt water seepage for the whole of the Netherlands is at least 1,000 million kg. Measurements by the

*In this section a short summary is given of the C.B.S. publication *Waterverontreiniging ten gevolge van verzilting, 1950–1970* (Water pollution caused by salination), The Hague, 1973.

Government Water Control Department and others reveal that the chloride carried by the Rhine at the point of entry into the Netherlands is approximately 10,000 million kg a year. About one third of this comes from the Alsace potassium mines and another third from the Ruhr District, while the rest is from industrial waste water and domestic sewage along the full length of the river and is partly of natural origin. Calculations show that the chloride carried in industrial waste water in the central western Netherlands is 18 million kg a year. The Cl^- content of domestic sewage is approximately 125 mg a litre. At an annual quantity of 30 m^3 per person, this amounts to some 40 million kg a year. Calculations also show that the chloride burden in the central western Netherlands originating from gas wells is 13 million kg a year, from precipitation 7 million kg a year and from fertilization 2 million kg a year.

The principal losses of function as a result of the sources of salination listed above (excluding salt water seepage, which has been taken as given) are as follows. Salination of the Rhine means inferior quality of the water as a raw material for the public water supply. This leads to measures of compensation in the preparation of drinking water. Furthermore, salination of the Rhine reduces the effect of flushing the polder reservoirs in the western Netherlands, resulting above all in financial damage to agriculture.

The financial damage, which consists mainly of loss of proceeds in the horticultural areas, has been estimated as follows. 1950 was taken as the year of comparison. With the aid of correlation calculations the connection was established between the Cl^- content measured in the Rhine and the Cl^- content in the Westland and in the area around Aalsmeer (two major horticultural and floricultural areas).

The Cl^- discharge of the Rhine, which increased steeply after 1945 in particular, was about 180 kg per second around 1950 and approximately 330 kg per second in 1969. As the multi-year average of the discharge is 2,200 m^3 per second, the amounts stated correspond to an average Cl^- concentration of approximately 80 mg per litre in 1950 and approximately 150 mg per litre in 1969. With the aid of the correlation found, it has been established that, as a result, the average Cl^- concentration in the polder reservoir water of the Westland rose between 1950 and 1969 from 148 to 195 mg per litre and in the polder reservoir water of the area around Aalsmeer from 118 to 165 mg per litre.

By means of investigations into the sensitivity of horticultural crops to salt, the reduction in proceeds per 100 mg of Cl^- per litre could be established for the most common crops. With the aid of this information, data on quantities brought in to auction and the above figures on the increase in the Cl^- content of polder reservoir waters, it was possible to determine simply the average reduction in annual proceeds as a result of the increase in the salt content of the Rhine between 1950 and 1969. This proved to be Dfl. 25 to 30 million a year.

The compensatory measure most commonly used for making the polluted surface water suitable again as raw material for drinking water is to keep it for a certain length of time in storage basins. As the quality of the surface water used declines, the size of the basin will have to increase so as to be able to distribute drinking water of the same quality. The most obvious method of establishing the effect of pollution on the costs of the water supply would be a comparison of cost prices in the period under consideration, 1950 to 1970. However, it should be borne in mind that the cost price is also affected by the fluctuations in the discharge of the river (dilution effect) and by the size of the demand for water.

For this reason, the choice has fallen on a theoretical calculation in which the two additional factors just mentioned have been eliminated. It has been investigated what costs were incurred in 1950 and 1970 in the preparation of drinking water from Rhine water by means of storage basins and ancillary installations, assuming a 10% dry year (fixed discharge pattern corresponding to a total annual discharge occurring on average once every 10 years) and assuming a capacity of 100 million m^3 a year at the 1970 price level. The total annual extra costs in 1970 in respect of 1950 as a result of the decline in quality of the Rhine water have been estimated in this way at Dfl. 15 million, of which roughly half can be ascribed to salination. The total extra investment required has been estimated at Dfl. 83 million, of which half can be ascribed to salination.

As the consumption of water is increasing greatly and as other sources (chiefly ground water) have a limited capacity, the rivers are becoming of increasing importance to the drinking water supply. This means that the compensatory costs that must be incurred to supply drinking water of good quality will rise drastically in the future unless the pollution is combated at source. Insofar as industry uses drinking water, the compensatory costs as a result of salination are already included in the above estimate.

The salt wedge in the New Waterway has made compensatory measures necessary. These consist in increasing the capacity of a pumping station and widening a number of waterways. It has been estimated that, as a result, the annual costs in 1969 were Dfl. 150,000 higher than in 1950.

There are plans to construct two canals to combat salination in Delfland and Rijnland. The canals must be seen as compensatory measures for both the salt wedge in the New Waterway and the salination of the Rhine. The canals will make it possible to flush Delfland and Rijnland with water from the IJsselmeer. The investments for these canals are estimated at Dfl. 200 to 250 million, with annual costs of approximately Dfl. 20 million (1970 prices).

The agricultural sector is taking only few measures against the salination of Rhine water. These include driving wells, spraying with drinking water and the construction of rain catch basins. The costs of these measures cannot be stated.

By storage of the salt from the French potassium mines the salt load of the Rhine can be reduced by about one third. This costs about 4 French francs per ton when storage takes place on the island of Fessenheim in Alsace. Since 7 million tons of common salt has to be disposed of every year, the annual costs of storage are approximately 28 million French francs (or Dfl. 18 million). If all the salt is stored, the annual costs of the present method of discharge can be deducted from this amount. The net amount then becomes Dfl. 15 to 17 million a year (1970 prices).

The investment required for the construction of a sill in the Nieuwe Maas against the further penetration of the salt wedge has been estimated at Dfl. 60 million, with annual costs of Dfl. 5 to 6 million.

In order to effect a considerable reduction in the penetration of salt water through sealocks and sluices, a number of measures have been taken, such as the installation of air-bubble screens. The total investment in these measures has been estimated at Dfl. 51.3 million, with annual costs of Dfl. 4.5 million.

Finally, to discharge the pumped-up salt cooling water used by Delft industry a pipeline has been laid to the sea. The investment in this is Dfl. 11.6 million, with approximate annual costs of Dfl. 1.4 million (1970 prices).

The above calculations can be summarized as shown in Table AII.7.

Construction of the elimination cost curve and the curve of compensatory costs and financial damage was based solely on the salination of the Rhine system.

With the aid of the data on storage of the salt from the potassium mines, the connection between the salt carried by the Rhine and the financial damage to horticulture, and also the compensatory costs in the preparation of drinking water, part of the elimination cost curve and the curve of compensatory costs and financial damage can already be drawn. To be able to give a greater range of the curves, data have been collected on the costs of measures for preventing salt discharges ($CaCl_2$ and NaCl) by the French and German soda works. It has been assumed that the other possibilities of elimination (e.g. in the German mines) involve higher annual costs than the measures mentioned above; from what

Table AII.7
Damage and costs of compensation and elimination as a result of salination (millions of guilders, 1970 prices).

	Capital investment[a]	Annual costs[a]
Financial damage		
Horticulture	—	25–30[b]
Compensatory measures		
Drinking water	41.5[c]	7.5[c]
Industrial water	U.Q.	U.Q.
Extension of pumping station and widening of waterways	—	0.15[c]
Desalination canals	200–250	20
Agriculture	U.Q.	U.Q.
Elimination measures		
Storage of salt from potassium mines	—	15–17
Sill against salt wedge	60	5– 6
Measures relating to sea locks and sluices	51.2	4.5
Discharge pipeline, Delft industry	11.6	1.4

[a]U.Q. = unknown quantity.
[b]1969 situation.
[c]Extra damage or costs in 1970 in respect of 1950.

follows it will be seen that, if this assumption is made, the data on the other measures are not needed in order to determine the optimum point of treatment.

The elimination cost curve is based solely on the annual costs. No assumption has been made about the period over which the measures that may be taken will extend. On the abscissa of the graph appears the chloride carried by the Rhine in kg of Cl^- per second (1 kg of Cl^- per second = 31.5 million kg of Cl^- per year); the ordinate gives the amounts of the total annual costs together with the costs of compensatory measures and the amounts of financial damage. As starting point for the elimination cost curve the 1970 situation has been taken.

The elimination measures taken into consideration for the construction of the *E* curve are arranged below in order of increasing annual costs.

For part of the soda production it is possible to change from the customary Solvay process, which uses sodium chloride as base material for sodium, to a process using caustic soda solution obtained in the electrolysis of sodium chloride. In the latter process no chloride is discharged. It is assumed that the production costs of the two processes are equally high. The costs of elimination are then nil. It cannot simply be stated for how much soda a change in process is still possible. That depends first of all on the demand for chlorine and the accompanying production of the by-product caustic soda solution. Both the required production of chlorine and the other uses for caustic soda solution depend on market conditions which often cannot be foreseen. The reduction of chloride discharges to be achieved by a change in process has therefore been put at x kg/sec. In connection with this two elimination cost curves have been drawn in Figure AII.2, *E1* and *E2*. *E1* indicates a situation in which no extra change of process is possible ($x = 0$). *E2* indicates the situation in which a change of process is possible for the production of 350 million kg of soda a year, as a result of which the discharge of chloride is reduced by 315 million kg per year, or 10 kg per second ($x = 10$). This reduction is shown on the horizontal part of the *E2* curve. For the rest the *E1* and the *E2* curve are identical.

By storing the common salt from the French potassium mines discharges of chloride into the Rhine can be reduced by 4,100 million kg a year, or by 130 kg per second. The annual costs of this have been

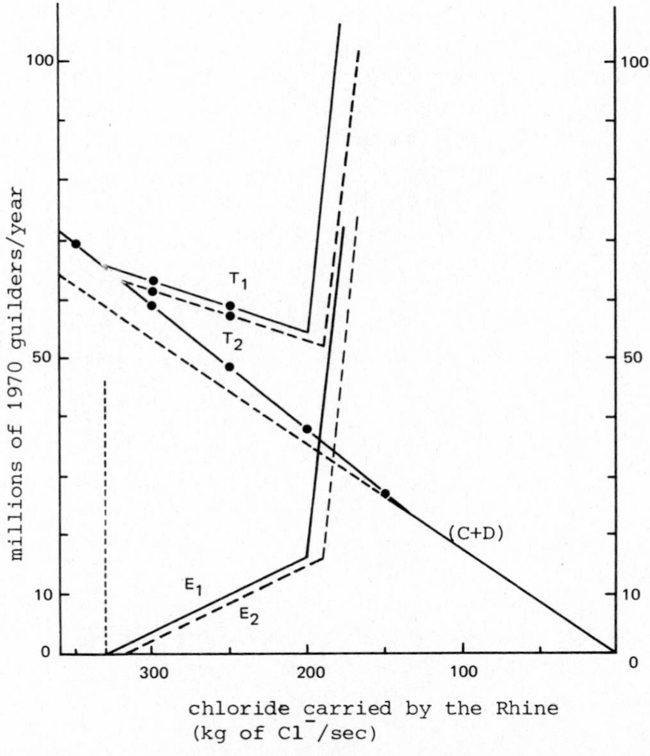

Figure AII.2. Weighing of costs and benefits of the prevention of chloride discharges into the Rhine.

estimated at Dfl. 15 to 17 million. With the aid of these data the less steep stretch of the *E1* and *E2* curve (from the abscissa to the kink) has been drawn.

The third possibility of elimination considered is the working-up and disposal of the calcium chloride that is discharged in soda production by the usual Solvay process. During this process NaCl is also released. Per ton of $CaCl_2 \cdot 2H_2O$ working-up costs are about Dfl. 125 at an annual capacity of 50,000 tons. As a result, the discharge of 0.67 tons of chloride is obviated. The elimination of 1 ton of chloride therefore costs Dfl. 190. If it is assumed that dumping in the sea in steel drums is a responsible method of disposal and the costs of this are put at Dfl. 40 a ton, the total costs of eliminating 1 ton of chloride are Dfl. 230. With the aid of this datum the steeply rising section of the *E1* and the *E2* curve has been drawn.

With the aid of the regression equations of the above-mentioned correlation calculations, which show the connection between the chloride concentrations of the Rhine on the one hand and the chloride concentration in the Westland and the area around Aalsmeer on the other, we have calculated that storage of the salt from the French potassium mines (as a result of which the chloride carried by the Rhine decreases by 130 kg per second) reduces the financial damage to horticulture by Dfl. 22 to 26 million. Assuming that the damage has a linear relation to the salt carried by the Rhine (this will more or less hold good in reality), this datum gives the straight part of the $(C + D)$ curve in Figure AII.2.* Superimposed on this is the curve showing the connection between the chloride carried by the Rhine and the compensatory costs – calculated as annual costs – of the storage basins that are needed to make the polluted surface water suitable again for the preparation of drinking water, insofar as these costs can be imputed to salination. This gives the $(C + D)$ curve in Figure AII.2.

The *E1, E2* and $(C + D)$ curves have been added together in Figure AII.2 (*T1* and *T2* curves). The latter curves indicate the total social costs. On the given assumptions an obvious minimum proves to occur. Without a change of process in the soda industry this minimum lies at 130 kg of arrested chloride per second. When, in addition, x kg per second chloride discharge is prevented by a change of process, the minimum of the social costs lies at $(130 + x)$ kg of arrested chloride per second.

The various cost data are not exact, but approximate. The question now is what effect inaccuracies in the cost data have on the place of the minimum. Only if the data used were so inaccurate that the left-hand part

*Any financial damage abroad was left out of consideration.

of curve *T* in reality fell instead of rising as the chloride carried increases would the actual minimum of the social costs be further to the left. Since the influence of the compensatory costs is only slight and the costs of elimination are fairly certain, a shift to the left would mainly be caused by too high an estimate of the financial damage. This estimate would then have to have been more than 40% too high. So great a deviation is improbable.

The curves in Figure AII.2 hold good for a situation relating to 1970. Since much of the greatly increasing demand for water will have to be met with Rhine water, the compensatory costs will almost certainly increase sharply. This means that, taking into account the developments since 1970, optimum treatment will almost certainly entail storage of the salt from the potassium mines.

*AII.4. Air pollution by the combustion of fossil fuels**

The combustion of fossil fuels (coal and coke, petroleum products and gases) is a major cause of air pollution. In the process of combustion a number of agents enter the atmosphere; these are listed in Table AII.8, in which also a brief summary is given of the principal losses of function that these agents cause.

The estimate of the emissions relates on the one hand to furnaces (domestic and other space heating, industry, power stations) and on the other to mobile sources (road traffic, rail traffic, inland shipping and air traffic). The emission estimate has been made by means of emission factors and fuel consumption. The emission factors depend on the fuel used, the method of combustion and, as regards road traffic, the manner of driving. Allowance is made for this in the estimates as far as possible. For estimation of the costs of elimination the techniques of treatment now operational were taken as a basis. Some fuels can be treated by more than one technique; for them, argued assumptions have been made. The results of the estimates are summarized in Table AII.9 on the conditions stated as a note below the table.

The table shows that, with the present techniques, the attainable emission restriction for sulphur dioxide is approximately 75%, for nitrogen oxides about 20%, for lead practically 100%, for carbon monoxide roughly 75%, for aerosols about 50%, and for hydrocarbons likewise about 50%.

*In this section a short summary is given of the C.B.S. publication *Luchtverontreiniging door verbranding van fossiele brandstoffen 1960–1972* (Air pollution by the combustion of fossil fuels), The Hague, 1975.

Table AII.8

Agents released, with principal losses of function.

Agent	Concentration in which the agent is of frequent occurrence in the Netherlands; daily averages ($\mu g/m^3$)	Principal losses of function	Concentration at which the loss of function proceeds to occur upon lengthy exposure ($\mu g/m^3$)
Hydrocarbons	Hydrocarbons excl. methane: 0–250 Methane: More than 1000	Hydrocarbons, with the exception of methane, play an important part in the formation of photochemical smog through their reaction with nitrogen oxides.	
		The occurrence of ethylene disturbs the growth of higher plants (growth hormone).	20
	Polycyclic hydrocarbons: 0.002–0.02	Polycyclic aromatic hydrocarbons are carcinogenic.	
Carbon monoxide	5,000–20,000	Carbon monoxide is absorbed via the lungs and combines with the haemoglobin in the blood, reducing the oxygen-transporting capacity; this entails an increased risk for some vulnerable sections of the population (e.g. cardiac patients).	50,000
Nitrogen oxides	15–75	Nitrogen oxides play a very important part in the formation of photochemical smog;	
		increase the chance of respiratory diseases among humans and animals;	Less than 120
		inhibit the photosynthesis of green plants;	500
		like sulphur oxides, cause accelerated corrosion;	—[a]
		oxidize organic compounds like dyes and fibres, as a result of which these fade or become weaker respectively;	100–300
		reduce the transparency of the atmosphere;	100
		have an unpleasant smell.	300–400
Sulphur oxides	100–300	Sulphur oxides cause respiratory diseases and, above all in combination with aerosols, can cause death;	100–500
		cause accelerated corrosion (effect greater than that of nitrogen oxides);	100–200

		attack calcareous stone (important with respect to, inter alia, buildings and sculpture);	100–500
		attack paper, materials made from (natural) fibres and dyes, which leads to damage in e.g. museums and archives;	250–500
		cause leaf damage in higher plants and death of among others lichens.	85
Aldehydes		Often possess a very unpleasant odour;	150–600
		irritate the mucous membranes.	300–3,000
Aerosols	25–200	Soot aerosols, not toxic in themselves, can greatly reinforce the effects of sulphur oxides by adsorbing the latter, among other effects.	100
		Elongated aerosol particles may cause asbestosis.	
		Aerosols containing polycyclic aromatics may be carcinogenic.	
		Aerosols containing sulphuric acid cause respiratory diseases.	Less than 300
		Precipitated aerosols may cause serious pollution of materials.	
		Aerosols cause a considerable drop in clarity of the atmosphere, so that visibility is reduced, whilst the climate may also be affected (though carbon dioxide probably plays a bigger role in this).	
Aerosols containing lead	1–5	Lead absorbed in the form of an aerosol may cause various diseases, among other things as a result of disturbance of enzymatic activity.	
		Precipitated lead aerosols can make agricultural crops and, indirectly, meat and milk from stock grazing on polluted grass unfit for human consumption.	
Oxidants (ozone and peroxyacetyl nitrates)	ozone: 0–70 PAN : 0–50	Oxidants attack rubber, dyes and fibrous materials;	20–100
		cause irritation of the mucous membranes and possibly respiratory diseases;	25–200
		cause damage to plants;	20–100
		have an unpleasant smell;	20–40
		play a part in the chemical reactions of photochemical smog.	

[a]Approximately 2.5 $\mu g/cm^3$ as nitrate.

Table AII.9

Emissions (millions of kg) and costs of elimination, 1972 (millions of guilders, 1972 prices).[a]

Type of measure	Capital investment	Annual costs	Emissions avoided for: Carbon monoxide	Nitrogen oxides	Sulphur dioxide	Lead	Aerosols	Hydrocarbons
Cyclones and electrostatic precipitators in coal combustion	3.2–7.4	0.74–1.03					17	
Electrostatic precipitators in fuel oil combustion	20–50	3.4–5.0					12	
Fuel gasification by power stations	60–120	12–24		1	42		1	
Gas oil desulphurization	90–135	32–55			94			
Desulphurization of fuel oil with								
3% or more sulphur	110–158	38–50			80			
2–3% sulphur	220–320	80–106			108			
1–2% sulphur	30–46	11.6–15.6			8			
Flue gas desulphurization in refineries in fuel oil combustion	90–130	34–46			150			
Restriction of nitrogen oxides in natural gas combustion in power stations	4–6	13–18		15				
Restriction of nitrogen oxides in fuel oil combustion in power stations	3–7	10–19		10				
Replacement of conventional petrol engine by stratified charge engine	530–580	130–260	1,450	33		2.1		85
Emissions without measures			1,850	310	620	2.2	58	175
Emissions after application of all measures			400	250	140	0.1	28	90

[a]The sums of money given hold good only for a fuel consumption as occurred in 1972 both by volume and by nature of the application. The data from the table are based on the measures now technically feasible at 'reasonable' cost (i.e., not the maximum technically feasible). Effects of fuel substitution (such as replacement of fuel oil by natural gas) and reduction of the level of activities have been left out of consideration.

Although the assumptions made could be well argued, other choices are of course possible. Consequently, a formula is given with which the costs of elimination can be calculated. For capital investment I (millions of guilders, 1972 prices) the formula is as follows:

$$I = 0.0041\,A + 0.0046\,B + 0.17\,C + 0.030\,D + 0.10\,E + 0.051\,F + 0.0015\,G + 0.0027\,H + 0.20\,K.$$

For the annual costs L (millions of guilders, 1972 prices), we can write

$$L = 0.0007\,A + 0.0007\,B + 0.034\,C + 0.011\,D + 0.035\,E + 0.021\,F + 0.0049\,G + 0.0078\,H + 0.054\,K.$$

where

A = millions of kg of coal of which the flue gases are treated with cyclones and electrostatic precipitators;
B = millions of kg of fuel oil of which the flue gases are treated with electrostatic precipitators;
C = millions of kg of fuel oil burnt in power stations with fuel gasification;
D = millions of kg of gas oil that are desulphurized;

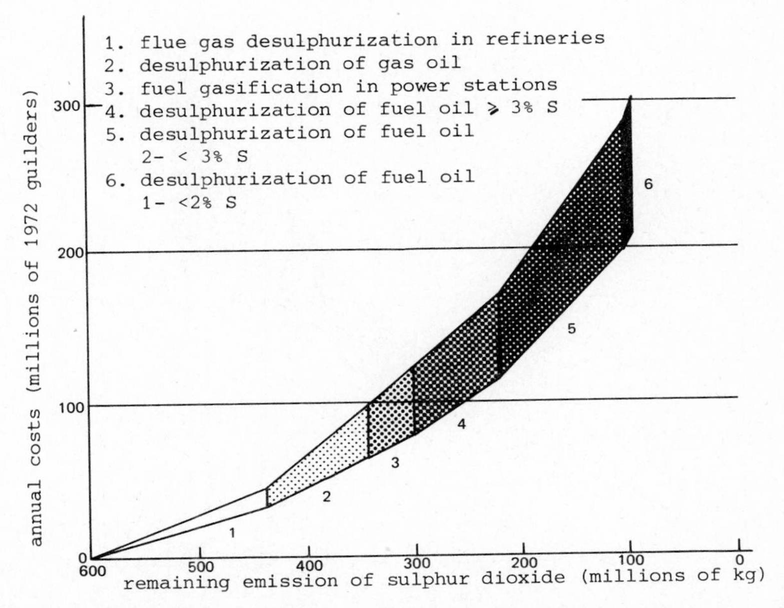

Figure AII.3. *Sulphur dioxide*: Annual costs of emission restriction as a function of the remaining emission.

E = millions of kg of fuel oil that are desulphurized (direct method);
F = millions of kg of fuel whereby flue gas desulphurization is applied;
G = millions of kg of natural gas for which emission of nitrogen oxides is restricted;
H = millions of kg of fuel oil for which emission of nitrogen oxides is restricted;
K = millions of kg of petrol for which the stratified charge engine is used in cars.

For the most important agents elimination cost curves were constructed (Figures AII.3 to AII.6). As in the case of biodegradable organic matter, these were based on increasing annual costs per unit of emission avoided in each of the treatment techniques. The uncertainty margins of the estimates are incorporated in the curves.

The same qualifying remarks must be made about the curves as about the elimination cost curves for biodegradable organic matter (Section AII.1): the curves are based on linear costs per branch of industry and per treatment technique; in practice, the chronological order should depend on the difference between benefits and costs (whereby the benefits must be estimated by the authorities in the absence of market data); fuel consumption relates to 1972.

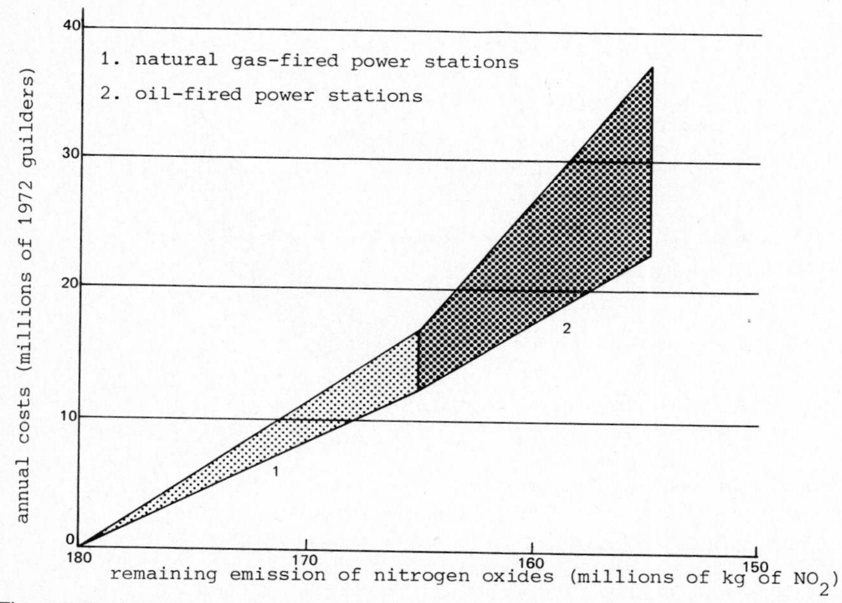

Figure AII.4. *Nitrogen oxides*: Annual costs of emission restriction as a function of the remaining emission.

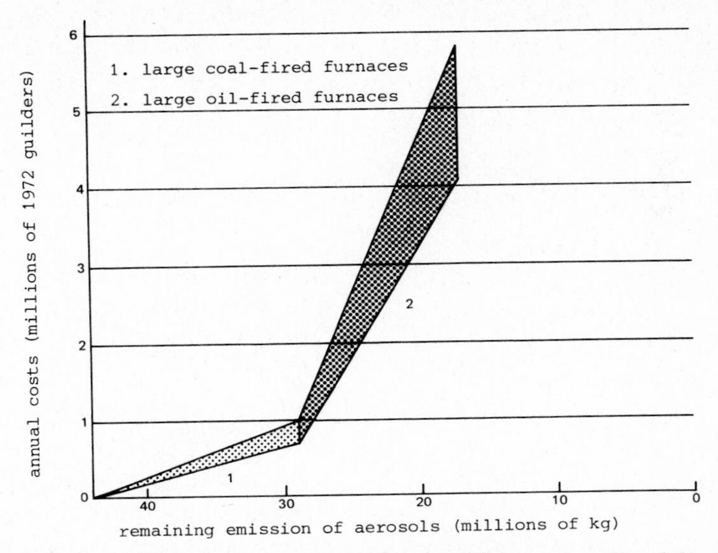

Figure AII.5. *Aerosols*: Annual costs of emission restriction as a function of the remaining emission.

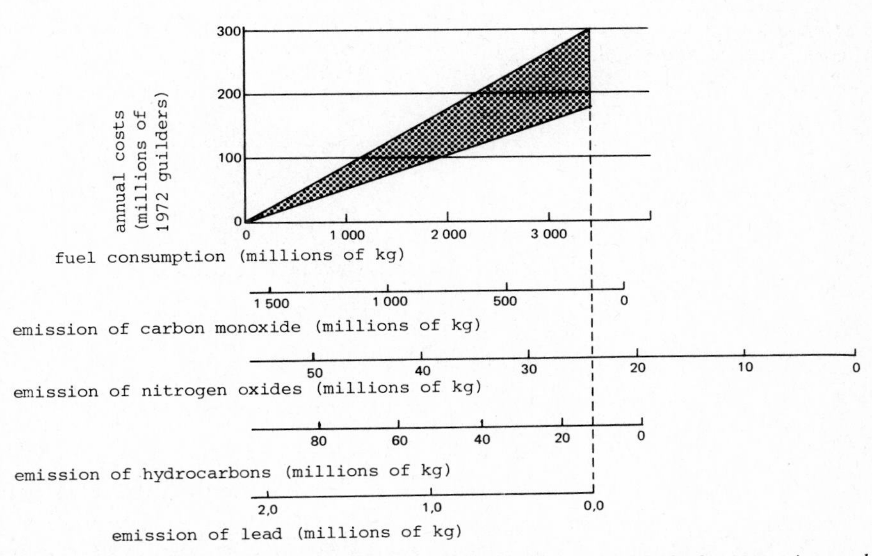

Figure AII.6. *Change from conventional petrol engine to stratified charge engine and unleaded petrol*: Annual costs as a function of the annual fuel consumption in stratified charge engines. On the additional axes the remaining annual emission by petrol-engined cars is shown.

LIST OF LITERATURE QUOTED

ACHTSTE Nota Inzake de Industrialisatie van Nederland. The Hague, 1963.
ALLAN, C.M. *The Theory of Taxation.* Harmondsworth, 1971.
ARGE, R.C. d'. *See*: A.V. Kneese.
ARTHUR, D. et al. A blueprint for survival. *The Ecologist* 2, 1972, No. 1.
ARVILL, R. *Man and Environment*. Harmondsworth, 1967.
AYRES, R.U. and A.V. Kneese. Production, consumption and externalities. *American Economic Review*, June, 1969.

BAKKER, K. Het verstoorde evenwicht. In: *Mens contra Milieu.* Baarn, 1970.
BARBREAU, A. *See:* G. de Marsily.
BEURS, C. de and R. Tweehuysen. *Tweede Rapport aan de Club van Rome Nader Bezien.* Commissie Maatschappij Modellen, T.N.O. Delft, 1975.
BIERSTEKER, K. *Verontreinigde Lucht.* Assen, 1966.
BLADERGROEN, W. J. Kinderspel. In: *De Wereld van de Kleuter*. Groningen, 1963.
BOULDING, K.E. The economics of the coming spaceship earth. In: *Environmental Quality in a Growing Economy*. Baltimore (Md.), 1966.
BOULDING, K.E. Fun and games with the gross national product – The role of misleading indicators in social policy. In: *The Environmental Crisis.* London, 1970.
BOULDING, K.E. Environment and economics. In: *Environment, Resources, Pollution and Society*. Stanford (Cal.), 1971.
BOUMA, F. *Evaluatie van Natuurfuncties.* Verkenningen van het Instituut voor Milieuvraagstukken, Vrije Universiteit. Serie A, No. 3. Amsterdam, 1972.
BOWER, B.T. *See* A.V. Kneese.
BRYSON, R.A. and W.M. Wendland. Climatic effects of atmospheric pollution. In: *Global Effects of Environmental Pollution.* Dordrecht, 1970.
BUCHANAN, J.M. *The Demand and Supply of Public Goods.* Chicago (Ill.), 1969.
BURTON, T.L. and M.N. Fulcher. Measurement of recreation benefits – A survey. *Journal of Economic Studies* 3, 1968, No. 2.
BIBLE, The.

CARSON, R. *Silent Spring.* Cambridge (Mass.), 1962.
C.B.S. Enkele berekeningen over het nationale inkomen van Nederland. In: *Speciale Onderzoekingen van De Nederlandse Conjunctuur.* The Hague, 1939.
C.B.S. *Het Nationale Inkomen van Nederland 1921–1939*. Utrecht, 1948.
C.B.S. *Statistische en Econometrische Onderzoekingen 2e/3e kwartaal 1958.* Zeist, 1958.
C.B.S. *Nationale Rekeningen, 1971*. The Hague, 1972.
C.B.S. *Waterverontreiniging met Afbreekbaar Organisch en Eutrofiërend Materiaal*. The Hague, 1972.
C.B.S. *Waterverontreiniging ten Gevolge van Verzilting, 1950–1970.* The Hague, 1973.
C.B.S. *Luchtverontreiniging door Verbranding van Fossiele Brandstoffen 1960–1972.* The Hague, 1975.
CLAPHAM, J. H. *An Economic History of Modern Britain, Free Trade and Steel, 1850–1886*. London, 1932.
CLAWSON, M. *Methods of Measuring the Demand for and Value of Outdoor Recreation.* Reprint No. 10. Resources for the Future, Washington (D.C.), 1959.
CLAWSON, M. and J.L. Knetsch. *Economics of Outdoor Recreation.* Baltimore (Md.), 1971.

COMMONER, B. *The Closing Circle*. London, 1972.
CONCEPTUAL, The, Framework of national income statistics. In: *National Income*. 1954 Edition. Washington (D.C.), 1954.
CORTEN, A.A.H.M. Beschermingsmaatregelen voor de Noordzeeharing: Te Weinig en te laat. *Visserij*, June/July, 1977.

DENISON, E. F. In: *Studies in Income and Wealth. Volume 10. Conference on Research in Income and Wealth*. New York, 1947.
DENISON, E. F. Welfare measurement and the GNP. U.S. Department of Commerce, Office of Business Economics. *Survey of Current Business* 51, 1971, No. 1.
DERKSEN, J.B.D. Zijn correcties van het begrip nationaal inkomen mogelijk en gewenst? *Economisch-Statistische Berichten*, 31 January 1973.
DIEREN, W. van and M.G. Wagenaar Hummelinck. *The Capital of Nature*. (In preparation).
DIGGLE, G. *A History of Widnes*. Widnes, 1961.
DOBBEN, W.H. van. Het vegetatiedek van de aarde en de invloed van de mens daarop. In: *De Groene Aarde*. Utrecht, 1966.
DREES Jr., W. and F.Th. Gubbi. *Overheidsuitgaven in Theorie en Praktijk*. Groningen, 1968.
DUESENBERRY, J.S. *Income, Saving and the Theory of Consumer Behavior*. Cambridge (Mass.), 1949.
DIJK, G. van and W. Smit. *Kleine Kansen, Grote Gevolgen*. Boerderijcahier 7601. T.H. Twente, Enschede, 1976.

EASTERLIN, R.A. *Does Economic Growth Improve The Human Lot?* Mim. paper. University of Pennsylvania, Philadelphia (Penn.), undated.
EICHHOLZ, G.G. *Environmental Aspects of Nuclear Power*. Ann Arbor (Mich.), 1976.
ERASMUS, D. *Betoog over de Lof der Geneeskunde*. Translated by L. Elout. Antwerp, 1950.

FABRICANT, S. In: *Studies in Income and Wealth. Volume 10. Conference on Research in Income and Wealth*. New York, 1947.
FIEDELDIJ DOP, Ph.H. Psychohygiënische factoren. In: *Criteria voor Milieubeheer*. Amsterdam, 1970.
FORRESTER, J.W. *World Dynamics*. Cambridge (Mass.), 1971.
FULCHER, M.N. *See*: T.L. Burton.

GALBRAITH, J.K. *The Affluent Society*. London, 1958.
GARBUTT, J. and H. Linnemann et al. *Mensen Tellen*. Utrecht/Antwerp, 1976.
GILLETTE, R. Nuclear safety: Calculating the odds of disaster. *Science* 185, 1974, 838.
GOEDHART, C. Waar de prijstheorie verstek laat gaan. *Orbis Economicus* 14, No. 1.
GRINTEN, P.M.E.M. van der and P.J. de Jong. Werelddynamica gezien vanuit de systeem- en regeltechniek. *Chemisch Weekblad*, 10 December 1971.
GRINTEN, P.M.E.M. van der and P.J. de Jong. Werelddynamica, een uitgangspunt voor een wereldbeleid? *Chemisch Weekblad*, 10 March 1972.
GROSSE, R.N. Problems of resource allocation health. In: *Public Expenditure and Policy Analysis*. Edited by R.H. Haveman and J. Margolis. Chicago (Ill.), 1970.
GUBBI, F.Th. *See*: W. Drees Jr.

HARTOG, F. *Toegepaste Welvaartseconomie*. Leiden, 1973.
HAYES, D. Nuclear power: The fifth horseman. *World Watch Paper 6*. Washington (D.C.), 1976.
HEERTJE, A. Welvaart en welzijn, een schijntegenstelling. *Intermediair*, 15 January 1971.
HENNIPMAN, P. *Economisch Motief en Economisch Principe*. Amsterdam, 1940.
HENNIPMAN, P. Nut, nuttugheid en objectieve gebruikswaarde. *De Economist*, 1943.
HENNIPMAN, P. Doeleinden en criteria. In: *Theorie van de Economische Politiek*. Leiden, 1962.

HENNIPMAN, P. De externe effecten in de hedendaagse welvaartstheorie. *Economisch-Statistische Berichten*, 20 March 1968.
HENNIPMAN, P. Welvaartstheorie of welzijnstheorie? *Economisch-Statistische Berichten*, 26 January 1972.
HERBER, L. *Crisis in our Cities*. New Jersey, 1965.
HICKS, J.R. The four consumer's surpluses. *Review of Economic Studies* XI, 1943.
HICKS, J.R. On the valuation of social income. *Economica*, August, 1948.
HUETING, R. Ruimtelijke ordening en het allocatievraagstuk. *Economisch-Statistische Berichten*, 21 May 1969.
HUETING, R. Moet de natuur worden gekwantificeerd? *Economisch-Statistische Berichten*, 21 January 1970.
HUETING, R. *Wat is de Natuur ons Waard?* Baarn, 1970.
HUETING, R. Milieu en werkgelegenheid. *Economisch-Statistische Berichten*, 5 March 1975.

ICERMAN, L. *See:* S.S. Penner.
ISARD, W. et al. *On the Linkage of Socio-Economic and Ecological Systems*. The Regional Science Association: Papers. Volume 21, 1968.
ISARD, W. *Some Notes on the Linkage of the Ecologic and Economic Systems*. Regional Science Association: Papers. Volume 22, 1969.

JANSEN, H.M.A. and J.B. Opschoor. *De Invloed van Geluidshinder op de Prijzen van Woningen – Verslag van een Enquête onder Makelaars in en rond de Haarlemmermeer.* Instituut voor Milieuvraagstukken, Vrije Universiteit. Werknota No. 15. Amsterdam, 1972.
JASZI, G. *Comments on F. Thomas Juster's 'A Framework for the Measurement of Economic and Social Performance'*. Unpublished paper prepared for the National Bureau of Economic Research Conference on the Measurement of Economic and Social Performance. Princeton (N.Y.), 4–6 November 1971.
JONG, P.J. de. *See:* P.M.E.M. van der Grinten.
JONG, W.M. de and G.W. Rathenau. *The Future Availability of Energy to the Netherlands.* Working Paper for the Wetenschappelijke Raad voor het Regeringsbeleid. December 1976.
JUSTER, F.T. *A Framework for the Measurement of Economic and Social Performance.* Princeton (N.Y.), 1971.
JUVENALIS, D.J. *Saturarum Libri.* Book III, verse 232 et seq.

KAPP, K.W. *The Social Costs of Private Enterprise.* Cambridge (Mass.), 1950.
KAPP, K.W. *Social Costs of Business Enterprise.* London, 1963.
KAPP, K.W. Social costs, neo-classical economics, environmental planning: A reply. In: *Political Economy of Environment.* Paris, 1972.
KAPTEYN, A. *See:* B.M.S. van Praag.
KEYNES, J.M. *Essays in Persuasion.* London, 1931.
KING, G. Natural and political observations and conclusions upon the state and condition of England. In: *Two Tracts.* Baltimore (Md.), 1936.
KING, W.I. *The Wealth and Income of the People of the United States.* New York, 1919.
KINGMA BOLTJES, T.Y. Stuurloos varen. *Water, Bodem, Lucht* 44, 1959, No. 3/4.
KLAASSEN, L.H. Niettes–welleszijn. *Economisch-Statistische Berichten*, 19 July 1972.
KNEESE, A.V. and B.T. Bower. *Managing Water Quality: Economics, Technology, Institutions.* Baltimore (Md.), 1968.
KNEESE, A.V. and R.C. d'Arge. Pervasive external costs and the response of society. In: *The Analysis and Evaluation of Public Expenditure: The PPB System.* A compendium of papers submitted to the Subcommittee on Economy in Government of the Joint Economic Committee, 91 Cong., 1 Sess., 1969.
KNEESE, A.V. *See:* R.U. Ayres.

KNEESE, A.V. Economic responsibility for the by-products of production. *The Annals of the American Academy of Political and Social Science* 389, May, 1970.
KNETSCH, J.L. *See:* M. Clawson.
KNETSCH, J.L. Outdoor recreation demands and benefits. *Land Economics* XXXIX, 1963, No. 4.
KOLKWICZ, R. and M. Marsson. Oecologie der pflanzlichen Saprobien. *Berichte der Deutschen Botanischen Gesellschaft* 26, 1908, No. 505.
KOLKWICZ, R. and M. Marsson. Oecologie der tierischen Saprobien. *Internationale Revue der Gesamten Hydrobiologie und Hydrografie* 2, 1909, No. 2.
KOMENDE, De, vijfentwintig jaar: Een Toekomstverkenning voor Nederland. Wetenschappelijke Raad voor het Regeringsbeleid. Rapporten aan de Regering No. 15. The Hague, 1977.
KRUG, L. *Betrachtungen über den National-Reichtum des Preussischen Staats und über den Wohlstand seiner Bewohner.* Berlin, 1805.
KUENEN, D.J. *Mens en Milieu.* Leiden, 1965.
KUENEN, D.J. Het recht van de mens op leefruimte. In: *De Rechten van de Mens.* Leiden, 1968.
KUENEN, D.J. Milieubehoud is zelfbehoud. In: *Mens contra Milieu*. Baarn, 1970.
KUZ, T. *See:* V. Smil.
KUZNETS, S. National income and industrial structure. In: *The Econometric Society Meeting, September 6–18, 1947, Washington, D.C.* Proceedings of the International Statistical Conferences, Volume V. Calcutta, undated.
KUZNETS, S. On the valuation of social income. *Economica*, February/May, 1948.
KWAST, B.A. and J.A. Mulder. *Beknopt Leerboek der Economische Aardrijkskunde.* Groningen, 1950.

LANJOUW, J. Waar gaan wij heen? In: *Het Verstoorde Evenwicht.* Utrecht, 1970.
LASSLO, E. et al. *Goals for Mankind.* New York, 1977.
LEDOUX, E. *See:* G. de Marsily.
LEONTIEF, W.W. Environmental repercussions and the economic structure: An input–output approach. *The Review of Economics and Statistics*, August, 1970.
LEOPOLD, A. The land ethic. In: *A Sand Country Almanac.* New York, 1949.
LINNEMANN, H. *See:* J. Garbutt.
LUNDHOLM, B. Interactions between oceans and terrestrial ecosystems. In: *The Global Effects of Environmental Pollution.* Dordrecht, 1970.

MARCUSE, R. *One Dimensional Man: The Ideology of Industrial Society*. London, 1964.
MARGAT, J. *See:* G. de Marsily.
MARGLIN, S.A. *Public Investment Criteria.* London, 1969.
MARKS, R.P. and S. Myers. Outdoor recreation. In: *Measuring Benefits of Government Investments.* Edited by Dorfman. Washington (D.C.), 1965.
MARSHALL, A. *Principles of Economics.* Eighth Edition. London, 1969 (First Edition, 1890).
MARSILY, G. de, E. Ledoux, A. Barbreau and J. Margat. Nuclear waste disposal: Can the geologist guarantee isolation? *Science* 197, 1977, No. 4303.
MARSSON, M. *See:* R. Kolkwicz.
MARTIAL. Book XII, poem 57.
MEADOWS, D.H. *The Limits To Growth.* New York, 1972.
MEASUREMENT, The, of Economic and Social Performance. Edited by Milton Moss. New York, 1973.
MEREWITZ, L. and S. Soslick. *The Budget's New Clothes.* Chicago (Ill.), 1971.
MESAROVIC, M. and E. Pestel. *Mankind at the Turning Point.* New York, 1974.
MESAROVIC, M. and E. Pestel. *Multilevel Computer Model of the World Development System.* IIASA Report SP-74-1. Luxembourg, 1974.
METELERKAMP, R. *De Toestand van Nederland, in Vergelijking Gebracht met die van Enige Andere Landen van Europa.* Rotterdam, 1804.

MEY, A. et al. *Encyclopedie van de Bedrijfseconomie.* Part I: Algemene Economie. Bussum, 1969.
MILJOENENNOTA 1970. Bijlage 15: Nota over de inkomensverdeling. The Hague, 1969.
MILL, J.S. *Principles of Political Economy.* London, 1862/1876.
MILLER, J.L. *See:* M. Miller-Sweeny.
MILLER-SWEENY, M. and J.L. Miller. *Bible Dictionary.* New York, 1952.
MISHAN, E.J. *The Costs of Economic Growth.* London, 1967.
MISHAN, E.J. What is wrong with Roskill? *Journal of Transport Economics and Policy* 4, 1970, No. 1.
MISHAN, E.J. *Cost–Benefit Analysis*. London, 1971.
MISHAN, E.J. The postwar literature on externalities: An interpretative essay. *Journal of Economic Literature* IX, 1971, No. 1.
MITCHELL Jr., J.M. A preliminary revaluation of atmospheric pollution as a cause of the global temperature fluctuation of the past century. In: *Global Effects of Environmental Pollution*. Dordrecht, 1970.
MITSCHERLICH, A. *Die Unwirtlichkeit unserer Städte.* Frankfurt am Main, 1965.
MULDER, J.A. *See:* B.A. Kwast.
MULISCH, H. *Bericht aan de Rattenkoning.* Amsterdam, 1967.
MUSGRAVE, R. A. Provision for social goods. In: *Public Economics*. London, 1972.
MYERS, S. *See:* R.P. Marks.

NASH, Hugh. Rasmussen report is demolished by Union of Concerned Scientists. In: *Not Man Apart*. San Francisco (Cal.), 1978.
NATIONAL Park Service (U.S.A.). *A Method of Evaluating Recreation Benefits and Costs of Water Control Projects.* August 1956.
NORDHAUS, W. and J. Tobin. Is growth obsolete? In: *Economic Growth: Fiftieth Anniversary Colloquium V.* New York, 1972.
NOTA Inzake Groei en Structuur van Onze Economie. The Hague, 1966.

ODUM, E.P. *Fundamentals of Ecology*. Third Edition. Philadelphia (Penn.), 1971.
ODUM, E.P. The strategy of ecosystem development. *Science* 164, 1969, No. 3877.
ODUM, H.T. *Environment, Power, and Society.* New York, 1971.
O.E.E.C. *A Standardised System of National Accounts.* Paris, 1952.
OOMENS, C.A. *A Note on the International Comparison of National Income Figures.* Unpublished paper for the International Association for Research in Income and Wealth, 1965.
OPSCHOOR, J.B. *See:* H.M.A. Jansen.
OPSCHOOR, J.B. Opinie-enquêtering en informatie. *Economisch-Statistische Berichten*, 19 May 1971.
OSBORN, F. *Our Plundered Planet.* Boston (N.Y.), 1948.

PEARCE, D.W. *Cost–Benefit Analysis.* London, 1971.
PEN, J. In: *Verslag van Werkzaamheden en Bevindingen over het Jaar 1964 van de Raad voor de Kunst*. Bijlage 3.
PEN, J. *Harmonie en Conflict.* Amsterdam, 1970.
PEN, J. Zeven methoden van antivervuilingsbeleid: Een poging tot systematiek. *Economisch Kwartaaloverzicht van de Amsterdam–Rotterdam Bank N.V.* March 1971.
PEN, J. In: *Haagse Post*, 8 March 1972.
PENNER, S.S. and L. Icerman. *Energy. Volume I: Demands, Resources, Impact, Technology and Policy.* Reading (Mass.), 1974.
PESKIN, H.M. *National Accounting and the Environment.* Edited by the Central Bureau of Statistics of Norway. Oslo, 1972.
PESTEL, E. *See:* M. Mesarovic.
PIGOU, A.C. *Income*. London, 1949.
PIGOU, A.C. *The Economics of Welfare*. New York, 1962.
PLATO. *Critias.*

PLOWDEN, S. *The Cost of Noise*. London, 1970.
POTMA, Th. *Energiebeleid met Minder Risico*. Report published by the Vereniging Milieudefensie. Amsterdam, 1977.
PRAAG, B.M.S. van and A. Kapteyn. Wat is ons inkomen ons waard? *Economisch-Statistische Berichten*, 25 April and 2 May 1973.
PRONK, S.E. and C.M. de Reu. De Wet Verontreiniging Oppervlaktewateren en zijn betekenis voor het milieubeheer in Nederland. *Benelux Economisch en Statistisch Kwartaalbericht*, No. 1,1972.

RATHENAU, G.W. *See:* W.M. de Jong.
RASPAIL, F.V. *Histoire Naturelle de la Santé et de la Maladie*. Third Edition, Part I. Paris/Brussels, 1860.
READER, W.J. *Imperial Chemical Industries: A History*. London, 1970.
REPORT on the Limits to Growth, A Study by the World Bank. Washington (D.C.), August 1972.
REPORT of Meeting held in Geneva, 19–23 March 1973. Statistical Commission and Economic Commission for Europe. Conference of European Statisticians. CES/AC.40/5.
REU, C.M. de. *See:* S.E. Pronk.
RICARDO, D. *The Principles of Political Economy and Taxation*. London, 1969.
RIDKER, R.G. *Economic Costs of Air Pollution: Studies in Measurement*. New York, 1967.
ROBBINS, L. *An Essay on the Nature and Significance of Economic Science*. Second Edition. London, 1935.
ROBBINS, L. *The Economic Causes of War*. London, 1939.
ROOS, F. de and D.B.J. Schouten. *Groeitheorie*. Haarlem, 1960.
ROSENSTEIN-RODAN, P.N. Grenznutzen. In: *Handwörterbuch der Staatswissenschaften*. Fourth Edition. Volume 4, Part 4. Jena, 1927.
ROSKILL, J. Commission on the third London airport. *Report*. Chairman The Hon. Mr Justice Roskill. London, 1971.
ROSTOW, W.W. *The Stages of Economic Growth: A Non-Communist Manifesto*. London, 1960.
ROYAL Commission on Environmental Pollution. *Sixth Report, Nuclear Power and the Environment*. London, 1976.
RIJKSBEGROTING voor het Dienstjaar 1971. Hoofdstuk XIII – Economische Zaken. Memorie van Toelichting.
RIJKSBEGROTING voor het Dienstjaar 1972. Hoofdstuk XIII – Economische Zaken. Memorie van Toelichting.
RIJKSBEGROTING voor het Dienstjaar 1973. Hoofdstuk XIII – Economische Zaken. Bijlage III: Economische gevolgen van de bestrijding van waterverontreiniging met afbreekbaar organisch materiaal.
RIJTEMA, P.E. *Een Berekeningsmethode voor de Benadering van de Landbouwschade ten Gevolge van Grondwateronttrekking*. Nota 587 of the Instituut voor Cultuurtechniek en Waterhuishouding. Wageningen, 1971.

SAMUELSON, P.A. A Pure Theory of Public Expenditure. In: *Public Finance*. Edited by R.W. Houghton. Harmondsworth, 1970.
SAMUELSON, P.A. *Economics*. Ninth Edition. New York, 1973.
SCHOUTEN, D.B.J. *See:* F. de Roos.
SCITOVSKY, T. Two concepts of external economies. *Journal of Political Economy* 62, 1954, p. 143.
SEARS, P.B. *Deserts on the March*. Oklahoma, 1935.
SIDDRÉ, W. De toenemende schaarste aan tijd. *Economisch-Statistische Berichten*, 25 August 1971.
SMIL, V. and T. Kuz. European energy elasticities. *Energy Policy*, June 1976.
SMIT, W. *See:* G. van Dijk.
SMITH, A. *The Wealth of Nations*. Volume I. London, 1970 (First Edition, 1776).
SMITH, A. *An Inquiry into the Nature and Causes of the Wealth of Nations*. Volume II. Homewood (Ill.), 1963.

SOSLICK, S. *See:* L. Merewitz.
STEVENS, J.B. Recreation benefits from water pollution control. *Water Resources Research* 2, 1966.
STUIVER, Minze. Atmospheric carbon dioxide and carbon reservoir changes. *Science* 199, 1978, p. 253 et seq.

TAUSSIG, F.W. *Principles of Economics.* Volume I. New York, 1915.
TESCH, J.W. et al. *Op Leven en Dood, Problemen Rondom de Chemische en Biologische Bestrijding van Plagen.* Wageningen, 1964.
TINBERGEN, J. *Does the GNP of a Country Indicate its Happiness?* This article has been dated 20 July 1970 and written for a Japanese journal.
TINBERGEN, J. Meetbaarheid van een rechtvaardige verdeling. *De Economist* 121, 1973, p. 2.
TOBIN, J. *See:* W. Nordhaus.
TREATMENT, The, of Environmental Problems in the National Accounts and Balances. Statistical Commission and Economic Commission for Europe. Conference of European Statisticians. CES/AC.40/4. 14 February 1973.
TREVELYAN, G.M. *English Social History*. London, 1945.
TREVELYAN, G.M. *Illustrated English Social History*. Volume IV. London, 1952.
TRICE, A.H. and S.E. Wood. Measurement of Recreation Benefits. *Land Economics* XXXIV, 1958, No. 3.
TWEEHUYSEN, R. *See:* C. de Beurs.

UNION of Concerned Scientists. *The Risks of Nuclear Power Reactors.* Cambridge (Mass.), 1977.
UNITED Nations. *Measurement of National Income and the Construction of Social Accounts.* New York, 1947.
UNITED Nations. *A System of National Accounts and Supporting Tables.* New York, 1953.
UNITED Nations. *A System of National Accounts*. New York, 1968.
UNITED Nations. *Yearbook of National Accounts Statistics, 1969*. Volumes I and II. New York, 1970.
UNITED Nations. *Yearbook of National Accounts Statistics, 1971*. Volume III. New York, 1973.
USE of Pesticides. Science Advisory Committee. Washington (D.C.), 1963.

VOGT, W. *The Road to Survival.* New York, 1948.

WAGENAAR HUMMELINCK, M.G. *See:* W. van Dieren.
WEMELSFELDER, J. Economie en menselijk geluk. *Economisch-Statistische Berichten*, 2 May 1973.
WENDLAND, W.M. *See:* R.A. Bryson.
WESTHOFF, V. Bodemerosie als bedreiging van de menselijke samenleving. In: *Natuurkundige Voordrachten*, New Series, No. 45, 1967.
WHITE Paper from the Secretary of State for the Environment. Cmnd. 6820. London, 1977.
WHITTAKER, R.H. *Communities and Ecosystems.* London, 1970.
WILSON, C.L. et al. *Man's Impact on the Global Environment, Assessment and Recommendations for Action.* Cambridge (Mass.), 1970.
WOOD, S.E. *See:* A.H. Trice.
WOODWELL, G.M. Changes in the chemistry of the oceans: The pattern of effects. In: *Global Effects of Environmental Pollution.* Dordrecht, 1970.

ZIELHUIS, R.L. Manipuleren binnen een ecosysteem. *Wetenschap en Samenleving*, No. 21, 1967.
ZIMMERMAN, L.J. *Arme en Rijke Landen.* The Hague, 1968.

INDEX OF AUTHORS*

*Italic page numbers – references; roman page numbers – mentioned otherwise; p.i. – personal information.